DOCTOR RABELAIS

By the same author

BIOGRAPHY, ETC.

François Villon; a Documented Survey
Ronsard
Charles V, Emperor of the West
The Soul of Marshal Gilles de Raiz
James Boswell, a Short Life (first edition published as *The Hooded Hawk*)
Four Favourites
The Anatomy of Dandyism; from the French of Barbey d'Aurevilly, drypoints
    by Hermine David
The London Spectacle; illustr. Feliks Topolski
The Stuffed Owl; an Anthology of Bad Verse (with Charles Lee)
A Christmas Book (with G. C. Heseltine)

DIVERSIONS

At the Sign of the Blue Moon
At the Blue Moon Again
On Straw, and Other Conceits
Welcome To All This
Take It To Bed
etc.

DOCTOR RABELAIS

by

D. B. WYNDHAM LEWIS

SHEED AND WARD · NEW YORK

Contents

Introductory Note

"Agnes thinks his books are rather amusing."
"Agnes would."

The clear cold tenor accents clove the summer afternoon peace of the Rue de la Lamproie with that finality so dear and familiar to admirers of what the late Hugh Kingsmill labelled "The Mupples", or British upper-middle-class, and the little group moved away. What had lured the clergyman with his trio of female relations from their quiet hotel (*English Spoken*) in Tours into the orbit of François Rabelais at Chinon was not apparent. Surveying the gates of No. 15, his distaste had been all too visible. Like Soames Forsyte, he seemed to be sniffing a dubious egg. It was then and there, a few years ago, on overhearing the finale above recorded, that I determined one day to dedicate to the unknown Agnes, obviously a woman in ten million, some modest future tribute to the Master, my friend and travelling-companion so long.

To add to the pile of paper already heaped on Rabelais' cenotaph calls for explanation and excuse. How many books have been devoted to him so far by learned men (hereinafter referred to as "the learned"), I do not know. In this field only St. Joan of Arc, on whom the catalogue of studies consultable at the Bibliothèque Nationale is a thickish volume in itself, continues possibly to outdistance him. Over several years I myself must have read a score or more Rabelaisian commentaries—essays, prefaces, monographs, critical editions, reviews, theses, correspondence, full-length studies—by authorities both British and French; making thereby an interesting discovery. However much the learned may vary in style and scholarship, practically all their works have a basic constant, dictated by an attitude fixed, axiomatic, unarguable, irrevocable, assumed in advance as the only one possible, and, as Friar John of the Chops would say, "matter of Breviary". To the overwhelming majority, in a word, of those of his commentators known to me, Dr. François Rabelais is a paladin of light against darkness, progress against reaction, and reason against superstition. One of themselves.

From this derives a species of adoration or *latria* which seems to me as droll as anything offered to Lord Belly by his worshippers in *The Fourth Book of Pantagruel*. For quite a number of the Doctor's hierophants his lightest belch or hiccup is relayed from Sinai direct. Since the pages that follow combine long, strong, enduring affection for one of the comic geniuses of all time with no particular reverence for the Rabelaisian Oracle booming *ex cathedra*, this book may be considered, in this sense, a departure startlingly new and breathlessly original.

Though his works continue a mine inexhaustible, nothing fresh seems discoverable henceforth about Rabelais' career—a statement to be qualified immediately by the recollection that there may be Rabelaisian treasure yet unearthed by diggers of Lesellier's calibre in the rich archives of the Vatican. Everything that can be known about him personally from other sources, at any rate, has apparently been collected and published by the *Société des Études Rabelaisiennes*. What I, with so many more, owe this monumental series and the work of Lefranc, Millet, Bédier, Plattard, Lesellier, Villey, Clouzot and others will be obvious. My own contributions to Rabelaisian research, if nobody has already published them, are quite minute. I take modest pride nevertheless in connecting Panurge, possibly for the first time, with the Old Italian Comedy, and I fancy none of my predecessors has gone into the question of where and how the Doctor picked up his astonishing command of sea-lingo (if Machinchose postulated the one in 1857, or Fichemoy-Lapaix established the other in 1903, it is too late to bother now). And again, no Rabelaisian authority known to me has found time or strength to grapple with that obscene old parrot Béroalde de Verville, whose *Moyen de Parvenir*, for which Dr. Rabelais was at one time falsely held responsible, contains at least one illuminating gibe at him. One further tiny discovery may be also new. The eternal playboy Panurge, though he bounces round like a lewd Peter Pan, is, I discover after some calculation, actually a man of middle age. I have found this reflection piquant and of wide application.

By way of further excuse for these pages it might be observed, apropos Dr. Rabelais' Obsession No. 1, that whereas a considerable number of the learned judging his case with Olympian aplomb have evidently never set eyes on a real live monk, it has been my privilege to know about a dozen of the species, British and foreign, drawn to the monastic life from many spheres of secular activity; ex-lawyers, ex-airmen, ex-physicists, ex-business men, ex-naval officers, even an ex-county cricketer. It is my impression that contact with men pursuing what a modern Rabelaisian authority operating from a famous British University describes as "an artificial mode of life" (how different from the gay, rich, natural life of dons) is helpful in any attempt to estimate the value of Dr. Rabelais' perpetual and violent tirades against a system in which he was such a glorious misfit. To this authority, incidentally, a trifle more research could reveal that "Frère Mineur" does not mean a friar under twenty-one.

In these pages the Doctor's portrait, therefore, will be discovered to be painted a trifle differently from the ritual Academy offering, though he remains, I trust, the same Doctor as he would remain if interpreted by Sargent, John, and Dali in turn. Interpretation I believe to be a hobby permissible to the amateur with no pretensions to scholarship and no more qualifications than affectionate intimacy with his subject. Such a type may even hit, accidentally or otherwise, on a few facets overlooked by the specialists, or obscured by their particular angles of lighting and approach. The amateur may likewise—who knows? —lack that terrible seriousness with which a supreme master of gaiety has been handled by so many predecessors in the field. God knows the Doctor lacks no owls in his train.

So this work may be taken chiefly as a tribute to a friendship long enjoyed at home, abroad, in the trenches of the Somme, in rough Channel crossings, on Highland braesides, in the Roman Campagna, in the houses of the rich at weekends (where the Four Books supply priceless solace), and all kinds of unlikely places. Two faithful companions, a couple of battered brown duodecimos, *Les Oeuvres de Mr. Françoys Rabelais, Docteur en Medicine*, published by Jean Martin at Lyons in 1588, are well accustomed to the probing suspicious glance of H.M. Customs, not to speak of their brethren of the United States. Being enriched with marginal notes and reflections in a crabbed but legible contemporary hand, they have a peculiar value for me. Among modern editions the folio of 1922, edited by Henri Clouzot and illustrated (how brilliantly!) by Joseph Hémard, is likewise in constant use. A brief list of authorities consulted, over and above those mentioned already or in the text, will be found at the end of this book. For the views, opinions, interpretations, likes, and dislikes expressed in it the responsibility is exclusively my own, and I may perhaps be excused for going a little deeper here and there, with specialist aid from both his Orders, into some aspects of Rabelais' religious position, or positions, than is usually done. Though in his contemporaries' estimation a doctor of medicine first, a scholar second, and a master of satiric comicality third, he was after all a friar, monk, and priest, of sorts, of the Catholic Church. To Dom David Knowles, O.S.B., of Peterhouse, Cambridge, and Fr. Howard Docherty, O.F.M., my thanks are conveyed herewith. I have likewise to thank the Librarian of the University of Sheffield for information concerning a precious Rabelaisian autograph in his possession.

A word on the translation seems to be called for.

Urquhart has naturally been used for the first three Books. The obscure eccentric Cromarty squire, superb but not, as will be perceived, always dependable, is a considerable artist more than a conscientious interpreter. Steele's friend Peter Le Motteux, who carried on with Books IV and V—which latter, being rejected by all the best modern authorities, I have duly separated from the Canon—is less superb and even less reliable, inherited Calvinist rancour tending to encourage undue embellishment and distortion. I have used him nevertheless. He combines with Urquhart to furnish Rabelais' naturalisation-papers, and the Doctor might have fallen into worse hands.

From Urquhart and Le Motteux, I take it, the unknown Agnes was wont to sip those delights which earned her the annihilating rap at Chinon. To the unknown Agnes these pages are offered in fellowship, sympathy, and admiration.

D.B.W.L.

London, 1957

I

"A Certain Jollity of Mind . . ."

I

TAKING HIS EASE IN HIS GREAT BRONZE CHAIR BY THE SMOOTH-
sliding Vienne and surveying his town of Chinon in Touraine,
Dr. François Rabelais wears in effigy, very properly, that large
and genial air commended by himself, after Hippocrates, to
brethren of the Faculty of Medicine striving towards a perfect
bedside manner. Without doubt the Doctor himself habitually
displayed *la face joyeuse, sereine, gracieuse, et ouverte* as he strode the
hospital-wards of Lyons and Metz in the 1530–40's. So far as
I can discover, its therapeutic value, a favourite Renaissance
theme, has never been questioned even by Molière at his naughti-
est. At that hilarious conference in *L'Amour Médecin* Monsieur
Filerin, the Faculty personified, does not scold his quarrelsome
colleagues for undervaluing this essential to exploitation, at least.

There is still a hospital in France where one may visualise the
smile of Dr. Rabelais operating in its ideal setting. This is undoubtedly, though the Doctor, alas, was never appointed there,
the magnificent Hôtel-Dieu at Beaune, now in its sixth century
of continuous service. Here, looking down the main ward from
the chapel screen, it is possible with a little imaginative goodwill
to catch a glimpse of a flying gown and two rows of sick staring
from their massive walnut beds after the great shining Rabelaisian
face with its commanding nose, nobly gilded by the Burgundian
grape, and gulping health from his passage like a draught of
Nuits. A more stupendous medical phenomenon than Dr. Rabelais
was bustling round Europe at this same period. It may be that
bull-necked, foul-mouthed Dr. Philippus Aureolus Theophrastus
Bombast von Hohenheim, genius, Cabbalist, and mystagogue,
self-styled "Paracelsus the Great", achieved no better immediate

results with a pinch of the Magisterium he carried with him always, drunk or sober, in the pommel of his sword "Azoth".

Those of Dr. Rabelais' patients who survived to remember their jolly physician in old age may have found it difficult to recognise him immediately in an engraving now at Versailles; *circa* 1601, from a lost portrait believed to be authentic. Mirth of a kind certainly hovers round the eyes and lips of the bearded imperious visage under the medical biretta, but it bids fair to be by no means Hippocratic. It holds, indeed, one might almost say, rich promise of what the French precision has classified as the *rire jaune*, first cousin to a snarl. In modern idiom, somebody is evidently due for a rocket. Somebody is about to be dowered with a few well-chosen epithets from the Doctor's immense repertoire of abuse, drawn from the library or the latrines. A fundamental good-humour would deprive his most outrageous verbal missiles of real harm.

Plenty of black eyes and bloody noses, metaphorically speaking, bestrew the Doctor's wake, but he does not wield the poisoned stiletto of a Voltaire or a Chamfort, and to mention him in the same breath as Swift, as is often done, seems to me monstrous. The Doctor displays plenty of the impetuosity of the Gaul, with a good dash of Gallic malice and even, when roused, some of that tigerish verve, so shocking to men of colder blood, which is as national a trait as the angelic sweetness of Gallic sanctity exemplified in a François de Sales and a Curé d'Ars. But there is no particle in Rabelais' composition of the black contempt for mankind which created the Yahoos. His heart is sound and his optimistic love of humanity and belief in its natural virtue such, indeed, that he cherishes quite sincerely the Renaissance impression that increasing secular knowledge will make it godlike. If, simultaneously with the denunciation of all war except a defensive one,[1] he is of the opinion that a little incidental bashing and bloodletting does no harm, and is great fun, this is a view held generally in his time. Hence the scientific gusto of the massacre at Seuilly, the beating-up of the Chiquanous, the murder of Dingdong, and a few other jolly rough-house episodes scattered through the Four Books. "Boys," one can hear the Doctor chuckle, preparatory to tossing

[1] On this topic, for one, he is not consistent, as will appear.

back an *horrificque traict* of Vouvray and dipping his quill afresh, "will be boys."

Indisputably a great deal of Rabelais' laughter is cruel. So, in varying degree, is all laughter provoked by the antics and misfortunes of one's fellow-men, and above all when no remedy is offered; a truth applying as much to the amiable Wodehouse as the corrosive Voltaire. The test here as everywhere is intention, and I think Rabelais mainly passes it. Two of his best-loved jests involve extreme human suffering and humiliation, but if their humours rarely cease to divert him he does not, like the devilish author of *Les Chants de Maldoror*, seriously look forward to seeing mankind at large devastated by such ills, on one of which, incidentally, Dr. Rabelais must have lavished his skill quite often during the years of hospital-practice. To him, I think, the comedy-appeal of both would derive from their representing a microcosm of the Fall. Cuckoldry, the stag's regalia—its diversions, as one of Sacha Guitry's characters reminds us, are infinite; "un cocu, c'est toujours comique". The eternal wittold, mocked in spring by every cuckoo, blandly unconscious of the ornaments decorating his foolish brow, seemed to the prince of Renaissance poets a theme gay enough for a summer afternoon's song in Arden.

> Take thou no scorn to wear the horn,
> It was a crest ere thou wast born . . .

A more genial note will come in with the Grand Siècle. When one of the actresses in the *Impromptu de Versailles* asks why on earth they should offend all the cuckolds present, cuckolds being the charmingest people in the world, a haughty and glittering audience undoubtedly rose as gleefully to the jest as Charles the Second's courtiers at Whitehall when the king called to the band for "Cuckolds All Awry", "the old dance of England". The same jape remains the mainstay of Palais-Royal farce today, though I believe the old astringent approach has returned.

From the great twin jest of the Powdering-Tub modern medicine has long since skimmed most of the cream. But the *Morbus Gallicus*, known to later generations of our hearty forbears as the French Distemper, or Covent-Garden Ague, was a great joke in

its time, and in Rabelais' day, we may recollect, still more or less
a novelty, having been imported into Europe from the New
World, as is usually supposed, round about the turn of the century. How merrily does the Doctor, in the Prologue to the
Second Book, commend his work to his "thrice-precious Pockified Blades" in their trials.

> O how often have we seen them, even immediately after they were
> anointed and thoroughly greased, till their faces did glister like the
> Keyhole of a Powdering-Tub, their teeth dance like the jacks of a
> paire of little Organs or Virginals when they are played upon,
> and that they foamed from their very throats like a Boare which
> the Mongrel Mastiff-hounds have driven in and overthrown among
> the foyles: what did they then? All their consolation was to have
> some page of the same jollie Book read unto them; and we have
> seen those who have given themselves to a hundred punchions of old
> Devils in case that they did not feele a manifest ease and asswage-
> ment of pain at the hearing of the same Book read, even when
> they were kept in a Purgatory of torment . . .

A winsome approach, even in Urquhart's rendering; the
original has an elusive, incomparable suavity and rhythm ("O
quantesfois nous les avons veu, à l'heure qu'ilz estoient bien
oingtz et engraissés à poinct", etc.). From this topic the Renaissance derived entertainment rich and ripe. When a violent
character like Ulrich von Hutten, Luther's ally and Erasmus'
adversary, published a treatise on the cure of syphilis and found
himself in due course in an advanced and all-too-apparent state
of decomposition, his bitterest friends might be forgiven for
shaking a shoulder. The great joke arrived in Europe three
centuries too late, unfortunately, for Rabelais' spiritual ancestor
Jean de Meung, whom otherwise I dare swear nobody could have
prevented, when that cynic took over the unfinished *Roman de
la Rose*, from introducing an obvious couple of low comedians
into Guillaume de Lorris' enchanted garden, among the fair
dames and their gallant chevaliers. "We", Bel-Cocuage and
Gale-Fleurie might have cried, grinning in the background,
"represent the *fin mot* of this high mystery of love of which your
poets and romancers make such a song. Look at us and laugh."
Such setbacks to human dignity are essentially farce-material.

The recurrent banana-skin whereby man, treading the path to a stupendous destiny, presents his backside suddenly to the pavement and his heels to the shuddering stars—where would the Comic Muse be without it? And the Muse of Rabelais, above all?

As M. Guitry remarks, laughter caused by this type of heartless joke is perennial. More usefully still Max Beerbohm, an ounce of whom I take on this question to be worth a ton of Bergson, went to the trouble some years ago of noting and analysing the jokes which chiefly arride the *homme moyen sensuel* in his modern British incarnation. His careful study of the comic Press produced the conclusion that two constants are involved, namely delight in cruelty and contempt for the unfamiliar. An indestructible formula, one might say. Its first half alone spans the ages, from Penelope's suitors bent double at the death-agonies of Irus *via* a popular raree-show like eighteenth-century Bedlam down to Kipling's sahibs reeling in paroxysms over rather small and tiresome practical jokes. In this sphere what the Victorians called "the march of mind" has of course operated to some extent. I fancy the average fun-lover of 1957 would find himself as little moved to hilarity by the twittering tiny feet of the newly-hanged serving-maids of the *Odyssey* as his Athenian prototype by those witty onslaughts on the unloved and unattractive British spinster which cause Gilbert-and-Sullivan addicts to roll in the aisle. Having brought refinement to torture itself, progress has influenced public taste in the same direction.

So much for Demos, for whose delectation Rabelais so lavishly caters with knockabout farce and lavatory-jokes and mayhem intensive and unlimited. But how account for the spell he can cast equally over the fastidious? Simultaneously to charm a frigid Jansenist like Racine, an aristocratic wit like Mme de Sévigné, the Catholic-Romantic Chateaubriand, and the anti-Catholic propagandist Kingsley is surely something of a feat, since the civilised do not commonly laugh, like the vulgar, at the same jokes. *Tot elegantes, quot cachinni*. Religion and philosophy and social background and education and temperament and experience of life and many other factors promote infinite diversity in this matter, as everyone knows. Sydney Smith's description of Malthus—"a good-natured man, and, if there are no appearances of approaching fertility, civil to every lady"—could hardly be savoured by anyone unacquainted with the Malthusian gospel, and only those cognisant, however vaguely, of the metaphysics of transubstantiation can appreciate the late Bishop Barnes's suggestion to prove it a myth by analysing a consecrated Host as the mathematical joke of the century. But Rabelais has appealed, and will probably continue to appeal, to the most unlikely minds. I register, with no attempt at explanation, his astonishing apparition, with a panegyric quoted from Scévole de Sainte-Marthe, in the *Annales Fratrum Minorum*, a Who's Who of illustrious literary Franciscans published at Rome in 1650 (*cum permissu*) by the Irish scholar Luke Wadding of that Order. Whether this tribute to a man regarded and approved still in highly respectable quarters as one of Rome's most formidable adversaries is connected in any way with the fact that none of Rabelais' innumerable editions has ever appeared on the Index I cannot say. A large and humorous clemency (*"Che che*, my dear sir, as we say at Rome . . .") like that of Paul III, who was so kind to him, may well have judged the French priest's fireworks to be excessively amusing, and no more harmful than the squibs of *il caro Pasquino*. So perhaps the laugh, as they say, is on the dons.

The spell of Rabelais certainly endures. In default of any better key to it the single word "ecstasy" suggests itself; ecstasy in its original Greek sense, a standing-out-of-oneself, total possession by a powerful Muse, the mark of all high literature. The Doctor is no portent as a thinker, and least of all as a French thinker. Clarity, precision, order—these are the last qualities to be looked for in his pages. Wisdom and tomfoolery, scholarship and obscenity pour from him—and in what imperial French!—like a great turbulent South American river sweeping to the Pacific in flood, bearing in its murky bosom rich silt, dead cows, virgin gold, ivory, apes, and peacocks, and every kind of ashcan-rubbish in inextricable confusion. To erect him on a Rodinesque pedestal as a master mind of the Renaissance is a quite modern foible. "Never has a man of such attainments", remarks M. Henri Clouzot, one of the Doctor's warmest admirers, "exercised less influence on his contemporaries." To them he was a brilliant medical man, a fine scholar, and a prolific entertainer of the commonalty.

Truly pitiful it is, therefore, to listen to the groans of learned men struggling to reduce Dr. Rabelais' system of cerebration to a formula. If he knew it himself, one may wonder how many of his original readers did, or even wanted to, being under the impression that the Doctor was not developing a treatise on Metaphysicotheologocosmolonigology in the Pangloss manner but amusing himself; relaxing after the day's labours in dressing-gown and slippers with a couple of bottles at his elbow and letting a harumscarum fancy go free. As he undoubtedly was, at least in the first two *Pantagruel* books, and to a large extent in all four. The Concept of Depth, as pedants would say, came to him in mid-career, when he changed his style, and proved retrospective. "It must be remembered that it was the author himself who later constantly read profound wisdom into his early merriment," observes a recent British authority. Olympianism does certainly succeed in stalking at intervals into the Rabelaisian circus-ring, and before the fun is resumed one or two hobbyhorses have usually been trotted out for exercise. To these many of the learned devote as anxious scrutiny as if they were the finest Arab bloodstock. One at least of them, as it happens, fell dead right under the Doctor's nose. In his own lifetime the Jesuits at the Collège du Trésorier launched a new scientific pedagogy, designed to produce "the complete man", which makes the rambling, unwieldy curriculum invented by the Doctor for young Gargantua look foolish. His ideal substitute for monasticism, again, the dream-Abbey of Thélème with its community of well-born neo-Platonic flirts and bucks, has been admitted to lack reason even by those who share his prejudice.

If any of the gallants or Ladies should say, Let us drink, they would all drink; if any of them said, Let us play, they all played; if one said, Let us go a-walking into the fields, they went all . . . .

To these newfangled nuns and monks, it will be perceived, their abbey's single rule, "Do what thou wilt", is an obvious stumbling-block, nor could any human beings on earth live together long on the Doctor's terms. One or two flaws have been detected likewise in his discussions of war, government, women, economics, and even some aspects of the religion of which he was professedly a priest, though in this last case some of the mis-representation is deliberate. *Ici l'on s'amuse.* Thus the Doctor is no very dependable pilot through Renaissance reefs and sand-banks. But one would rather be run aground by him, still laugh-ing, than be brought to strange ports by some of his soberer contemporaries.

Of that perpetual Rabelaisian laughter it may be said, I think, that those who love the Doctor most are willing to concede that there are times when it becomes a little strident, a little tiresome, inviting the reflection that as with Democritus before him, up-roarious amusement at other people's foolishness would seem to co-exist with a convenient unawareness of some of his own. This is a well-known foible of the satirical tribe which must, while the world lasts, be manfully endured, and there is actually a point at which it seems as though the Doctor is on the verge of cheerfully admitting it. Having described himself in the Prologue to the Fourth Book as hale and jovial, "sound as a Bell, and ready to drink", he pauses, and proceeds to foil expectation.

> Would you know why I'm thus, good People? I'll e'en give you a positive answer—such is the Lord's Will, which I obey and revere; it being said in his Word, in great Derision, to the Physician neg-lectful of his own Health, Physician, heal thy self.

So much for that. The physician has diagnosed and found nothing wrong with himself. The Lord's will simultaneously, as is quite clear, confirms Dr. Rabelais' authority to castigate and laugh, and when one of the castigated returns a few thwacks as lusty as his own he will be quite genuinely shocked and incensed ("Dogs! Hypocrites! Cannibals!" . . .). Thus heartlessly does the Comic Spirit sometimes desert her favourites, nor are the greatest exempt. What happened when anyone ventured to hit back at Voltaire or Smollett everyone knows; the welkin rang with indignant screams. So also with Dr. Rabelais, and such an amiable weakness lessens neither his stature as an artist nor the affection he continues to inspire; still less the tonic value of that Atlantic gale of health, joy of life, and frank high spirits blowing through the Four Books of *Pantagruel* and the surge and thunder of that incomparable prose, as stimulating today as in the Re-naissance, an age which like our own had very little to laugh about. Hence the response he evokes from virile intellects in every age from Du Bellay down to Hilaire Belloc, who loved Rabelais dearly all his life, read him to the end of it, and eulogised him in a memorable essay.

So we may come, none too soon, to Rabelais' own word for his philosophy. He calls it "Pantagruelism", its essence being "a certain Jollity of Mind, pickled in the scorn of Fortune"; a very sound working philosophy indeed, and to a sick and agitated world crouching at present under the shadow of total annihilation a highly commendable one.

> Eh gai! C'est la devise
> Du gros Roger Bontemps.

Like the world of Rabelais, Béranger's had its drawbacks, cholera-epidemics and bloody insurrection among them. To laugh in the Paris of the 1830–40's, which so often seems to crackle continuously with blasphemies and musketry, was certainly meritorious. Yet like the Rabelaisian blend, Béranger's Pantagruelism prompts a question, more than ever pertinent since the splitting of the atom, which might be put to every apostle of public gaiety. What, master, is your excuse? Under which king, Bezonian? Unless, sir, you are to be relegated to the class of chimeras bombinating in a vacuum, mere noise-machines emitting anything from the automatic roars of a Tapley to the arid cackle of an Anouilh, kindly produce a reason for this mirth. Béranger thus made to stand and deliver has nothing very vital to offer us in the year 1957, his Roger Bontemps being one of the many illegitimate offspring of Jean-Jacques Rousseau; a child of Nature disporting himself under the indulgent eye of some vaguely-conceived Good Fellow in the sky, of the kind fathered on Khayyàm by FitzGerald; a type as outdated as last year's film-queen. Rabelais' gaiety is a different matter. The springs of his laughter have an irony so exquisite, so glorious, that I think only now, within the last few years, can it be appreciated in its full perfection.

The Doctor is, in fact, in his prevailing mood, a typical Victorian liberal agnostic born before his time, believing in the self-sufficient perfectibility of man, natural progress, and natural virtue to begin with. For him the Renaissance is the dawn of inevitable millennium; while the last clouds of medieval ignorance and imbecility vanish in sunlight mankind marches onward and upward towards some splendid if not clearly-defined peak of earthly beatitude. Except that the Victorian progressist was often under the cosy impression that he had already arrived, the Doctor may be seen at times to lack nothing but the top-hat and whiskers of a Macaulay or a Cobden. Natural progress, natural virtue—if this is strange doctrine to be held by a Catholic priest, or for that matter by any professing Christian, one may recall that the Doctor was for most of his life only nominally in either category, and that greater Renaissance humanists than he did not share these whimsies. And since he was not to foresee that natural progress would flower four centuries later in the discovery of forces capable of blasting all life to smithereens, and liable at any moment to be so used, he can hardly be blamed for those alleluias which, impinging on a modern ear, so pleasingly enrich the harmonies of a great comic symphony.

Pantagruelism remains, meanwhile, a philosophy intact and precious, unaffected by time or circumstance; still gay and pickled in the scorn of Fortune and, perhaps, more effective with one or two added ingredients which the Doctor overlooked.

It was of course not his unique discovery, nor even in his own time exclusive to men of his own cast of mind. In the year of the publication of *Gargantua* a most noble, admired, and finished Pantagruelist and master of gaiety died with great goodwill, joking on the scaffold, in defence of the spiritual supremacy of the Holy See.

> Dear Jester in the Courts of God—
> In whose spirit, enchanting yet,
> Wisdom and love, together met,
> Laughed on each other for content! . . .[1]

With another canonised Pantagruelist of the day he may even have brushed elbows, during his endless prowls in Rome, in the Via della Carità: a young Florentine of that quarter whose favourite cry of "Allegramente!" may be taken to express the quintessence of the Rabelaisian philosophy raised to its highest

[1] Francis Thompson, "To the English Martyrs".

possible power. The disciples of Philip Neri certainly knew good reason to be merry. Is it extravagant to bracket the Doctor for a moment with the Apostle of Rome—*lux sanctae laetitiae*, as Newman calls him? Both were dynamos of gaiety, each took all things human for his province, and it would seem today that the Italian had the better right to laugh.

2

How weary, stale, flat, and unprofitable
Seem to me all the uses of this world . . .

Thus does Hamlet's cry sum up the enormous ennui of the Renaissance, of which we hear so little. Nor does he despair alone. In the most elegant of silvery Latin and in the choicest of Greek Erasmus had long before him expressed a nausea for existence almost as complete as that of a Jean-Paul Sartre, if such comparison is possible. "This most criminal age . . . The unhappiest and most depraved of ages imaginable . . . Thrice-wretched Erasmus, most miserable of all men . . ." Final dis-illusion came to this idol of the Renaissance in his early forties, but the *taedium* had set in much earlier. All the flashes of wit and gaiety lighting up the *Moriae Encomium* ("The Praise of Folly"), the little book which captivated all Europe in 1509 and was dedicated to More, of all men, seem to me merely to emphasise what Dr. Johnson would call inspissated gloom, though I am aware that worthy men can still take it to be the continuous jest Erasmus in his elusive way pretends. Only the fool and the humbug are happy; any man who would take life's bitterness seriously would deprive himself of life; all is folly and unreason, civilisation is a horror, nothing is worth living for—this was the message, rapturously received. Is there any man alive, Erasmus asks years later in one of the *Colloquies*, who cannot in perfect truth agree with the saying that "the best thing is never to have been born, the next best to die at birth"? Europe's most illus-trious and feline scholar was the unhappiest of men. If his de-pressions chime oddly with the harvest-choruses of the Whigs, how do they go with the whoopings of Dr. Rabelais as he dances so indefatigably before the Ark?

To its greatest lyric poet the Renaissance did not seem a particularly sunny age either, as Ronsard testifies in his maturity,
brooding over wholesale strife, wreckage, loot, sacrilege, bloodshed, and the riving-asunder of Western Christendom. Unlike
Rabelais, Ronsard does not raise his glass to Millenium. Of
finer fibre, he is freer from illusion. Whether the two ever met
is not known. Their only recorded juxtaposition occurred at the
funeral in Le Mans Cathedral of Guillaume du Bellay in 1543;
Rabelais was nearly fifty and Ronsard twenty, and they may
never have exchanged a word. At the Renaissance banquet their
attitudes are strikingly different. Nobody enjoys himself more
uproariously than the Doctor, yet one sees Ronsard in his prime
noting the fading flowers and the waning waxlights with moody
distaste and yawning with lassitude.

Tout est perdu, Nicolas, tout s'empire... [1]

Though this long lament was written during the French wars of
religion, some twenty years after Rabelais' death, the orgy had
begun to pall long since on not a few aching heads and hearts.
Towards the 1520's it was plain that something had gone badly
awry. The cultural revolution called the Renaissance—actually
the third since Charlemagne—which had been so enthusiastically
fostered and furthered by half-a-dozen lettered and art-loving—
too art-loving—Popes, with the assistance of an international
intelligentsia of which fair young Giovanni Pico della Mirandola,
whose physical beauty, noble blood, and astonishing brains
justify Pater's hailing him the Prince Charming of the Renaissance,
might be called the most decorative flower, had been diverted to
a considerable extent into other channels. The neo-pagans had
triumphed, and a modern French scholar aptly divides the
Renaissance, viewed from the standpoint of the Christian civilisation of the West, into four distinct phases: a honeymoon with first
disillusions, an autumn of ripe fruits and dead leaves, and a brief
St. Martin's summer waning into a winter in which "la Renaissance assagie, baptisée, meurt des excès de la Renaissance
païenne."[2]

---

[1] "All is lost, Nicolas; all grows worse . . ." (To Simon Nicolas, Secretary-Royal.)
[2] Louis Bouyer, *Autour d'Erasme*, Paris, 1955.

The pagan movement was nothing new in Rabelais' time. As far back as 1471 the lawyer Lorenzo Valla, Rector of the University of Rome, had furnished adepts with a manifesto in the shape of a highly-significant volume of dialogues called *De Voluptate*, with a face-saving finale of no great conviction or import. Four hundred years before Swinburne the skies of an enchanting pagan world of blue and gold devoted to beauty, happiness, and the gratification of every fleshly impulse are seen in Valla's pages to turn sick and grey at the breath of the pale Galilean; *air connu*, a song of ancient Greece contrasting curiously with the malaise of its poets, their moanings over the fleetingness of youth and beauty, their horror of inevitable death. ("Either erotic anatomy or grumblings about old age," as Professor Gilbert Norwood described the Anthology.) The still-current Sunshine Myth, hymned by Antonio Beccadelli in Valla's book with the lyrical intensity of an incantation, took enduring root, and in some aspects fruited lavishly in circles more fashionable than that of the scholars and bookmen. Polite historians do not dwell on such outward manifestations of Renaissance Hellenism as sodomy, a vogue which claimed not a few grave, portentous Corydons like the eminent Elizabethan labelled παιδεραστής in Aubrey's *Brief Lives*, and the public display, abetted by *la haute couture*, of the naked female bosom; a spectacle, to be repeated under the French Directoire, which cannot have been invariably delightful to the connoisseur.

Such excessive dalliance with the Hellenic genius was inevitable in some quarters. Every movement of the kind has its lunatic fringe. It need hardly be observed that the best humanists, and the Christian ones perforce, sipped the heady new wine more rationally and fell into no such excesses; the life and death of St. Thomas More, greatest of them all, demonstrate to what heights Renaissance man was capable of rising. A certain amount of emotionalism should not be misconstrued. The scholar in one of Erasmus' *Colloquies* who confesses himself on the verge of crying: "St. Socrates, pray for us!" is simply expressing, in a company of kindred minds, his joy at finding a noble pagan soul so closely akin to a Christian one. The silver lamp kept burning day and night before the bust of Plato in Marsilio Ficino's study at Florence illustrates a similarly generous enthusiasm.

It may equally in his case, it occurs to one, have expressed a trifle of that attitude to which many of what may be called the Left Wing Renaissance intelligentsia were prone; a tendency, curiously naïve, to regard themselves as conquistadors of an intellectual New World, *coheredes* and *sodales* in their sphere with Columbus and Balboa, Cortes and Pizarro, claiming total annexation and exploitation-rights. Yet the Early Fathers were steeped in a purer Platonism than theirs, and what more Hellenic than that unquenchable spirit of rational inquiry, fundamental to Catholic thinking, of which the thought of Aquinas affords a monumental example?

In any case the unfortunate human race did not seem to be thriving on the new discoveries. Long before Rabelais' maturity crystal dawn had given place to thunderclouds, visions of imminent Millenium to chaos involving bloodshed on a larger-than-medieval scale. The old united Christendom was dead, slain by the Black Death and the Great Western Schism, oddly so called; the new world was confused and bewildered and rent by savage conflict. The flight from medieval pity and charity so frequently encountered in Rabelais' pages is arrestingly demonstrated in the greatest work of the sublimest poet of the age. Straight from purgatory, still being cleansed there by suffering from "foul crimes done in my days of nature", the Ghost in *Hamlet* calls for bloody reprisals like any bravo of his time or gunman of ours. "If thou didst ever thy dear father love, Revenge his foul and most unnatural murder . . ." Post-mortem vindictiveness of this kind Dante would rightly reserve to the damned in hell. Shakespeare has yielded to the Zeitgeist, if only temporarily. To *Hamlet* will succeed *Measure for Measure*, the medieval Catechism translated into pure and noble poetry. Rabelais is not the only Janus of the Renaissance.

The flight from pity is an outstanding mark of the period. A typical mob of the Middle Ages ready to tear a monster like Gilles de Raiz to pieces after his arrest would be moved equally to join in the penitent's prayers and tears at the gallows-foot. The Renaissance mob—for example during the sack of Rome— knew no such weakness. Its spirit is well conveyed in the ferocious jollity with which Frère Jean des Entommeures liquidates the invaders of the vineyards, as in the merry drowning of the sheep-merchant by Panurge. In Rabelais' laughter is heard the callousness of the new age. Today the spectacle of souls sped violently into eternity with a guffaw is a routine with which every cinemagoing child is familiar. Before the sixteenth century, we may reflect, it was extremely rare. Thus Rabelais in this particular aspect is undoubtedly a "progressive". The fact should tend to encourage honest but faint-hearted lovers of bawdy lured by hearsay into buying one of those smudgy English translations commonly found nestling among the contraceptives and aphrodisiacs in shady little shops, only to recoil in an agony of boredom from strange locutions and appalling wads of Renaissance scholarship.

It is easier to sympathise with these weaker brethren in Pantagruelism, perhaps, than with a *chapelle* of pedants on their knees before an imaginary giant of Renaissance thought. Whether Rabelais, though well aware of his powers, ever conceived himself, as is the foible of successful literary men, to be one of the real Samurai I strongly doubt. Barring a correspondence in his early days with the illustrious Budé, whose hobby was the encouragement of promising young men, he enjoyed no discernible communion with any leading intellectual of his age. Was the letter he addressed to Erasmus out of the blue in 1532, that paean of respectful adulation ("Salve itaque atque etiam, Pater amantissime, Pater decusque Patriae . . .") ever acknowledged? The great Erasmus, protégé of Popes, friend of Kings, premier scholar of Europe, now in his late and ailing sixties and due two years hence to decline a cardinal's hat, may not have deemed this contribution to his enormous fanmail from an obscure admirer in Lyons worth answering, and indeed may have died unaware of Dr. Rabelais' existence.[1] It is a thousand pities these two never knew each other. Over and above what benefits the Doctor continued to derive from Erasmus' prose, intimacy with a subtler wit might have induced him to temper some of his cruder buffooneries and possibly, even, to reconsider his position here and there, since long before his end Erasmus discovered the Renaissance dogma of human self-sufficiency to be a delusion, his last utterance being a cry to the Mother of God: "O Mater Dei, memento

---

[1] Erasmus died in 1536. The first of Rabelais' works to be published under his own name, *The Third Book of Pantagruel*, came out ten years later.

mei!" Next to Erasmus' friendship I can think of only one major corrective Rabelais missed through no fault of his own. The victory of Lepanto, whereby the western world was saved from destruction solely by the energy of the Holy See, would have done him, as it did so many noisy *mangeurs du Pape*, a world of good in the matter of the revising of prejudices and the re-orientation of abuse. ("Laugh *this* off," as Don John of Austria might have said grimly to the creator of the Papimanes.) But Lepanto came at least seventeen years too late to metagrabolise Rabelais, unfortunately.

Throughout the greater part of his life Catholic Christendom seemed to be fighting a rearguard action. Over large areas of northern Europe the new heresies kept making steady headway, backed as they were by princes and their satellites enriched by robbery from the Church and greedy for more. There had been a time when revolt against the Holy See might well have been nipped in the bud and its champions reconciled, together with the Greeks. But Rome had failed to grasp its opportunities and it was now too late; the new sects were too numerous, self-assured and hostile, and the Greeks implacable. The last faint chance of repairing the once-seamless robe vanished when Henry VIII's cousin Reginald, Cardinal Pole, moved by a scruple of humility, declined the tiara proffered "by acclamation" in 1550. The all-but-second English Pope combined a spotless character with the urbanity of royal blood, high learning, and the skill of a practised diplomat. In Peter's chair Pole, if anybody, could have reduced the sixteenth-century German Reformation to the dimensions of all the half-forgotten heresies in our history which have come and gone. *Dis aliter visum.* Having afforded the English for the last time, it would sometimes seem, the spectacle of a Papal Legate sweeping in his barge up the Thames, while all the bells of London rang for joy, to absolve the Queen and both Houses of Parliament, kneeling, from heresy and schism, Reginald Pole had barely succeeded to the See of Canterbury in 1558 when he died.[1] Of the eight Popes ruling Western Christendom in Rabelais' lifetime only two were of the calibre of a Pole. Adrian VI, that dour and silent Dutchman (1522-3),

---

[1] In a previous reign a British Government arrangement to have him assassinated by the hand of Sir Thomas Wyatt, during a diplomatic mission in Spain, had misfired.

had barely been able to tackle the fringes of the Papacy's most obvious priority-problem, the reform of the Curia, before he died, to the huge relief of all concerned. With the accession of Paul III (1534–50) this respite ended. Over and above the establishment of a Commission of Reform, approval of the energetic new Society of Jesus, and the summoning of the Council of Trent, Paul III's programme included a last attempt, still possible for a statesman of his quality, to come to terms with the Renaissance and restore the unity of Christendom. He, too, died before half his determinations could be put into effect. It was a dozen years after the presumed date of Rabelais' death that the first Pope of the Counter-Reform arrived at last, in the frail and formidable person of St. Pius V, the Pope of Lepanto. By that time Reform and Renaissance had gone their way.

Meanwhile, all the world had stood dumbfounded at the news of the sacking of the capital of Christendom (May, 1527) by forty thousand half-starved Imperial troops, the scum of Europe, under the renegade Constable de Bourbon; a week's nightmare of massacre, debauchery, loot, sacrilege, and general running-amuck after the Constable's death in which his Lutherans, true descendants of the Goths, especially distinguished themselves. Only the devotion of the Papal Swiss Guard, who gave two hundred of their lives for him in a desperate battle, saved Clement VII himself from being murdered before he could escape to Sant'Angelo. To not a few exultant prophets in Germany and Switzerland, and to numbers of faint hearts everywhere, this spectacle seemed to foreshadow the imminent demise of the Papacy after barely fifteen centuries' existence. "We are waiting", wrote the Imperial ambassador to his master amid still-smoking ruins, "to know how Your Majesty intends the city of Rome to be governed, and whether it is to be some sort of Apostolic seat or not." But if the Emperor Charles V was deeply shocked by his responsibility for this disaster, the cultus of Pagan Rome, co-existing with neo-Hellenism and in its way quite as virulent, enabled numbers of the European intelligentsia to bear the prospect of the Papacy's end with fortitude.

These enthusiasts too were flourishing and vocal. Had not a clique of dons of the University of Rome, under Lorenzo Valla's immediate successor, who called himself Pomponius Laetus and

trapesed about the city in antique dress, toyed for a time in 1468
with reviving the old republican *Romanitas*? Such clowning was
never Rabelais' form. That sardonic humour of his would have
moved him undoubtedly, had he been present, to laugh with
the Roman mob at the ridiculous Pomponius deambulating, to
use the appropriate jargon of Pantagruel's Limousin scholar, the
quadrives and compites of the Urb in toga and caligules. Nor,
though the builders of new St. Peter's, *architetti della reverenda
fabrica*, from Fra Giocondo down to Michelangelo, were as
ruthless with pagan remains as Constantine had been before
them—the remark is that of the eminent archaeologist Lanciani—
did the Doctor ever join in those ritual Left Wing lamentations
for vanished glory which were so fashionable at this time, when
nothing was more chic than a Roman pilgrimage taken for the
express purpose of turning one's back on all the chief shrines
and basilicas and pacing the Forum, or *Campo Vaccino*, among
the sheep and goats in bitter anguish for—mostly imagined—
splendour then buried deep under the grass.

> Nouveau venu, qui cherches Rome en Rome,
> Et rien de Rome en Rome n'apperçois . . .[1]

Even a convinced if morose Catholic like Joachim du Bellay
could give way to academic tears among the ruins.

> Rome n'est plus; et si l'architecture
> Quelque umbre encor de Rome fait revoir,
> C'est comme un corps par magique sçavoir
> Tiré de nuict hors de sa sepulture.[2]

Like Gibbon brooding over the Capitol a couple of centuries
afterwards ("attached to the old Pagan Establishment", as he
explained to Lord Sheffield), the Renaissance pilgrim of this
type, surrounded by the rich full-blooded life of the Eternal City,
was blind and deaf to anything dated after the last of the Antonines.
Not so Rabelais, as his Roman letters attest. At the same time
one may readily allow that in the year 1527 he would not be

[1] "Newcomer, seeking Rome in Rome, and finding nothing of Rome in Rome . . ."
[2] "Rome is no more; and if some shadow of Rome is still evoked by brick and
stone, it is like a corpse dragged by art-magic from the tomb at night." (*Les Anti-
quetez de Rome*, Sonnet V.)

overmuch concerned for the fate of the Papacy, being at the time, so far as can be ascertained, in his brief crypto-"Evangelical" phase. Though the Holy See's habit of surviving cataclysms of every dimension was not yet the open wound it is nowadays to practitioners of what is called the best contemporary thought, its recovery from the Bourbon tornado may have disappointed Rabelais as much as it did his fellow-priest Calvin, who reached the limit of endurance five years later and quitted the Church.

Pessimism concerning the future of Western Christendom among that vast majority of educated French Catholics uninfected by any Renaissance virus was certainly excusable during the first half of the reign of François I, when France seemed likely to go the way, at best, of Henry VIII's England. Playing a confusing and subtle game of his own in the blind-man's-bluff of European diplomacy, François was combining normal Gallicanism with marked indulgence for the growing Calvinist groups at home which his sister Marguerite then openly protected and encouraged. Favour came abruptly to an end in 1534, when increasing truculence from the Royal protégés, in the shape of threats and insults, the destruction of statues of the saints and the defiling of churches, culminated on the night of October 17–18 in the "Affair of the Placards". A series of fresh threats and odious mockeries of the Blessed Sacrament, printed in Switzerland, were posted up in public places at Paris and five other cities, one being attached to the door of the King's apartments at Amboise. Such a wave of anger swept through France as swept Athens after the mutilation of the Hermae, and François changed his mind. "Perceiving," says Jacques Bainville, "that the adherents of the Reform, with some lack of judgment, were about to lay hands on him, he disengaged himself without brutality", and order was restored, not without the unpleasant consequences for a few of the trouble-makers which that phrase then implied and the law provided. But if François ceased to indulge the Reform, he remained in his relations with the Holy See the stiffest of Gallicans, like Henri II after him, and Léon Daudet's deduction from those vigorous swipes at the Roman Curia in the Fourth Book that Rabelais became the Crown's chosen propagandist seems sound enough. Cardinal du Bellay introduced the Doctor into the Royal entourage in the late 1530's; he was the ideal pen-pusher for the purpose. No question of religion was involved in this clash with Rome, as need scarcely be added; it was part of the recurring family trouble over the definition of spheres of authority and the collection of dues—what is nowadays called the Business Angle, which gave Luther his opportunity.

Hence the carefree zest with which the Doctor bombards the Temporal Power; a zest contrasting quaintly with his anxiety, resembling that of a small boy with a too-ready catapult, to placate a glowering Sorbonne by purging his first two popular works of anti-Sorbonnical gibes and introducing a wise and weighty Catholic theologian into the Third. Given his temperament, a few more Vatican windows than the Curia's were naturally liable to suffer in the process. If such indiscriminate energy seems odd in a priest who addressed the Holy See personally on three occasions with filial humility, and was treated with marked benevolence by Paul III, the period can show far odder behaviour. An historic case of the liberal outlook is that of another of Rabelais' patrons, Odet, Cardinal de Châtillon, who turned Calvinist and, excommunicate but still garbed in his Roman scarlet, married publicly; for which affront to his religion Ronsard cancelled the dedication to Châtillon of one of his volumes of verse. Unlike Marguerite de Valois, who by poetic justice received the Last Sacraments from a friar of that Franciscan Order on which she expends such venom in her *Heptameron*, the cardinal-apostate never recanted, and might have continued to wear the livery of the Sacred College in domestic bliss with *Madame la Cardinale* till the end of his life, had it been a peaceful one. Is this eccentricity much more marked than that of the Catholic great lady, sister to Ronsard's love Isabeau de Limeuil, who died with a fiddler at her bedside playing by order *La Défaite des Suisses*?

As a hundred more instances could be cited to show, Rabelais' age is a tumultous and, in comparison with the Middle Ages, a mentally unbalanced one: perfidious, ostentatious, arrogant, avid of licence, malignant, essentially greedy, gross, and violent. But as Lucien Romier has remarked, with its violence went fine gestures, and even in the art of murder it had style. Its fount of all the arts of living was Italy, where the peak of human achievement attained in three different media by Michelangelo did not spare that godlike nose from being bashed by Torregiano with equal vigour and grace. A famous textbook of good manners, *Il Cortegiano*, by Baldassare Castiglione of Urbino,

> That grammar school of courtesies
> Where wit and beauty learned their trade
> Upon Urbino's windy hill,

and a European best-seller before the 1560's, set the note for the polite. Style is observable in every department of Renaissance self-expression; in the goldsmithery and rascalities of a Cellini, the motets and songs of a De Lassus and a Janequin, the inlaying of beautiful armour, the daily measurement of English Jesuits being slowly lengthened on the rack, the dedications of a Copernicus, the enormous and intricate ballets at the Louvre, the splendour of the Loire châteaux, and in that great flood of sonnets pouring, it would sometimes seem, from the pen of every Renaissance man capable of holding one, from Shakespeare and the masters of the Pléiade down to a Government spy and agent-provocateur like Anthony Munday, who likewise wrote very passable lyrics, and figures in the Oxford Book of English Verse. Even rival Reformers hurling threats and insults at each other studied their style; some of Luther's outbursts are as choice as anything out of Rabelais.

All this care for form derived from the patronage of the artist in every medium by ruinously-expensive Courts, not to speak of a wealthy rising bourgeoisie. No higher standard in living has ever been maintained, despite the high cost of this performance, due to Spain's exploitation of her New World gold and silver mines. Yet even more striking than the monstrous luxury in dress we contemplate in Renaissance portraits is, I think, the faces of the sitters; so often disturbing, so often faintly sinister. When, above a doublet fit for a jovial millionaire pearly-king, the spectator is fixed by, for example, the snakish eye of a Bacon[1] or a Cecil, a certain cool shock results, however swiftly one may remind oneself, and on very good grounds, that such trappings may in some cases have hidden a fine lousy shirt. By its recorded faces the Renaissance gives its secret away to a large extent. With

---

[1] "Dr. Harvey tolde me it [Bacon's] was like the Eie of a viper." (Aubrey, *Brief Lives*.)

B

a great deal of epicene splendour go many hard, crafty, brooding, enigmatic, sneering, cruel, or merely piggish eyes; a feature not exclusive to this or any other age, but oddly at variance with such creations of Whiggish fancy as the Noble Elizabethan, a confection only a trifle more whimsical than Rousseau's Noble Savage. It takes no great effort to discern in many portraits of the period those seeds of doubt, despair, and dissolution which have flowered so richly some four centuries later.

Or even flowered at the time. A swift multiplication of sects, some of them barely sane, and phantasmagoric as a dream of Hieronimus Bosch, began in Luther's own lifetime, as Ronsard points out with sardonic relish to Calvin's lieutenant Béza. These, and the emergence of a string of self-proclaimed Messiahs from the bloodthirsty Anabaptist lunatic John of Leyden in the 1530's to (so far) the Rev. Mr. Smyth-Piggott in the 1890's, are no less a natural result of the Renaissance than the frenzy of chauvinist nationalism, affecting even what Kipling's sahibs called the Fuzzy-Wuzzy, which has split our present world into a mosaic-pattern of reciprocal offensiveness and hate. Worship of the God-State—the cornerstone of Lutheranism, as Dean Inge once remarked—has so long been an established religion that it is difficult to imagine that civilised men were ever shocked by it. Like Luther's authorisation of bigamy to the Landgrave of Hesse, it was one of those innovations which for a time command only the adhesion of a select group of advanced thinkers, but in due course spread outwards and downwards, according to the law of inevitable progress, until they are accepted by all who have emancipated themselves from outworn dogma. A curious weakness is detectable in Luther, as in Melanchthon, Bucer, and other German thinkers of the period. They knew spasms of fear on viewing some results of their labours. "All the waters of the Elbe," wrote Melanchthon to a friend, "cannot supply enough tears to weep the disasters of the Reform." "These things," confessed Luther to Zwingli, referring to chaos, crime, and suicidal mania prevailing in liberated Germany, "terrify me." There was a blacker moment when Luther spoke to this same Swiss confrère and rival of submitting to a General Council of the Church, but this impulse soon waned. It is interesting to think what might have happened to European history had it conquered him.

Of the three absolute princes whose ambitions intensified the troubles of the Western world in Rabelais' time only François I, King of France, his first royal patron, may concern us here. Titian's portrait possibly flatters François I a trifle. The anonymous portrait at Hampton Court may be a truer likeness. With a curiously lustful sidelong leer on his narrow-eyed, black-bearded, ovoid features the Valois is squeezing a slim feminine waist, at this particular moment his wife Eleanora's, as she looks up at him coyly, holding a caduceus toy. The royal leer is, one feels, about to merge at any moment into a wink at the spectator. But the *roi artiste et galant homme* was a great deal more than a sensualist. Like his rival Henry VIII an athlete and a man of culture, unlike Henry a born soldier, he combined furious gallantry in battle with boasting and rhodomontade in a very Gallic manner. Insatiable of *la gloire*, a passionate and apparently discerning patron of the best artists of his age, French and Italian —did he not pay his honoured guest Leonardo twenty thousand pounds, in modern money, for the Gioconda?—he patronised literature and scholarship likewise in princely wise. The Collège de France remains his monument still, however much it disappointed Budé's dreams, and to the appointment of Claude Garamond as Royal Printer typographers owe those fine founts of Greek, Roman, and Italic which glorify the first Plantin printings. As the personification of the French nation at one of its best periods, strong, vital, prosperous, a power in Europe, infinitely diverse in regional laws and customs as in costume, yet united in a national bond of moderation and good sense, François has perhaps no equal save Louis XIV. His elegant clothes, studded with jewels and stiff with gold or silver embroideries, are as much the deliberate expression of a keen and supple intelligence, on which religion sat very lightly, practising the art of absolute kingship, as his patronage of Rabelais and his entire lack of conscience in European diplomacy—his allies included the Turk and the Algerian pirates—which was all a Machiavelli could have desired. It is characteristic of François that having been described in public by the Emperor Charles V, after a particularly blatant doublecross, as a cad (*lâche*), having instantly challenged the Emperor to a duel, and having had his challenge promptly accepted, he dropped the matter. Much as he loved a fight,

superb swordsman as he was, he knew when to deny himself a
pleasure for a greater diplomatic gain.

Such is Rabelais' first royal patron, and with such a one behind
him the most reckless satirist could congratulate himself. As it
happened, there were forces in France which even an absolute
monarch did not care to try too far. It is possible that the Doctor's
prudent flight to Metz amused the cynical king on his dying-bed
as much as anything in *The Third Book of Pantagruel*.

3

For some three centuries it has been a matter of routine among
the learned, following La Bruyère, to label Rabelais an enigma,
which he undoubtedly is; and the best modern authorities continue to contradict each other vigorously over his state of mind.
If, as Gaston Boissier said, there are two Ciceros, there are at
least six Rabelais. Clearly a freethinker, declares M. Abel
Lefranc of the Collège de France, himself of that persuasion and
incorporating in his recent definitive edition of the Works the
final word, so far, in Rabelaisian research. By no means clearly,
demonstrates M. Etienne Gilson, who enjoys the advantage over
M. Lefranc of an intimate acquaintance with the science of
theology. To Ferdinand Brunetière Rabelais is no mystery at all,
being a natural pagan *dans le sens étendu, dans le sens large, dans le
sens profond du mot*. On the fringes of the great floating dust-cloud
of Rabelaisian commentary—like Dante he has fascinated cranks
of every description—may be glimpsed a variety of strange labels
attaching to him, though I do not recollect his having been so
far proved, like Dante, a Waldensian pastor, a crypto-Freemason,
or an anarchist. A study by a Cambridge don of the 1920's
seems to make him a kind of uninhibited Cambridge don, in the
Porson tradition, whereas in the eyes of Léon Daudet he has every
mark of a militant Action Française leader born before his time.
Among the smoothest of all modern judgments on the Doctor
seems to me to be that of the late Professor George Saintsbury,
who found in him "nothing incompatible with an orthodoxy
which would be recognised as sufficient by Christendom at large,
leaving out of the question those points of doctrine and practice
on which Christians differ"; which embraces the whole roaring

chaos of Protestantism very satisfactorily. It may, therefore, be cheerfully assumed by lovers of Rabelais with no pretension to scholarship that the truth about the Doctor is still anybody's guess.

There is no doubt, however, about the size of the Rabelaisian Enigma. A cloud of unknowing envelops even the Doctor's beginning and end. Though his family was of the solid legal middle-class, so jealous of *paperasserie*, no record exists of the date of his birth. When and where he died, a famous man, is unknown also. Even the place of his burial is conjectural; according to the only evidence, an eighteenth-century anthology of epitaphs, his grave lay under a fig-tree in the cemetery of St. Paul near the Bastille, long since obliterated under the Rue des Jardins-St. Paul. A story, dated a century earlier, that he was buried in the nave of St. Paul's church, which stood in this street until the Revolution destroyed it, seems to be hearsay. His career bristles at intervals likewise with question-marks, as does his entire personality, or what one of his *bêtes noires*, the Subtle Doctor, Duns Scotus, whom he never read, would call his "this-ness", *haecceitas*. How, for example, does one reconcile the arrogant young Franciscan rebel, drunk on classical Greek and apparently at daggers drawn with his Order, with the diligent priest of Clement VII's indult authorising his exchange to the Benedictine habit? How much religion remained when Dom François, having qualified in medicine, that fruitful breeding-ground of materialism, was authorised from Rome once more to exchange into the secular priesthood? How deep were his sympathies with known apostates like Étienne Dolet and Bonaventure des Périers, for some time his boon-companions, and with the friends and allies of Geneva— in due course to be pilloried by him as *les demoniacles Calvins, imposteurs de Genève*—in the circle of Marguerite de Valois, and how significant is his shrug at Scaliger as "a thorough-going atheist"? And once more, those gibes at the Temporal Power, Rabelais' contribution to the Gallican campaign of the 1540–50's, which fill the Fourth Book—how far do they mask hostility to the Spiritual? And if the savage and posthumous Fifth Book is not, as the best modern scholars agree, Rabelais' work at all but a Calvinist broadside, how far may his literary remains have provided ammunition for Rome's enemies?

Many more questions will loom as we proceed. To one of the chief of them the only reasonable answer seems to have been suggested by Léon Daudet. That high-spirited violence, that recurring recklessness in vituperation, that mighty spate of verbalism may surely be taken to have some direct connection with the Septembral Juice of which Rabelais is so indefatigable a propagandist? He was, as Daudet points out, a typical son of Touraine, where a more or less continuous state of mild alcoholism from dawn to dusk is not uncommon among the rural population, or was not some years ago.[1] To assume that his perpetual paeans in praise of wine are pure "literature" therefore seems to me, as to Daudet, absurd. Without being in any sense a sot the Doctor may well, I think, have put the bottle to very regular use, with much benefit to his pen. The jovial epitaphs by Ronsard and Du Bellay assume this quite clearly, as do one or two attacks during his lifetime. They could hardly have lacked some basis.

> Une vigne prendra naissance
> De l'estomac et de la pance
> Du bon Rabelais, qui boivait
> Toujours cependant qu'il vivoit . . .[2]

Ronsard's long jest indeed depicts a Rabelais of Flemish rather than Tourangeau breed; red-faced, roaring, sleeves tucked up, rolling flagon in hand among the pots and pans, *comme une grenouille en la fange*. Legend? Poetic licence? Who can tell? Bishop Richard Corbet in Aubrey's *Brief Lives*, like Rabelais "a very learned and ingeniose man", was wont to doff gravity very efficiently whenever he and his chaplain locked themselves into the wine-cellar. "Then first he layes down his Episcopall hat—*There lyes the Doctor.* Then he putts off his gowne—*There lyes the Bishop.* Then 'twas, *Here's to thee, Corbet*, and *Here's to thee, Lushington.*" Similarly may Dr. Rabelais (who could have written Aubrey's lines) have discarded a normal decorum at intervals and given himself whole-heartedly to the *Dive Bouteille*, and that notable connoisseur M. André Simon has rightly reserved him a place in his *Bibliotheca Gastronomica*[3] among the leading œnophils of the ages.

---

[1] *Flambeaux*, 1927.
[2] "From the belly and paunch of the good Rabelais, who drank continuously as he lived, a vine shall spring . . ."
[3] London, The Wine and Food Society, 1953.

So, turning Rabelais' pages, one may not unreasonably visualise their author as regularly pausing to refocillate—Aubrey's engaging verb—his spirits and style with a swingeing draught of the wine of his country. And if, in current prose, the Doctor may occasionally grieve the judicious by appearing a trifle "lit", he is sound enough in principle, as a cloud of witnesses agree; among them the great Blackstone, writing with a bottle of vintage port ever at his elbow, and drawing the energy and fortitude required to reduce the corpus of British Law to relative coherence from the same unfailing source to which men of genius have applied from Horace down, utilising the finest brain-tonic known to man more or less rationally according to temperament and opportunity. Much leaden pedantry and frigid mumbling might have been obviated, it occurs to one, if a few of the Doctor's expounders had done the same.

Clearly the theory advanced by Daudet, himself a man of medicine and letters, solves not a few of Rabelaisian problems over which many bald heads continue to nod, assiduously and without avail. It explains not a few of the Doctor's contradictions, incoherencies, obscurities, hiatuses, quirks, confusions, lapses in continuity, and announcements of portents which never happen. More than once the Doctor forgets his promises or suddenly changes his mind. Laboriously to dig for some abstruse explanation like a pig rooting for truffles seems a painful waste of time, the inevitable result being a string of hypotheses. The learned fight notably shy, I have always observed, of the possibility that Doctor Rabelais was ever under the influence of the grape he so constantly praises and recommends, literally and in metaphor, at the top of his lungs. We do not actually know that the Doctor tipped the bottle lavishly. We only know that he says he did— for example in the final chapter of the Second Book:

My Head akes a little, and I perceive that the Registers of my braine are somewhat jumbled and disordered with this Septembral Juice [ceste purée de septembre] . . .

And again, from the Prologue to the Third:

Stay a little till I suck up a Draught of this Bottle; it is my true and only Helicon; it is my Caballine Fountain; it is my sole

Enthusiasm. Drinking thus I meditate, discourse, resolve, and conclude. After that the Epilogue is made, I laugh, I write, I compose, and drink again.

Henry James did not describe his writing-technique with daintier concision, and it is difficult to conceive the reluctance of so many grave and good men to grasp this jovially-proferred key to not a few Rabelaisian puzzles.

And it is (God forbid) no intention of these pages to grieve the learned, to whom the Doctor extends such a comfortable benediction in his first Prologue, in words that may well end this chapter. "Be frolick now, my Lads, cheer up your hearts and joyfully read the rest, with all the ease of your body and profit of your reines; but hearken joltheads, vietsdazes, or dickens take ye, remember to drink a health to me for the like favour again, and I will pledge you instantly, *tout aresmetys.*"

The last two words are, I find, a locution from Gascony, meaning "Right away".

II

Grey Friar

I

ROOKS IN THE WALNUTS, STARLINGS IN THE VINES, A FARMSTEAD
called La Devinière, a grove of willows, the workshop of Jean
Denyau the wheelwright in the nearby hamlet, the cakes of
Lerné, three miles away, which eaten fresh from the oven with
muscat grapes are "celestial food for Breakfast" and of notable
value to the costive—these are the chief memories of Rabelais'
childhood scattered through the Four Books, with an especially
tender recollection, as may well be imagined, of the home vine-
yard. Do we gather from the shout of "O lachryma Christi!
c'est de la Devinière!" at Gargantua's birth-feast that the
domestic product was sweet and white, recalling the Neapolitan
vintage? An amusing little wine, no doubt? Brusque, a trifle
tactless? The Doctor himself does not indulge in esoteric fiddle-
faddle ("It's all alcohol to me!" one can hear him cry, shocking
some dévot in the Belloc manner), nor is he even interested, like
the eminent Arnaud de Villeneuve, one of his predecessors at the
Faculty of Medicine of Montpellier, in the therapeutic aspects
of the grape. Nor, so far, have I discovered any monograph
since his time discussing the impact of the Septembral Juice,
watered or otherwise, on his infant metabolism. It might—who
knows?—have been as significant as the influence of geometry
on the child Pascal.

La Devinière, which the majority of authorities accept, following unshakable local tradition and his own references, as
Rabelais' birthplace, stands still intact three miles to the south-
west of Chinon in Touraine, in a countryside practically un-
changed after four hundred years.

It is a small, plain fifteenth-century house of stone, with farm-
yard and outbuildings. Taken over by the State within recent

years as an historical monument, it has so skilfully been restored, refurbished, and turned into a spick-and-span museum of Rabelaisiana that the Doctor would barely recognise it. A spacious original hearth adorns the oak-beamed living-room occupying the entire ground floor, all neat nowadays as a new pin. Above are two rooms with a loft. In the larger of these, said to be the room of Rabelais' birth, a number of rustic *graffiti* used to decorate the dusky walls, among them a long-since illegible scribble in cursive Greek by some past devotee seized with the Renaissance spirit. These have been banished, together with the little round pillars which when I first knew La Devinière bordered the exterior stone staircase leading to the upper floor, over which extends the penthouse-roof, supported by a couple of long slender pillars of square stone. But from the top of the steps the eye is refreshed by the same gracious landscape which was the theatre of the Picrocholian War. Dozing in summer-afternoon sunshine, the long gently-undulating meadows with their brooks and springs, their groves and clumps of walnut, willow, and oak, a distant belfry or two on rising ground above its cluster of mellow red-tiled steadings, typical Chinonnais country, lie infinitely serene and sedative. Viewed as I last saw it not long ago, with thunderclouds massing ominously over the wide sky and one last dazzling oblique sunray lighting up the tall white fairy-tale château of Coudray-Montpensier in the middle fore-ground, the scene seemed of a sudden to tremble with the same electrical vibrations which so affected the two scholarly Oxford ladies who had that adventure in Marie-Antoinette's Trianon at the beginning of the century, and the clucking of distant hens was charged with mysterious expectancy. The moment passed. It is not given to everybody to take a backward step in Time.

The unrecorded year of Rabelais' birth has been conjecturally fixed, after much learned argument and contradiction, at 1495, in the reign of Charles VIII; his friend the poet Clément Marot was born in the same year. Rabelais' father, Maître Antoine, was a prominent lawyer of Chinon, owning a large house in the town, the farm of La Devinière, a fine estate at Chavigny-en-Vallée, ten miles down the Loire, and other land at Seuilly and on the Anjou border. Hence even if he were not actually born at La Devinière, the child François may be taken to have spent more than one long summer holiday at that well-loved homestead with its tenant-farmer. Since the preposterous Rabelais Legend, which will be surveyed in its place, makes Maître Antoine an innkeeper, his indignant shade must be propitiated with a correct *état civil.* He was a licentiate in law, Seneschal of Lerné, and an advocate of the *siège royal* of Chinon, acting for some time as Deputy Lieutenant-General and senior barrister in the Courts; in other words a man of parts and substance and a leading citizen. His house in the Rue de la Lamproie was, judging by its successor on the site, now numbered 15, a spacious one, with, presumably, the same wing on either side enclosing a paved entrance court-yard. His wife, *née* Frapin, came from Angers in Anjou, where her brother Joseph was living till well into young François' adolescence. Maître Antoine Rabelais had two other sons, Jamet and Antoine, both older than François, and a daughter. None of them figures even in local history.

Extremely little is known of François' childhood. Born at La Devinière, he would have been baptised in the little parish church of Seuilly, less than a mile away. At the now-ruined Benedictine abbey in the same hamlet, over which on rising ground to the south towers, today as in his time, the mirific château of Coudray-Montpensier, he is believed to have received his earliest schooling; the monastery's vineyards will be the scene in the First Book of Frère Jean des Entommeures' epic clash with the invading forces of Picrochole, King of Lerné, and the remains of spacious cellars still testify to their extent. It would seem that the child stayed at Angers now and again with his uncle. In the original prologue to the Fourth Book is a reminiscence of Uncle Joseph Frapin's gift for composing and singing fine merry carols, *beaux et joyeux noëlz*, in the Poitevin dialect. On a wall of the lower hall of his house on St. Laurence's Mound was pictured an exploit of his one-eyed talking jay, Goitrou by name, a bird a child would long remember, famed for its zeal in urging all and sundry to drink, and still more for leading a flock of local jays into battle against a flock of invading magpies and gloriously routing them "at the Malchara Cross". Rabelais makes this affair a presage of the defeat of the Bretons by Charles VIII in 1486, since magpies' tails resemble more or less the *hermines* in the ducal arms of Brittany. It is one of his duller stories, winding slowly to the

point that the jay Goitrou's battle-cry, "Crocquez pie!"—
"Gobble the magpies!"—passed into a local proverb meaning
"Drink deep and drink hearty". From all this one might gather
that Uncle Joseph Frapin was, as his nephew turned out to be,
a stout man at the bottle; possibly the only one in a starchy legal
clan. His nephew styles him *seigneur de Sainct George*, so he may
have owned some land.

With this everything that is known of Rabelais' infancy comes
to an end, and amateurs of what is called "child-psychology"
will need a very strong glass indeed to detect much of relevance
in the childhood of either of his two giants. Doubtless baby
François "wallowed and rowled up and down" as lavishly as
baby Gargantua; it must have been difficult to keep him off
the manure-heap at La Devinière. One may see him likewise
staring owlishly from the open doorway at Denyau the wheelwright whistling at his work. Early affection for this obscure
rustic craftsman—the name is still a local one—who makes Gargantua's first oxcart and "fair greate" wooden horse is discernible
in the Doctor's remembrances after thirty years and more. That
François' infant rages were instantly quelled and pacified by
"the sound of Pintes and Flaggons", on hearing which he "would
on a sudden fall into an Extasie, as if he had then tasted of the
joyes of Paradise", seems to me extremely likely. The significance
of those pleasant clashings and tinklings would be learned at the
right time. Perhaps, like baby Pantagruel, when he grew tired
of his cradle he smashed it. For him too, perhaps, were made
rattles of blown-up hogs'-bladders, such as serve for "the Play,
Pastime and Disport of little Children"; and perhaps he, likewise, was later given a tiny crossbow with which to shoot at
small birds. By this time one could also see him conning his
first hornbook on a bench at Seuilly.

Manfully resisting the temptation to derive a lifelong resistance
to discipline automatically from early repressions, known or unknown, I think it can be legitimately assumed, in the absence of
evidence, that Maître Antoine Rabelais' rule of his household,
however kindly, may have been strict. What the Renaissance
child of this class had to endure in England is set down in charming John Aubrey's *Description of the North Division of Wiltshire*,
into which Aubrey weaves memories collected from old Mr.

Tyndale, his neighbour, who had been a child in the reign of Elizabeth Tudor. "From the time of Erasmus," notes Aubrey, "till about twenty years past"—a period ending roughly in the late 1550's—the English gentry and upper bourgeoisie brought up their children with such severity that "the child perfectly loathed the sight of his parents, as the slave his torture . . . Gentlemen of thirty and forty years old were made to stand like mutes and fooles bareheaded before their parents". On such occasions boys might have to stand at attention for a couple of hours with "one hand at the band-string, the other behind them"; girls were frequently beaten by their mothers with the half-yard-long handles of "prodigious fans" for failing to do likewise; if their strength failed they might ask permission to kneel on a cushion brought by a serving-man. Whether a similar régime prevailed in French households I have not discovered. There is no hint of it in the early recollections of Pierre de Ronsard, whose relations with his parents were close and affectionate, but his case may not be typical. Except for jolly Uncle Joseph Frapin, Rabelais never alludes to any of his family, even obliquely; which probably has no significance whatsoever.

One thing about his childhood can be taken for granted. A considerable amount of it must perforce have been spent in the house in the Rue de la Lamproie, Maître Antoine Rabelais' residence during term-time, or most of the year. This ample house gave place a century or so later to another, itself now venerable. A marble wall-plaque recalls the vanished home of Rabelais; the *courette* behind the tall wooden gates must be its only surviving relic. Yet delicious little Chinon has not been so raped and mangled by Progress, so far, as unduly to dismay a great revisiting shade. Though Innocent the pastrycook's shop in the Rue du Grenier-à-Sel, which Panurge remembers in the great storm, was swept into Limbo long ago, the medieval Hostel de la Monnaie, or Mint, in the same street remains, with the fifteenth-century archway of the nearby underground tavern called the Painted Cellar, and most of Chinon's little narrow crooked streets preserve their old names, cheek by jowl, of course, with that Danton-Diderot-Gambetta-Hugo-Rousseau-Voltaire sequence with which the bravos of the Third Republic afflicted every beautiful ancient town in France. With royal, almost

visible contempt every one of the gracious medieval and Renaissance houses so carefully preserved in the Rue Voltaire repudiates
that destroyer's name. Windbag Gambetta is fortunately banished to a boulevard of his own on the outer fringes of the town,
and if it is an annoyance to find lachrymose Jean-Jacques of
Geneva in possession of a stretch of one of Chinon's two main
thoroughfares, Dr. Rabelais would be pacified, I think, on finding
his own name on the other. He would certainly be far from
displeased to note a highly reputable *Omelette Gargamelle* offered
permanently by Chinon's principal restaurant, and to discover
that the red wine of Chinon in its half-dozen variants (that of the
Grille especially) lacks none of its traditional smoothness or the
delicate wild-strawberry aroma he loved so well.

   The spell of his essential Chinon I am by no means alone in
finding recurrent and considerable. Arthur Machen has conveyed its first impact on him in the 1890's in words inseparable,
to me, from memories of the town. "The train passes through
Chinon Forest, and you leave the station and come out into the
sunlight. Here is a narrow river valley: the clear Vienne in the
middle of it; to the left a gentle rising land, rich with vines; to
the right a long, golden, precipitous cliff, golden in such a sunlight as we never see in England. As in the backgrounds of the
old Italian masters, the trees stand out clearly, vividly, distinctly
against the sky; so was it at Chinon. That long, mouldering, and
golden cliff was surmounted by the walls of the old castle, golden
and mouldering also, irradiated; and from the river to the cliff
the town climbed up; narrow ways, winding ways, steep ways,
and every here and there the grey-blue *tourelles* of the fifteenth-
century houses piercing upwards, and the dark mass of the forest
stretching far and far away beyond."[1] And for Machen, as for
every man of sensibility, the mellow sun of the Chinnonais casts
across all that countryside for ever the long gigantic shadows of
Pantagruel, Friar John, and Panurge, "the three who are yet
one, who came to him, we must conjecture, in clouds and darkness and uncertainties, as he listened to the new song of the
vineyards, and the vine and the outpoured wine". Something of
vanished gaiety still hangs in the air over Chinon. I have, indeed,
known a moment, in the courtyard of the Boule d'Or inn of a

[1] *Things Near and Far*, ch. iv.

starry autumn night, when Orion seemed to be cracking his belt with enormous mirth, amid the laughter of the spheres. *En cestuy temps, qui fut la saison des vendanges* . . . But the singers have departed, and there are no more songs.

> Do not expect again a phoenix hour,
> The triple-towered sky, the dove complaining,
> Sudden the rain of gold and heart's first ease. . . .

Under the moon the shapely old houses of the Grand Carroi, the Rue Marceau, and the Rue Voltaire with their gables, crockets, corbels, buttresses, round or octagonal *tourelles*, and mullioned lights continue to tantalise the questioner with that air, common to all such, of withholding impenetrable secrets and dreams incommunicable. Of these Balzac managed to catch a glimpse. If the *Contes Drôlatiques* have not the veritable Rabelaisian bouquet they are often pretty near it. The native background of Aloysius Bertrand's *Gaspard de la Nuit*, again, that minor classic of the Romantico-Gothic revival, has always seemed to me to be Chinon more than a half-imagined Dijon. For the rest of us these old stones preserve all their mysteries inviolate. Less reticent are the remains of the royal castle high on the cliff dominating Chinon town. Twice in history brilliantly floodlit by Clio, Muse of Publicity, it stands, despite a sore banging in the wars of religion and a final dismantling by Richelieu, tremendous and impressive still with its massy remaining towers and bastions. In the now roofless Great Hall which witnessed St. Joan's first encounter with the Dauphin, the mantel against which Charles may have leaned, half dazed with joy, as he talked to her is still in its place, desolate, battered by weather, a national monument odiously neglected. Seventy years later in the same hall, Cesare Borgia, Duke of Valentinois, handed to Louis XII the Bull from Rome annulling the King's marriage with holy, meek, malformed Jeanne de Valois, recently raised to the altars. In Brantôme's pages the trumpets ring out again and the bull-emblazoned Borgia bannerols precede the duke and his glittering suite of cavaliers in cloth-of-gold as they ride slowly up Chinon's higher main street. François Rabelais was then, so far as conjectural calculation avails, about three years old. Maître Antoine Rabelais must certainly have been among the town's notables officially welcoming the gorgeous Borgia ruffian, who it appears today has been, like the rest of the family, somewhat mishandled by the Whigs—but what un-Whiggish figure in history has not? The child François must have heard all about this signal event many times as he grew up. He will not recall Cesare's visit to Chinon in the Books, or even in those surviving letters from Rome some years hence.

When he last looked up at the castle from Chinon's streets we do not know. There is a quip in the Prologue to the Second Book about his just having returned by Pantagruel's leave from a visit to his cow-country, *pays de vache*, to see if any of his relations were alive. If this means anything, he must have been in Chinon some time in 1533–4; there is no evidence of any later visit. The only surviving document bearing his undoubted signature, namely the Montpellier University matriculation register, attests that in 1530 he was still attaching *Chinonensis* or *Chinonnais* to his surname, in the provincial style of the time, but in the fine autographed set of Galen now in Sheffield University Library he has dropped it, and I suspect the sudden panegyric of Chinon in one of the last chapters of what some call the "Fifth Book" was merely popped in by its unknown author to lend his work a more authentic air.

> Which is the oldest City in the World? ask'd Pantagruel. 'Tis Chinon, Sir, or Cainon in Touraine, said I. I know, return'd Pantagruel, where Chinon lies, and the Painted Cellar also, having my self drunk there many a Glass of cool Wine; neither do I doubt but that Chinon is an ancient Town; witness its Blazon; I own 'tis said twice or thrice,
>
> > *Little Town,*
> > *Great Renown,*
> > *On old Stone,*
> > *Long has stood ;*
> > *There's the Vienne, if you look down ;*
> > *If you look up, there's the Wood.*

An ensuing whimsy about Chinon's antiquity, attributing its foundation to Cain, is not a bad shot at the Doctor's manner, but it seems to me that by 1550, when the Guises took him up, he

had become too much a citizen of Rome and Paris and a protégé
of the great to retain much sentimentality for his native town,
to which there is no reference in the Four Books barring Panurge's
cry at sea.

But Chinon certainly remembers him, and his presence broods
over it palpably. Anyone desiring to tread there in his actual
footsteps can, I think, assume without fear of denunciation by
lurking pedants that the boy may often have accompanied his
father from the house in the Rue de la Lamproie to the lawcourts near the present Town Hall, and he may well be imagined
thus, pacing circumspectly and attentive to the discourse of
Maître Antoine, whom one pictures as being constantly button-
holed in the street by grave personages municipal and legal, and
saluted on every side. That familiarity with the law and that
command of legal patter which stick out everywhere in the Four
Books may be traced, I imagine, to a source as early as this. In
Mr. Justice Bridlegoose's exposition of the manner in which
imperfect lawsuits are cared for and tenderly brought to their
proper dimension, as cubs are licked into shape by the mother-
bear, is it difficult to hear the satiric echo of more than one
portentous voice droning at Maître Antoine's table in term-time?

. . . but when there are heaps of these Legiformal Papers packed,
piled, laid up together, impoaked, insatcheled, and put up in Bags,
then is it that with a good Reason we may term that Suit to which,
as pieces, parcels, parts, portions and members thereof they do
pertain and belong, well-formed and fashioned, big-limmed, strong
set, and in each and all of its Dimensions most compleatly membred.
Because *forma dat esse rei, L. si is qui ff. ad leg. Falcid. in C. cum delicta
extra de rescript. . Barbat. cons.* 12, *lib. II.* And before him [etc.,
etc., etc.].

It is unfortunate but inevitable that so much of Rabelais'
early history should have to consist of a very few known facts
and a whole string of conjectures gleaned chiefly from his works.
Even Chinon's indefatigable historian, M. Gabriel Richault, has
been unable to discover anything in particular about his remarkable fellow-townsman at this period, which is perhaps not surprising. The Local-Boy-Makes-Good cultus is a comparatively
recent thing. Were Rabelais flourishing today the Chinonnais

would undoubtedly be exploiting him with all the zest of the
canny men of Kirriemuir, who were pointing out the—or at least
a—Window in Thrums and selling the tourist souvenir-pin-
cushions while the distant sobs of the Anglo-Saxon were still
being borne, like the Mock Turtle's, on the evening breeze. A
Renaissance town took its phoenixes more calmly. In those days,
also, literary gentlemen did not publish their autobiographies at
twenty-five.

2

At a period when children all over Europe were packed off to
a university at the age of ten, a custom continuing for nearly
another century, the question of young François Rabelais' future
must have become a topic at the dinner-table in the Rue de la
Lamproie round about the year 1504.

He is not to be destined for any university; which considering
his temperament may be just as well, the contemporary academic
life being rough and its discipline severe. Missing this experience
will not, however, deter him from that onslaught in the First
Book on the celebrated Collège de Montaigu, in the University
of Paris, which could have been added to the chatter of Old
Gaffer Hearsay in the Land of Satin. Thus vehemently does
Gargantua's tutor Ponocrates deliver himself to the child's
father, Grangousier:

> My sovereign Lord, think not that I have placed him in that lowsie
> Colledge, which they call *Montague*; I had rather have put him
> amongst the gravediggers of Sanct Innocent, so enormous is the
> cruelty and villany I have known there; for the Galley-slaves are
> far better used amongst the Moor and Tartars, the murtherers in
> the criminal dungeons, yea, the very dogs in your House, than are
> the poor wretched Students in the aforesaid Colledge; and if I
> were King of Paris, the devil take me if I would not set it on fire
> and burne both Principal and Regents, for suffering this inhumanity
> to be exercised before their eyes.

It would seem that apart from listening to some of the tavern
gossip of the Sorbonne quarter the Doctor based this diatribe on
his idol Erasmus' objurgations in the "Ichthyophagia" chapter
of the *Colloquies*. In his late twenties Erasmus went up to Montaigu

for a few terms to read for a degree in theology on a senior bursary procured him by his patron the Bishop of Cambrai, and loathed the place from roof to cellars. Bad wine, putrid mutton, barbarous conversation, bleak and grimy rooms, mould in the eggs, ice in the washing-bowl—the great man vents his spleen *à l'érasmienne* twenty years later like a mother's ewe-lamb suffering his first term at a tough British public school. Even for its dons Montaigu was a redoubtable experience, being a college run for divinity students on the lines of apostolic poverty with hard work, hard fare, super-Trappist discipline, and plenty of punishment. It may be noted that neither of Erasmus' most illustrious fellow-alumni of the Renaissance period, Loyola and Calvin, has a word to say against the régime.[1] Life at Montaigu, like life at eighteenth-century Eton, demanded what is called "guts", with which Erasmus was not over-equipped. In any case Montaigu was hardly a target for outsiders. Unquestioning acceptance of Rabelais' abuse as evidence argues in some of his commentators an attractive simplicity.

However, Maître Antoine ruled out the universities, doubtless having reasons for so doing. He was certainly not inhibited by questions of expense or any other domestic complications. As families went at the time his own was abnormally small, and as he was a reasonably prosperous man of assured position, the disposal of his sons cannot have presented him with problems which harried struggling contemporaries of the same social class carrying the responsibility for anything from six children to sixteen. Fortunately or unfortunately, the Renaissance father, like the Victorian Papa, knew one infallible outlet for surplus or expendable male offspring. The Victorian paterfamilias (compare Dickens *père*) solved his problem by heaving out a few of his progeny one by one to the uttermost parts of a then far-flung and highly-convenient Empire to rule the Native. The last resort of his Renaissance prototype (compare Luther *père*) was the nearest monastery, and whatever anonymous hack wrote the bitter anti-Catholic diatribe known to those of the learned who still accept it as *The Fifth Book of Pantagruel* scores a legitimate

---

[1] Compare, as textbooks say, the sensitive Ronsard, who at the age of ten endured without squealing a couple of terms at the Collège de Navarre, where the régime was almost as hard.

point for once in this connection. Pantagruel asks where all the
monastic birds on Ringing Island come from. Master Aeditus
replies that they come from two countries called "Want-o'-
Bread" (*Joursanspain*) and "Too-many-of-'em" (*Tropditieux*),
flocking to Ringing Island every year and leaving their parents
and relations behind.

> This happens when there are too many Children, whether Male
> or Female, in some good Family of the latter Country, insomuch
> that the House would come to nothing if the Paternal Estate were
> shar'd among them all. For this cause, Parents use to rid themselves
> of that Inconveniency by packing off the Younger Fry, and forcing
> them to seek their Fortune in this Isle . . .

Why Maître Antoine disposed of his youngest son in this
manner is the first of the many mysteries overhanging Rabelais'
whole life. One would imagine a shrewd legal eye would have
discovered already what was to be obvious to anybody a few
years hence, namely that few boys in the kingdoms of France
and Navarre could less patiently endure any species of yoke. In
the chapter of the Fourth Book in which Panurge on the high
seas so briskly drowns the abusive sheep-merchant Dindenault,
or Dingdong, with all his sheep, there is a significant passage with
some bearing on this. "Hark you me, my Friend John," says
Panurge to Friar John after the affair, "never did Man do me
a good Turn but I return'd or at least acknowledged it. No, I
scorn to be ungrateful, I never was, nor ever will be. Never
did Man do me an ill one without ruing the Day that he did it,
either, in this World or next. I am not so much of a Fool either."
For which Frère Jean des Entommeures, miraculously recollecting
his cloth for once, rebukes him. "Thou damn'st thy self like any
old Devil. It is written *Mihi vindictam*,[1] etc., matter of Breviary,
mark ye me; that's holy Stuff." If Panurge may be deemed here
to be using, as often, his creator's voice, that vindictive streak
may have been discernible in the boy already, promising little
for a monastic future. He must at any rate, one is relieved to think,
have been the complete antithesis of the tiny coxcomb Eudemon,
"not as yet twelve yeares old" and an epitome of all the virtues,
who is brought into an early chapter of the First Book to shame

[1] "'Vengeance is mine,' saith the Lord," etc. (Rom. xii. 19)

the child Gargantua's ignorance by delivering a long, smooth, impeccable Latin panegyric in his presence, and seems to have minced straight out of *The Bad Child's Book of Beasts*.

> This child is dainty as the Cat,
> And as the Owl discreet.

Instead of kicking this insufferable little prig through the roof young Gargantua falls to blubbering "like a Cow", from which a psychiatrist might possibly diagnose a belated guilt-complex in his creator. But since the Doctor's great object is to show up Gargantua's earliest pedagogues as illiterate nincompoops one may perhaps reject any secondary complications here.

No Eudemon in deportment at all events, one may safely swear, was the youngest Rabelais boy. Had he proved difficult to handle already? In a deed confirming the division of Maître Antoine Rabelais' estate, dated January 26, 1534, his son François is not mentioned. From this at first glance some family trouble might be guessed; but such omission was routine, every person taking monastic or conventual vows being dead in civil law and thus debarred inheritance. The puzzle of François' noviciate seems insoluble. Could it ever be imagined that the boy was himself pining for the religious life, a saint in embryo?

The parental decision made, young François Rabelais was duly dedicated to the Church. According to an Angers lawyer of the early seventeenth century, Bruneau de Tartifume, whose authority has been generally accepted in default of any other, Maître Antoine proceeded to put his youngest son into the noviciate at the Franciscan friary of La Baumette at Angers, fifty miles north-east of Chinon. Why the choice of Angers, with Tours so near, is again mysterious, except that it was a thriving University town, and some Frapin relatives lived there. To Angers therefore Maître Antoine, possibly having some legal business there in addition, carried his son, and left him with the Master of Novices. La Baumette was a house of the Strict Observance.[1] It was also

---

[1] A label applied in the late thirteenth century to Franciscan houses adhering to the Rule in the matter of ownership, which St. Francis prohibited. Finding this too difficult in practice, the Conventuals obtained Rome's permission to own property collectively. The Observants continued to vest ownership in the Holy See.

a *studium generale* for the Province of Anjou—a house of studies such as the Franciscans, with some other Orders, maintain in leading University towns, including then as today Oxford and Cambridge, to enable their student-friars to read for a degree. Like all Franciscan houses La Baumette was ruled by a Warden, *Guardianus*, in English-speaking countries now referred to as "Father Guardian". The Master of Novices and his youthful charges formed a little enclave of their own.

Standing at the gate near the lower bridge of Angers, the friary was a fifteenth-century foundation of René, King of Provence, named after the famous Provençal sanctuary of La Sainte Baume. Only its chapel survives, much altered. How long François Rabelais lived in this house is unascertainable. He may have been still there in 1518. He had certainly left before 1521. It is not likely that his new life of duty and schooling left him much leisure for looking at the still-attractive town, or that his Master of Novices permitted it. A street there now bears his name. Of the Angers of his day remain the Cathedral, the church of St. Serge, the skeleton of King René's château with twelve enormous bastions, St. John's Hospital and a few other relics of an impressive past. In the chapel above-mentioned the arms of his future patrons the Du Bellays are painted on a windowpane, but it is not likely that he had any contact with this eminent family at La Baumette, and a conjecture that Guillaume du Bellay, his future hero, was his fellow-novice, has been proved untenable, Guillaume being a student in Paris at the time. It is conceivable on the other hand that Maître Antoine Rabelais had some professional connection with the family, whose fine manor still stands at Gizeux near Bourgueil, about eighteen miles from Chinon. If so, this might explain Maître Antoine's choice of La Baumette, of which house the Du Bellays were benefactors. But nothing is known—a refrain to be repeated, alas, more than once in these pages.

Little of Angers appears in the Four Books. Two of the town's three present bridges over the Maine, the Pont de la Haute Chaîne and the Pont de la Basse Chaîne, perpetuate the memory of the massive chains slung ac oss the river by order of King René in 1518 to defeat smugglers; which chains Rabelais will remember when he wants something strong enough to keep the gigantic Pantagruel in his cradle. Another recollection of Angers, the plague of 1518, terminates Pantagruel's brief stay in the Second Book. La Baumette itself is mentioned in passing once, in connection with some stables hewn in the chalk, or *tuf*, as the local custom was, of the hillside overlooking the river. The story of Uncle Joseph's jay may attach to the next ten years or to infancy.

So the main door of La Baumette closes behind Maître Antoine Rabelais and he returns at length to Chinon, having committed what one may trust to be the only important error of judgment in an honourable career.

3

With a few years still to wait for our first authentic glimpse of him, does it take much reconstructive effort to see an alert and lusty novice in the habit of the Friars Minor, which has not varied through seven centuries, striding down an Angevin cloister, washing up crockery, sweeping floors, cheerfully banging pots and pans in the friary kitchen?

During his noviciate-year young Rabelais wears, as today, what the Rule of St. Francis calls the probationary habit, *pannus probationis*, of rough grey-brown serge or sackcloth, with a short cloak or *caparon* serving as a hood, if required, out of doors. This habit, issued to him with underwear in duplicate, is belted round his loins by the triply-knotted, symbolic, perpetual rope which in France has long since attached to his Order the folk-label of "Cordeliers". Beneath it he wears the woollen tunic and shorts in which he sleeps, and unless, "compelled by necessity", he has sought permission to wear shoes, which seems unlikely, his feet go bare and sandalled in all weathers.

His day is amply filled from dawn to nightfall. Recitation of at least part of the Office, attendance at Mass, and other obligations combine with hours of schooling, manual labour, and domestic chores to send him to bed, one may assume, healthily sleepy. At any time during his noviciate and, with a dispensation, during the three years following, he is free to quit the Order and liable equally to be expelled from it; and since Rabelais remains a friar for at least ten years, taking final vows and Holy Orders at the appointed times, it may reasonably be deduced that the gentle yoke of Francis will take some time yet to become an intolerable burden to a proud-stomached young scholar. Curbing a quick satiric tongue and speaking courteously to all (*honeste loquentes omnibus*) was, I should judge, young François' major trial to begin with, since he was forbidden to criticise even the easy-going world he had just quitted. "I warn and exhort the brethren," says St. Francis, "not to despise or judge those they see clad in soft or coloured apparel, and using choice food and drink (*cibis et potibus delicatis*); rather let each judge and despise himself." The enormous junketings of Pantagruel and his companions all through the Four Books are evidence that Friar François Rabelais ultimately found no difficulty in conforming to the first half.

His gift for friendship must have been exercised at La Baumette as elsewhere. Like the average religious house in any age, La Baumette was neither a sink of iniquity nor a nest of saints, but a community of men of varying age and temperament striving to live together in amity under vows for the service of God and their neighbour, as men have successfully managed to do, taking rough with smooth, for so many centuries. The crusty and the crabbed would have their proportion in Rabelais' community as in any other, but to assume that the "Grr! you swine!" of Browning's hypothetical Spanish cloister expresses anything but a singular phenomenon in monastic life would be unduly to flatter a rich poetic fancy.

On the other hand the general reputation of the Friars Minor, numbering many thousands then as now, was low enough at this period. Since the Black Death had wiped out half the regular and secular clergy of Western Christendom, and, it seemed at times, the better half, this enormous mendicant Order above all had attracted a fair number of black sheep; many of them, as St. Thomas More said, no better than tramps.[1] Being closer to the proletariat of Europe than any other Order, espousing its cause and providing its most popular preachers, the Franciscans naturally took the brunt of the attack when criticism flowered at the Renaissance into widespread hostility and hate. To every storyteller of the period, from the King's bluestocking sister

---

[1] A strong spiritual revival beginning some forty years before the Council of Trent and affecting nearly every religious Order is often overlooked. See Daniel-Rops, *L'Eglise de la Renaissance et de la Réforme*, vol. iv.

Marguerite de Valois down, to the neediest hack trotting in the wake of sub-Rabelaisian entertainers like Béroalde de Verville, Bonaventure des Périers, Noël du Fail, and a half-dozen more, the footloose Cordelier is Target No. 1; a dirty, sneaking knave, clown, hypocrite, glutton, seducer, thief, and all-round blackguard. In sheer venom—for some of Rabelais' onslaughts end, surprisingly, with a half-indulgent smile for *les béats pères*—the Princess Marguerite in her Platonico-Calvinist phase can outdo them all; one at least of the stories against friars in her *Heptameron*, the Eleventh Novel of the Second Day, would sicken a scavenger and delight an existentialist. To combine the invention of a dirty schoolboy with the lofty mysticism of *A Godly Medytacyon of the Cristen Sowle*, as her chief literary work appeared in Elizabethan English, is a typical Renaissance feat.

Much of this chorus of disapproval was justifiable enough, and merely echoing a number of medieval saints and not a few satirists with no sectarian axes to grind, and of less malice than is often assumed. A refined modern mind is apt to distort and magnify the intention of masters of gaiety like Boccaccio and Chaucer exploiting what has been called the perennial Catholic family joke. At its most pointed it is frequently of clerical inspiration. At its homeliest it may be exemplified in the Summoner's gibe, evoking such hilarity on the road to Canterbury, about the twenty thousand friars in hell.

> "Hold up thy tail, thou Sathanas," quod he;
> "Shewe forth thyn ers, and let the frerë see
> Where is the nest of frerës in this place . . ."

A little discrimination is very desirable in this matter. Not every merry friar was another Fra Cipolla out of the Decameron. The typical Franciscan of the Middle Ages lived, as M. Plattard justly observes, "in joy, a joy which blossomed into somewhat coarse jests". Such was that celebrated, almost legendary Florentine figure of the thirteenth century, Fra Salimbene di Adamo of the Order of Friars Minor; mirth-loving, wine-loving, frank and free enough in speech to bring, like so many of the medieval Franciscan preachers, a blush to a genteel Catholic cheek today, but for all this a sterling Christian and an excellent friar. The *sel franciscain*, remarks M. Gilson, one of Fra Salimbene's firmest friends, is too little known and appreciated.

A great deal of the flood of Renaissance malevolence against the religious Orders is what is called today "ideological", and it was unfortunate for the blameless that two monastic misfits of such eminence as Erasmus and Rabelais led the pack. One might reflect simultaneously, for fairness' sake, that neither of these brilliant lampooners drew on his own experience of the cloister. The Austin Canons Regular of Steyn may with one or two exceptions have appeared stupid to Brother Desiderius Erasmus—they had even more to endure from youthful arrogance, it seems, than the Franciscans of Fontenay—but he can call them neither slack nor degenerate. The two Franciscan houses which sheltered Rabelais observed their Rule, as did the Benedictines of Fontaine-le-Comte under his admired friend Antoine Ardillon, *le noble Abbé*. Both Rabelais' and Erasmus' exercises on the monastic theme may, in fact, be taken to spring from spiritual pride, a galling early discipline, and a quite dashing disregard for justice. To all wholesale contemporary invective one of many antidotes is the case of the monks of the London Charterhouse, selected by Henry VIII for death as a community precisely on account of the exemplary holiness of their lives. It may be discounted a little further, perhaps, by recollecting the satirist's prevailing weakness in every age. In moments of ecstasy he is apt to let his pen run away with him. This applies even more to a neurasthenic wit like Erasmus than to the bustling Rabelais, and indeed a couple of years before his death Erasmus to some extent repented and atoned for years of spiteful fun with a glowing eulogy, addressed to a Carthusian monk, of "those who, being truly dead to the world, have dedicated themselves to God" [1] Not so Dr. Rabelais, who continued to supply the Reform with ammunition to the end and was obviously never pulled up by the reflection that such a magnificent projection of anti-monastic fantasy as Frère Jean des Entommeures might be cited evermore as a model product of the contemporary cloister. ("Tant pis!" one hears him grunt. "So what?") Just as reasonably might Mr. Pecksniff be accepted as a specimen Fellow of the Royal Institute of British Architects. There may be quarters where he is.

[1] Preface to the Psalms of Haymo of Fulda, 1534.

However, the Mendicant Orders by Rabelais' time had certainly become a grave problem, and Rome was so seized of the fact that the reforming Commission of cardinals *de emendanda Ecclesia* set up in 1536 by Paul III recommended letting them all die out and replacing them with new foundations. From this drastic solution the exemplary energy of one new Order at least of the Counter-Reform reprieved them, and Ignatius may almost be said to have won the day for Francis and Dominic.

We return to Friar François Rabelais, following his Rule in a decent house, and not, one suspects, without difficulty. Of the three vows of poverty, chastity, and obedience, the third may have given this highly egocentric young friar most trouble. His novice-master may not have led an easy life with him. In every page of his vast work can be felt a pragmatical and imperious temper. Not from such wood is carved a Francis or a Bonaventure.

Meanwhile he took voraciously to his schooling, as no one even remotely familiar with his works will need to be told. Studying the newcomer on the benches before him, the Master of Novices at La Baumette undoubtedly perceived within a week or two that a born scholar had arrived, a coming asset to the Order, a new Duns Scotus, possibly, another Roger Bacon or Alexander of Hales. Some twenty-five years later their outstanding pupil will overwhelm his Franciscan pedagogues and their textbooks with abuse and mockery, reserving a special guffaw ("barbouillamenta Scoti") for the Subtle Doctor, protagonist alike of the Immaculate Conception and the Theory of the Formal Distinction; the same who three hundred years after Rabelais moved Gerard Manley Hopkins to admiration.

> Of reality the rarest-veinèd unraveller; a not
> Rivalled insight, be rival Italy or Greece;
> Who fired France for Mary without spot.

Hopkins had firmly grappled and comprehended the Scotsman, than whom no dialectician of his formidable race may be more justly compared with a Capablanca reigning at the chessboard. Compared with that of Duns Scotus, so I am credibly informed by persons on easy terms with the celebrated eighteenth-century

Scottish philosophical school, the cerebration of Hume appears amateurish; likewise that of the respectable Reid and the no-less-respectable Dugald Stewart. One is apt to suspect that thinkers who have dismissed the Subtle Doctor down the ages with that roar of "Dunce!" coined by discomfited Oxford antagonists seven hundred years ago have not taken the trouble Hopkins took. Among them may certainly be counted Doctor Rabelais, for a reason which will very soon emerge. Today, when most minds qualified to judge agree with Hopkins ("One of the most able and acute philosophers Britain has produced", is a recent verdict on the Subtle Doctor)[1] the gibes of the Renaissance assume a quaintly Fourth Form flavour. For Rabelais, as for many other flouters, there is, nevertheless, some excuse. Long before his time the system of Duns Scotus had been displaced in schools of his Order by a hotchpotch of chopped logic and an arid formalism, the work of hack-commentators. The like had befallen Scotus' fellow-Franciscan William of Ockham, whose Surrey village has long since forgotten him, but whose powers were lately extolled over the British radio by a select company. It was remembered on the eve of his sixth centenary that Ockham had been the Emperor's man against the Papacy, and moreover had had some of his "terminist" theory all but condemned, in his own day, at Rome.

On the mind of a youth nourished with the chaff and dregs of Nominalism the impact of the New Learning, so called, would naturally be shattering; notwithstanding which Rabelais retained all his life despite himself (*testibus* the Four Books) the scholastic mode of reasoning, with not a little of its technical language. Undoubtedly he would have dismissed the *Opus Oxoniense* of Duns Scotus, had he encountered it, with the same derisive hoots as the *Summa* of Aquinas, since it remains his fixed impression—a prevailing one—that everything connected with the medieval Schools is the idiotic pastime of barbarians. Such naïveté is not exclusive to the Renaissance. Rabelais would, were such a fancy possible, have been by no means the only surprised listener to benefit from a disputation in the Thomist mode on the moral issues of nuclear warfare broadcast by a trio of Dominicans in London not long ago.

[1] *Medieval Philosophy*, by Frederick C. Copleston, S.J., London, 1952.

Shortly a notable combatant, as we may well guess, in those
formal Latin disputes in hall on a given theme which sometimes
developed into a free-for-all, young Brother Rabelais continued
to devour everything the Franciscans of La Baumette had to teach
him; passing, like Villon at the Sorbonne before him, from Aelius
Donatus to Alexandre de Villedieu and Alain de Lille, thence to
Cato the Censor, from him to Bruslefer and Tateret, and so
through the traditional elementary curriculum, not omitting the
rules for good manners at table and elsewhere which were com-
pulsory likewise. A clever fellow, the Master of Novices must
have reported in due course, with a notable appetite for learning
(notable undoubtedly in refectory as well); a lover of conflict
and laughter in lecture-hall as at recreation; no ascetic, no
mystic, no seeker after seraphic perfection, no ecstatic out of the
Fioretti; a testy and somewhat difficult type, apt to collide with
the Rule. Every monastic school and every seminary past and
present knows the breed. Brother François nevertheless was
persevering. In the intervals of cramming himself with knowledge
and perfecting his Latin he had been, as the Rule provides,
"received to obedience"; taking simple vows covering the next
three years, assuming the hooded habit, and still able, with a
dispensation, to change his mind at any time. He did not do so,
and proceeded in due course to final vows, by which time he
must have decided to prepare for Holy Orders, with his superior's
sanction. In 1521, at the age of about twenty-six, he was a priest.

Here we come up against the Enigma once more. Clearly
Rabelais did not take Orders at La Baumette. A letter of 1521
yielding the first real news of him shows that he had some time
previously transferred to the Franciscan friary of Fontenay-le-
Comte, in Lower Poitou. When, or why, is not known. A deed
has been discovered, dated April 5, 1519, relating to some
property in Fontenay purchased on the friary's behalf and bearing,
among those of a dozen witnessing friars, the presumed signature
of Rabelais. If this proves his residence at that date, it has no
bearing on his status; he could still have been in one or other of
the four Minor Orders, which are those, progressively, of porter,
lector, exorcist, and acolyte. On March 4, 1521, at any rate, the
cloud lifts at last. On this day we find Friar François Rabelais
addressing a highly respectful letter from Fontenay, in both

classical languages, to the eminent, influential, and paternal Guillaume Budé.

Budé, the most illustrious Hellenist and humanist in France and a European celebrity, was at this time Secretary to the King. He practised a benevolent hobby, the encouragement of promising young men of letters, and his correspondents were innumerable. Among them happened to be a young fellow-friar of Rabelais' at Fontenay, one year his senior and a good Greek scholar, Pierre Amy by name. Since 1520 Amy had been urging his friend, who had since arrival at Fontenay also become a passionate Grecian, to write to the great man, to whom Amy had already mentioned him as an enthusiast for the "Attic Minerva". This Rabelais at length summoned up courage to do. His first letter is lost, but Budé, a busy man, acknowledged receipt of it to Amy. After a pause Rabelais wrote another, composed with exquisite care. This is the letter of March 4, 1521, and to this Budé at length replied very kindly, with compliments on the young friar's style. By now, in fact, Rabelais, a first-class Latinist, was rapidly becoming a master-Grecian as well, with a good smattering of law thrown in.

And he was now also, as Budé's reply reveals, a priest, recently ordained, of the Catholic, Apostolic, and Roman Church; stamped with that mystical invisible seal which no human frailties, lapses, betrayals, crimes, or even total apostasy can efface; *sacerdos in aeternum*, hands anointed, lips dedicated; qualified henceforth, even if suspended, deprived, or excommunicate, to transubstantiate and to shrive; as much a priest as any con- temporary saint in Orders like John, Bishop of Rochester, due a few years hence for glorious martyrdom. How illuminating, how valuable, how essential to a biographer would be some first-hand evidence, such as we have concerning Talleyrand, of the exact state of mind in which Father François Rabelais said his first Mass.

Was he—even he—on this solemn occasion devout, awed, and recollected, as a new young priest should be? Or is there some- thing of autobiographical import in the description in the First Book of his bustling hero Friar Jean des Entommeures as a *beau desbrideur de messes, beau descroteur de vigiles*? Étienne Gilson has remarked how recognisably the opening of the Preface of the

Mass, "Vere dignum et justum est, aequum et salutare, nos
Tibi semper . . .", which Rabelais must often have said or sung
in these early days, echoes in a phrase from one of his prologues,
"Non doncques sans juste et équitable cause je rends graces à
Dieu"—"Therefore not without just and equitable cause do I
render thanks to God." This does not necessarily imply devotion.
It may be a trick of memory. Renan occasionally mingles long-
remembered Mass-harmonies with his doubting and dejected
prose, the "damp diction of M. Renan", as Huysmans called it,
in like fashion. Young Father Rabelais' mental state on a given
morning in the 1520's as he ascended the altar steps repeating the
Aufer a nobis is, alas, impossible to conjecture; as indeed it is,
in this connection, at any time.

From the kind of vague materialism and the Deist commonplaces permeating the Four Books—the fleeting references to
Christianity can be practically numbered on one hand—the only
deduction is, I think, that "our good Father Pseudo-Evangelico-
Papistico-Anabaptistico", as the jeering Béroalde de Verville
calls him,[1] is not so much allergic to Catholic spirituality down
the ages as insensitive—a creature like the John Bull of the *Apologia*,
"neither of heaven or hell", less capable of certain vibrations
than a Borgia. Atrophy of the spiritual nerve-centres seems a
reasonable diagnosis. This would not prevent his carrying out
his sacerdotal duties for a time, as claimed in his appeal to Rome,
with perfect conscientiousness, even if he never recognised a
scintilla of their significance. In the France of the Encyclopaedia
he might well have revolted like Talleyrand. "They'll regret it!"
—the terrible fit of rage and despair in which the cynical young
rake pitchforked into the priesthood by a devout mother's folly
(and long enough poor Madame de Talleyrand lived to regret it)
celebrated his first Mass stands on record as an all-time warning
against misguided piety. Renan's case seems less comparable.
Having succumbed to German sophistries the rebel never returned at long last, like Talleyrand, but continued with obstinate
Breton melancholy to blend denial with nostalgia, as when those
memories of the Litany of Our Lady of Loreto break so poignantly
into his moving prayer to Pallas Athene on the Acropolis. "Tiens,
déesse, quand je me rappelle ces chants mon coeur se fond, je

[1] *Le Moyen de Parvenir, circa* 1590.

deviens presque apostat . . ." If an old friend like the Président
d'Épesse is correctly reported, Rabelais was brought back at last
by a twitch on the same invisible line which restored the aged
Talleyrand. But if he was ever shaken, like Renan, by lost beauty
I take leave greatly to doubt.

4

"Epistula tua . . . utriusque linguae peritiam singularem
redolens", wrote Budé in reply to Rabelais in the spring of
1521. "Your letter exhales a singular mastery of both [classical]
languages." The young man had been showing off, in Greek
especially. He continued to do so in several more letters to Budé,
a couple of whose replies have survived. They are distinctly
encouraging and not a little pedantic, with a glint or two of
dignified humour, since his new protégé has permitted himself,
amid discreet flattery of his patron, a respectful jest or two, such
as a Greek epigram on the highborn blind at Court, whose idol
Plutus needs a Budé to operate. It is to be noted that Budé does
not share the contempt of so many of the new intelligentsia for
the monastic life. Budé in fact deemed it ideal for a rising man
of letters, and wrote to Pierre Amy to this effect in 1520. Daily
contact with the Divine, remoteness from family and other
worldly complications, a thought-inspiring solitude, *solitudo in-
vitatrix mentium ad commentandum*, and—evidently his young friend
had been grumbling—limitation on personal liberty itself are
all privileges enabling a monk or friar to outstrip the ordinary
layman on the road to knowledge very swiftly. One may detect
a grimace on both faces as Amy reads this passage to his fellow-
friar, joint satisfaction and Rabelais' exaltation at the honour of
Budé's notice notwithstanding. A more enigmatic expression
may have flitted across Friar François' features on noting Budé's
reaction to a mock attack by himself on his friend Amy. "Where,"
wrote Budé, himself in jest (or was he?), "is that fraternal charity,
the bond of the monastic life, the foundation-stone of the religious
Orders, the cement of a community (*glutinam unanimitatis*) which
in your recent oration you were ready to declare almost divine?"
The great Budé seemed to be labouring the point overmuch,
perhaps. A joke was a joke, and the monastic bond was not the
most agreeable topic Friar François could think of.

However, an agreeable new life, relatively speaking, seemed to be opening before him. Nothing remains of the friary of Puy-Saint-Martin at Fontenay-le-Comte. It was sacked and destroyed by the Calvinists in 1568; the present town-hall stands on or near its site. Like La Baumette it was a house of the Strict Observance, founded in 1408 and attached to the Franciscan Province of Poitou-Touraine; which might vaguely explain Rabelais' transfer had it not become seven years later, on application to the Council of Constance, an independent house, "the better to observe the Rule". From the fact that it sheltered a Chapter-General in 1457 one may deduce that Fontenay was a larger and more important house than La Baumette. Apart from Rabelais, the only friar on its rolls whose name has survived is one Philippe Bertin, dealt with by the law for heresy in 1448; hardly a favourable presage, as Etienne Gilson remarks. In this house Friar François Rabelais will remain till 1524.

Whether or not the friary itself was a pleasant change from La Baumette, the town of Fontenay offered Rabelais, very soon after arrival, an alluring prospect, in the shape of an introduction by Pierre Amy to a choice humanist and literary circle which met regularly at the house, or in fine weather in the laurel-grove, of a prominent local lawyer, Maître André Tiraqueau. As the capital of Bas-Poitou and a *siège royal* under a Lieutenant-Seneschal, Fontenay-le-Comte swarmed with lawyers of all shapes and sizes. It was a comely, flourishing market-town with prosperous cloth-making and tannery industries and some good Gothic building, very little of which survives. Except that women were excluded from its symposia, Tiraqueau's circle might be considered an adumbration, so to speak, of the Hôtel de Rambouillet and similar cultured cenacles in the century following. Oddly enough, or perhaps not very oddly, one of its principal topics for discussion was woman and her status under the marriage-law, on which Tiraqueau had published a couple of weighty Latin treatises. Contemporary feminists cannot have cared for Maître André Tiraqueau. *Kinder, Kirche, Küche*—he holds very firmly with Bismarck that woman's place is the home, and she the junior partner. A little time before the introduction of Rabelais to the Tiraqueau circle a lettered magistrate of St. Jean d'Angély,

C

Amaury Bouchard, had written against this view, and a dignified arglebargle was in progress.

Could it be barely possible (if one may ask without offence) that Maître André's laurel-grove of a summer evening was not quite so portentous an academy as the learned and serious invariably assume? Might some contemporary Molière have possibly detected a trifle of comedy-relief in this assemblage of small-town notables, lawyers, and dilettanti prosing and debating over their wine? If their host, to begin with, possesses such Molièresque traits, discernible in his writings, as a solemnly-approving judgment of his own worth and an indignant touchiness when contradicted, his magistrate father-in-law, Artus Cailler, a prominent figure in the town, seems almost ready to step on the stage with Armande Béjart. A "person of importance in his day", holding the office of Criminal Lieutenant of Poitou, Maître Artus undoubtedly received as many bows and congees, as he paced the main street of Fontenay, as his Spanish confrère in Browning.

> My father, like the man of sense he was,
> Would point him out to me a dozen times;
> "St—st!", he'd whisper, "the Corregidor! . . ."

Since, in addition, the Criminal Lieutenant had married a very young girl and trained her with precision according to the precepts laid down in his son-in-law's first treatise (1513) on marriage, his place in a contemporary *École des Femmes* is more than indicated. Among the voices in Maître André's laurel-grove, as dusk fell and the bats began to swoop, the shrill pipe or the measured cadences of a Monsieur Tibaudier, a Monsieur Trissotin, or even a Monsieur de Pourceaugnac would not sound out of place to any observer of provincial life.

Whether or not any such engaging grotesques graced Tiraqueau's assemblies—other habitués whose names have come down to us are Jean Brisson, *avocat du Roi*, Hilaire Goguet, Seneschal of Talmont, and the magistrate Amaury Bouchard, already mentioned—to assume a dull pomposity as their normal characteristic is certainly to err, and damnably. Living in a freespoken age and calling a spade a spade, Maître André's guests would not infrequently permit themselves, at the expense of an enigmatic sex, a reflection or two which today might seem in dubious taste outside a clinic. There are plenty such in the great dissertation on cuckoldry by the physician Rondibilis in the Third Book; notably in the long psycho-physiological passage beginning: "When I say Womankind, I speak of a Sex so frail, so variable, so changeable, so fickle, inconstant and imperfect", etc., etc. Rondibilis is supposed to be drawn from one of Rabelais' later acquaintance, Dr. Rondelet of the Faculty of Medicine of Montpellier, a noted ichthyologist, but his type, *hilaris et facetus*, is universal. In the printed page the voice of Dr. Rondibilis is clearly heard; deep, rich, and drolly deliberate. Quite possibly he had a twin practising at Fontenay.

From Friar François' fond recollection of these nights and banquets of the gods will blossom, years later, the enormous serio-comic brouhaha over Panurge's projected marriage which fills half the Third Book, and to which even the bells of Varennes contribute their confusing counsel, clamouring in the distance: "Marie-toy, marie-toy, marie, marie, marie, très-bien t'en trouveras, veras, veras"; which at close quarters is heard to be: "Marie poinct, marie poinct, poinct, poinct, t'en repentiras, tiras, tiras, cocqu seras." Among the voices of Panurge's counsellors those of the theologian Hippothadée, Rondibilis aforesaid, and the "pyrrhonian" philosopher Trouillogan sound to me like faint but distinct echoes from the Fontenay garden. It is a pity that for the most part our Urquhart so inadequately renders the laconic and exquisitely-non-committal Trouillogan as he drives Panurge into a dancing fury.

> PANURGE: Que m'en conseillez vous?
> TROUILLOGAN: Rien.
> PANURGE: Me marieray je?
> TROUILLOGAN: Je n'y estois pas.
> PANURGE: Je ne me marieray donc poinct?
> TROUILLOGAN: Je n'en peux mais.
> PANURGE: Si je ne suis marié, je ne seray jamais cocqu?
> TROUILLOGAN: J'y pensois.
> PANURGE: Mettons le cas où je suis marié.
> TROUILLOGAN: Où le mettrons nous? [etc., etc.].[1]

[1] P: What is it that you advise and counsel me to do?—T: Nothing.—P: Shall I marry?—T: I have no hand in it.—P: Then shall I not marry?—T: I cannot help it.—P: If I never marry, I shall never be a Cuckold?—T: I thought so.—P: Put the case that I be married.—T: Where shall we put it? [etc., etc.]

Thus, I fancy, must one or the other of Tiraqueau's legalists
have fenced with and side-stepped his interlocutors. Nobody
present can have enjoyed such verbal duels more, or joined with
keener relish in the logomachy arising from this and every topic
discussed—and any question of ethics, law, philosophy, or the
humanities could make an evening's diversion for these dilettanti
—than young Friar François Rabelais, who may without much
difficulty be seen seated with his friend Amy on the fringe of the
group; bolt upright, with intent glittering eyes, a smile hovering
on his lips, his hands, when not occupied with a goblet, tucked in
his sleeves in the monastic style, alert to catch and return the
flying allusion. Like young Samuel Johnson among the dons of
Pembroke, he may have made his début by surprising his elders
with a quotation from Macrobius, or some authority equally
recondite.   At all events he continued to impress the company
to such an extent that his host pauses twice to pay him a compliment in the second edition (1524) of his *De Legibus Connubialibus*.
"Or so our François Rabelais, Friar Minor, a man highly lettered
in Greek and Latin, permits himself to conjecture", writes
Tiraqueau in a note against Bouchard apropos Lucian's cynicism
about an orator's first business being to please the women. And
again, mentioning a translation of Herodotus[1] on which his young
guest is apparently now engaged: ". . . a man of consummate
ability in the Greek and Latin tongues, and in all learning far
beyond what one might expect at his age; a man above all the
ordinary prejudices, *not to say the excessive scruples*, of his Order."
This last tribute (italics mine) points, I think, to not a few racy
observations on his brethren offered by young Friar François for
the diversion of the company when the wine was circulating, and
foreshadows some of that trouble for the satirist which was imminent even now. He had become by this time a distinct orna-
ment to the Tiraqueau cenacle. Some complimentary Greek
verses of his, comparing his host to Plato and duly printed by
Tiraqueau, show that Friar François had a fitting sense of those
reciprocal literary courtesies which have come to be so crudely
described as "logrolling".
     Thus ensconced in a club of choice spirits, admired and ad-
miring, Friar Rabelais could hardly be blamed for uttering that

[1] This has not survived.

familiar slogan of the Clique ("We few, we happy few . . .")
which he will develop to Tiraqueau some eight years later in a
long Latin letter from Lyons. In this letter is heard that darkness-
into-light refrain which sums up the whole Renaissance credo.
It must have been a recurring cliché under the laurels at Fontenay-le-Comte:

> How comes it [writes Rabelais to his former host] that in the midst
> of the light illuminating our time, in which by a special bene-
> faction of the gods we see the rebirth of every kind of useful and
> precious knowledge, there are still people to be found everywhere
> who will not or cannot clear their eyes of that thick and more-
> than-Cimmerian fog of the Gothic age [*densa illa gothici temporis
> caligine plus quam Cimmeria*], and lift them to the sun? . . .

Et patati, et patata. The same theme, though "the gods" will
merge into a single Deity of vaguely Platonic provenance, will
echo from at least two of the Four Books, and from Gargantua's
letter to Pantagruel in Book II with the blandest assurance:

> . . . for that time [the Middle Ages] was darksome, obscured with
> clouds of Ignorance, and savouring a little of the infelicity and
> calamity of the Goths, who had, wherever they set footing, destroyed
> good literature, which in my age hath by the divine goodnesse
> been restored to its former light and dignity [etc., etc.].

As it happened, a Gothic fog of some density was taking shape
on Friar François' horizon at this moment—we are nearing the
end of 1523—and Tiraqueau's hospitality would soon be affording
precious refuge and solace, if indeed it could still be enjoyed.
The admiration of Maître André's circle was not, it seems, shared
by Rabelais' superior, whose relations with the ardent classicist
under his roof were on the verge of becoming strained. So far
there had been no objection in principle to any young friar's
devoting himself, within reason, to the spare-time study of
classical Greek. But it could be overdone. Of the dangers lurking
in excessive enthusiasm for any man bound by sacred vows St.
Peter Damian, himself a passionate classicist in his youth, had
written five hundred years before Friar Rabelais: "The songs
of the poets beguiled me, the philosophers dazzled me with their

golden phrases, the Sirens enchanted my soul nigh unto death.
The Law and the Prophets, Gospel and Epistle—the whole
glorious speech of Christ and His servants seemed to me a poor
thing and empty . . ."[1] Towards the end of 1523, or a little
later, an unforeseen happening obliged the Father Guardian of
Fontenay at length to take a stiff view. In accordance with a
recent ruling of the Faculty of Theology of the University of Paris,
commonly called the Sorbonne, a body authoritative but neither
infallible nor (as may be well understood) universally popular,
Friars Rabelais and Amy were ordered to cease their Hellenic
studies forthwith, and their Greek books were confiscated.

5

For ninety-nine per cent of Rabelais' commentators in modern
times, so far as I can gather, the issue at Fontenay-le-Comte is
simple and crystal-clear. Monkish ignorance and obscurantism
persecuting progress, enlightenment, and learning—not a few
of them break almost into a sacred dance inspired by this attractive
theme. There is a case nevertheless for the Guardian of Fontenay,
and it may be stated for once. The Sorbonne's ruling apart, the
obligations of a Friar Minor do not include the passionate pursuit
of secular learning for its own sake, and obedience to the Rule
is a solemn vow before God. The Order has produced its scholars,
and famous ones, but not of the kind Friars Rabelais and Amy
were bent on becoming. That they had been given extra time
for Greek studies before the ruling one may reasonably doubt;
that they had asked, and been refused, is quite possible. On the
other hand a patient Father Guardian had certainly granted his
two problem-cases some favours. His permission would be necessary to attend those regular assemblies *chez* Tiraqueau, which
would clash with attendance at the night-Office in choir and would
make likewise, since the two friars may frequently have returned
some time after the rest of the community was asleep, for dis-
turbance of the "great silence" and unpunctuality at Matins.
Extended leave of absence, moreover, had been granted Friar
Pierre Amy at least once; we find him staying with Amaury

---

[1] *De Perfectione Monachorum*; quoted by Helen Waddell, *The Wandering Scholars*,
London, 1927.

Bouchard at Saintes in Saintonge for some weeks, doubtless grumbling to Bouchard, as he did to Budé, about the hardships of the Franciscan state. At the same period Rabelais struck up a warm friendship at Saintes with a genial resident magistrate named Briand Vallée, with whom he will stay some time at Bordeaux four years hence, so it may be assumed that he had been granted leave with his fellow-friar, presumably not on the business of the friary but his own.

It is not on record that either of them had been evading his monastic duties. There is, however, plenty of indirect evidence of Rabelais' state of mind. The opening diatribe against monasticism in the First Book includes at least one complaint which would interest a psychologist. "True it is," says Gargantua scornfully, "that with a tingle tangle jangling of Bells they trouble and disquiet all their neighbours about them." Much earlier, in Janotus de Bragmardo's burlesque oration for the return of the bells of Notre-Dame, occurs the first adumbration of this grievance. Bragmardo quotes one Pontanus, "the secular Poet", who lived near the Cathedral and

wish't those bells had been made of feathers, and the clapper of a foxtail, to the end that they might have begot a chronicle in the bowels of his Braine, when he was about the composing of his carminiformal Lines.

Again, from Chapter LII of the First Book, describing the foundation of the dream-Abbey of Thélème:

. . . and because in all other Monasteries and Nunneries all is compassed, limited, and regulated by hours, it was decreed that in this New Structure there should be neither Clock nor Dial.

From which Gargantua goes on to grunt, in his creator's behalf:

Now can there be any greater dotage in the World than for one to guide and direct his courses by the sound of a Bell, and not by his owne judgment and discretion?

Such campanophobia, to coin a solecism in the carefree scientific manner, is significant, I think. Whoever wrote the "Fifth Book", published under the title of *Ringing Island*, must have thought so too, since he developed this allergy into a major theme. Attempted psycho-analysis of the illustrious dead is one of the more futile of literary pastimes, and I have little difficulty in spurning any temptation to link an anti-bell complex (see "Anxiety-Hysteria") with a guilt-complex eventually deriving, inevitably, from our old friend the Oedipus-complex, so firmly attached to so many great suffering shades in recent years. But it may at least be assumed that the testy scholar working on Herodotus in his cell must have paused very often to curse a sudden clanging summons to choir or refectory, recreation or bed, even more fluently than he would execrate the periodical jangles from the belfry announcing to the countryside the Offices from Matins to Compline, with an extra carillon for Mass. How a community of men diversely occupied could be otherwise notified of the passage of time and their varying duties is difficult to conceive. "You're in the Army now," Friar François might justly have been reminded; and probably was.

At the root of this fuss about bells it takes no Freud to discern a temperamental hostility towards discipline of every sort, illustrated richly in Rabelais' writings and career. His superior, if a man of any intelligence at all, must have been aware of this from the beginning. It may very well be that both Rabelais and Amy had turned a deaf ear to a bell or two, or obeyed its summons in their own good time. In which case the Guardian could have pointed out to them with perfect reason that if their sole concern was to read classical Greek undisturbed, a Franciscan friary was obviously no place for them.

One well-known neurosis, I think, any skilled superior might have diagnosed in both, though I have never seen it mentioned in this connection. Restlessness and discontent in the cloister may be, and often have been, conditioned or amplified by that old lurking enemy of the spiritual life which our forefathers called "accidie", *accidia*, a kind of creeping languor, fatigue, and temporary paralysis of the soul. How its octopus-like embrace affects the victim is sufficiently described by Chaucer's Parson: "He dooth alle thyng with annoy, and with wrawnesse [indignation], slaknesse, and excusacion." Against this misery even the best monk may have to fight at times. A man of imperious temperament and no vocation would be its easiest prey. He need not be a paranoiac (see Havelock Ellis) like Friar Martin Luther screaming and tumbling on the floor at Erfurt to find "accidie" poisoning his whole existence.

Such likely contributory factors, curiously ignored by the learned, seem to me to have their place in any attempt to assess the rights and wrongs of the crisis which was to end Rabelais' connection with the Franciscan Order, and which may be ultimately resolved into a clash between authority and private judgment; a microcosm of the conflict which had lately split Germany and Switzerland, and to some small extent France, into two hostile camps. In this case Authority's demands were clear enough. The professed, and still more the ordained Franciscan is required to say or hear daily Mass, to recite the sevenfold daily Office with his brethren, to fast all through Lent and on all Fridays, to own no money or property, to practise modesty, gentleness, good manners, and charity towards all men to work with his hands for his sustenance and his community's, and to eschew pride, idleness, envy, detraction, murmuring, and solicitous interest in the things of this world. He is bound likewise to cherish his brethren, to serve the sick and poor, to preach only by permission, to avoid "suspicious intercourse" with women, and implicitly to obey the lawful orders of his superiors from the Minister-General down. In the matter now vexing Rabelais and Amy St. Francis seems to provide a loophole, in his generous way:

> Let not the unlettered strain after learning [*non curent nescientes litteras, litteras discere*] but let them consider how they ought to desire above all to have the Spirit of the Lord and his holy operation [etc.].

Both friars might, and undoubtedly did, suggest that they were not precisely among the "unlettered". Their superior could advance a more immediate issue. Enthusiasm for Greek, as the Sorbonne had intimated, was now suspect. He probably had no need to explain why. In earlier centuries the original language of the Gospels still lingering in the Mass and the Good Friday liturgy had been as much the common language of the Church as

Latin; but since its revival at the opening of the Renaissance
Greek had been so sedulously exploited by neo-pagans and others
of the disaffected as to have become, as it were, a master key to
subversion, which its subtleties encouraged *ad infinitum*. A typical
example of its uses in the wrong hands was the text-twisting
whereby the Calvinist scholar Berquin got Erasmus into trouble,
despite more than one papal brief confirming his Catholic orthodoxy. In the view of the theologians of the Sorbonne, who
were probably not entirely the degraded clowns exposed by
Rabelais in the Four Books, the fall of Byzantium had introduced
into the West that capricious and dissolvent Greek spirit to which
Roman order is the traditional enemy, all attempts at reconciliation notwithstanding. There was also, perhaps, something
to be added about the morals of classical Greece as displayed in
the not very evangelical pages of Sappho and Anacreon. Aristotle
was a different matter. Him the Middle Ages had (so to speak)
baptised, canonised, and naturalised not only via the Arabic
and the Syriac but—by the hand of the eminent Grosseteste for
one—from the original. What was perturbing the Sorbonne about
the Greek revival in the 1520's was its exploitation by scholars
more or less hostile in the interests of scriptural and dogmatic
criticism increasingly destructive.

To a later age which has seen the German Higher Criticism
itself tower, totter, and crash like the Giant Loupgarou the alarm
of the Sorbonne may seem slightly ludicrous. But the attack was
then a new one, and not to be ignored. Erasmus' commentaries
on the Greek text of St. Luke's Gospel had been extremely startling
to the Faculty of Theology;[1] even more his *Ratio Verae Theologiae*.
Neither of these works would perturb any Catholic theologian
in the least today; indeed, Erasmus' basic orthodoxy in fact and
in intention, papal testimonials apart, has been recently confirmed once more by a French Oratorian scholar whose admiration is as keen as his critical faculty. But in Rabelais' time
Lutherans and Calvinists were going much further with the dis-
secting-scalpel than Erasmus; humanists with a following in
France like Berquin and Lefèvre of Étaples were already rejecting
all dogma in favour of a "Bible-only" dogma of their own, soon
to become axiomatic in countries of the Protestant ascendancy.

[1] Although Leo X accepted the dedication of his Greek New Testament (1516).

On such a scale hostility to the Faith of the West was something quite unknown. Therefore, decided the Sorbonne, we must deal with this matter at the root; since this rising tide of recklessness derives chiefly from the present rage for Greek, let us place a general ban on Greek studies, so far as possible. Such a move, recalling the banning of Greek five centuries earlier, on much the same grounds, by the Mahometan theologians of Arab Spain, was a less reasonable one than the routing of the innovators by argument. Unfortunately the only argument recognised by the Sorbonne at this moment was drawn from those already-noted dregs of Nominalism at which every humanist of importance in Europe shrugged his contempt. Not until the middle of the century were Cajetan in Italy and Vittoria in Spain able to readjust the intellectual balance by restoring Aquinas to primacy. By that time a great deal of the damage was irreparable.

So the ban on Greek letters was issued and enforced—though not completely, since the Hellenists had the king's support and that of not a few prelates—within the jurisdiction of the Faculty of Theology. One may judge that the position at Fontenay, at any rate, was put by the Guardian to Friars Rabelais and Amy briefly and with point. The Rule came first. Service of God before service of Greek—elementary, surely? They may be imagined standing stiff and silent to attention in the Guardian's room, side by side, hands tucked in sleeves. As it was a superior's duty when necessary to correct his friars, in the words of St. Francis, "humbly and charitably", so it was for the corrected, "remembering that for the love of God they have renounced their own will", to submit and obey, "saving only in what may be opposed to their conscience, or to our Rule". A certain heat may have been engendered nevertheless before the interview ended; voices raised, possibly; a few shrugs and gestures exchanged. For Amy one cannot answer; though capable of sudden revolt, as will appear, he is the dimmer figure. But it seems a hundred-to-one-likely conclusion that the glowering eyes of Friar François Rabelais premised, as soon as he received permission to speak, a smart brush with authority, and possibly not the first. "How can I govern others, who cannot govern myself?"—in the cry to Pantagruel of his great creation Friar John there surely rings the accent of Rabelais himself? Impetuous temper and youthful conceit may well have conquered him on learning that his precious Greek volumes had been removed already from his cell, presumably for good. A brisk clash had been predictable sooner or later. Coming in these circumstances. it was to exasperate Rabelais so permanently that no literary figure of his age will excel him in the sport of friar-baiting. Taking shape in his stormy brain at this moment, perhaps, are a few of the choicer insults which a thousand demagogues will exploit and millions of innocents take for gospel evermore, so that the simple word "monk" or "friar" will bring automatically before their mental vision a shaven hypocrite, glutton, lecher, bibber, and mumbler of meaningless Latin amid a jangling of noisy bells. "If you can conceive how an Ape in a family is always mocked, and provokingly incensed, you shall easily apprehend how Monks are shunned of all men, both young and old . . ." It is true that Rabelais will add a reservation—"I mean those lither, idle, lazie Monks"—and distinguish these from "our good Friar John . . . he travels, he labours, he defends the oppressed, comforts the afflicted, helps the needie, and keeps the close of the Abbey". But as Friar John turns out to be devoted to none of these Christian labours, one can hardly blame the simple for declining to make any distinction at all.

"Are we alive after all this satire?" Dr. Johnson once asked his circle in mock apprehension. Monasticism has survived the onslaughts of Rabelais and his fellows with no great difficulty. Yet one may well suspect that the Guardian of Fontenay-le-Comte, listening to a furious striding down the corridor and the banging of a distant door, had no conception of what he had just started.

6

Ohé! Proh pudor! ὀτοτοτοτοτοῖ! Heus! . . . Back in their respective cells, Friars Rabelais and Amy seize their pens. Their illustrious patron must be advised of this outrage without delay. One hears two hard-driven quills squeaking energetically. Is it irreverence to be reminded somehow of those indignant protests in the sacred names of Literature, Democracy, and Progress which were wont in more carefree days to appear in the London

Times, over a dozen eminent signatures, whenever some obscure British novelist was pushed off a kerb in Italy or Spain?

From Budé's replies, in Greek and Latin, suitably grieved and astounded, and elaborately ignoring the Sorbonne, one perceives that his protégés had not wasted their ink. To Amy, his ewe-lamb, Budé writes at considerable length on February 24, 1524, a little time after the event. He has been truly shocked to learn that two such zealous adepts of the classics, whose erudition (so swiftly acquired!) should be an honour to their community, have been persecuted by sworn enemies of elegance and letters. Every friend of learning would be ready, so far as in him lies, to rush to their assistance, as to that of all aspirants to universal knowledge. And so forth and so on. However, Budé concludes, dropping the pitch an octave or two, now that the persecutors have realised how their conduct is viewed by persons of the highest eminence, including—let us not forget that Budé is Secretary-Royal—the king himself, he understands the trouble is over. Budé's young friends have emerged from this trial with all honour. Let them persevere in their studies with new zeal.

To Rabelais came Budé's reply a little later. A briefer letter. The eminent Hellenist has cooled down considerably. He apologises for not writing before, but he did not know where Rabelais might be found, nor Amy, who, it seems, has quitted Fontenay recently for some destination unknown. Budé has just heard from one of the most enlightened and honourable personages in the Franciscan Order—and the news overjoys him—that their Greek books and papers have been restored to his young friends, and they now enjoy liberty and tranquillity in their studies as before. How this fits in with the opening of his letter is not clear, nor does he explain it. He proceeds to give Friar Rabelais a résumé of some of his own tussles with the mulish theologians of the Sorbonne. Of these types he speaks more in sorrow than anger. They actually judge the divine Homer to be full of impieties! And Budé's letter ends.

So pressure has been brought to bear, the storm is over, and, possibly to his relief, Budé has not had to call on the friends of learning to rise in a body. Friar François Rabelais may have been feeling relieved likewise. He has his books again, and everything considered, the late hubbub involved more glory than discomfort.

Though bereft of his comrade and feeling his loss—"Damon and Pythias", Budé had styled them, Amy being likewise a second Pylades and another Pirothous—I see him settling down to Herodotus once more with the reflection that things might have been worse. A trifle of envy at Amy's superior *panache* pricks him simultaneously, unless I misread between the lines of his own version of this episode years later.

Something of the manner of Friar Pierre Amy's exit from Fontenay—seemingly a dashing one, in the best monastic traditions of the Victorian novel—may be gleaned from Chapter X of the Third Book, which is devoted to a discussion of divination by the *sortes virgilianae*. This was an old-fashioned foible still popular with the Renaissance intelligentsia. One opened a volume of Virgil haphazard or threw the dice to decide the page; a line leaped to the eye, and one obeyed the oracle. Rabelais recounts the affair briefly but, abetted by our excellent Urquhart, in spirited fashion:

> When Mr. Peter Amy did in like manner explore and make trial if he should escape the Ambush of the Hobgoblins, who lay in wait all to bemawl him, he fell upon this Verse in the Third of the *Aeneids*,
>
> > *Heu fuge crudeles terras, fuge litus avarum!*
> > Oh flee the bloody Land, the wicked Shoar!
>
> Which Counsel he obeying, safe and sound forthwith avoided all these Ambuscades.

It is all suitably, as we say, hotted up, even to Urquhart's rendering of Virgil; for "bloody" might equally be read "severe", and for "wicked", "covetous". However, the pagan oracles had spoken clearly enough, and Amy shook off the dust of Fontenay forthwith. Whether he vanished by day or night, over the garden wall or through the main door, is not on record, but he arrived soon afterwards, "safe and sound", at the Benedictine house of St. Mesmin, near Orleans, where he had friends. Here he took up his quarters and applied himself once more to Hellenism. Such a procedure is explicable only by the assumption that the Abbot or Prior of St. Mesmin was sufficiently warm an ally to risk trouble with his diocesan for harbouring a runaway religious, and of another Order and Province at that. Trouble of this kind indeed seems to have loomed at length. Some eight months later, in October 1524, we find Amy living in Lyons among a group sympathetic to the Reform, and no doubt still flourishing Budé's letter ("What an outrage against the Muses! How one would like to chastise these superiors who cultivate ignorance under the name of orthodoxy! . . ."—the good Budé simplifies the situation, we perceive, like many sympathetic observers after him). Thereafter Amy vanishes from circulation. Presumably he left the Church altogether when some of his Lyons friends took this step.

Rabelais, meanwhile, continuing, perhaps a trifle more judiciously, with his Greek at Fontenay, seems to have been restless and dubious about the future. That he had considered breaking his vows like his friend—throwing his frock to the nettles, in the picturesque French phrase—and taking the consequences, is a fascinating semi-certainty. To a man of such vagabond humour it must have occurred more than once in the night-watches that across a not-too-distant frontier, in Zwinglian Switzerland or Lutheran Germany, a refugee of his quality could look for a very cordial welcome. The same would apply very soon to England, where even in the sceptical eighteenth century a solitary ex-monastic recruit to the Establishment like Père Le Courayer could become overnight the pet of bishops and the *chouchou* of the cultured. In France, on the other hand, an absconding friar was quite liable to find himself doing penance on bread-and-water in some episcopal prison or in some rigorous monastery, usually Cistercian, for any period deemed suitable by ecclesiastical authority. To Rabelais, who, as will amply appear, preferred the comfortable life, such an arrangement would undoubtedly appear a prospect to be dismissed swiftly from his thoughts. He was not of the stuff from which the martyrs are woven. A Calvinist solution, moreover, could never have appealed for a moment to his jovial and refractory nature; a fact very comprehensible to anyone who has encountered the stony frigidity of its typical French incarnation, in comparison with whom the glummest of Scots or Dutch adepts—not to speak, I am told, of the glowering *predikant* of the Boer hinterland—seems an impulsive chatterbox.

And everything considered, and however easy of achievement, a future in Geneva, least Pantagruelist city in Europe then as now, would have been for Friar Rabelais, one may reflect in sympathy, a quite appalling error of judgment. At best such a refugee would be expelled by the Dictator in about half the time it took Calvin to rid himself of that most mirth-loving and wine-loving of song-birds, Clément Marot, whose presence among Geneva's puritans is irresistibly suggestive of a canary among crows, and whose religion was not Calvin's.

> Amour, tu as esté mon maistre,
> Je t'ay servi sur tous les dieux . . .[1]

Marot indeed contrived to keep sufficiently sober during his stay *chez* Calvin to finish translating the Latin Breviary psalms into mellifluous French verse. A Rabelais would have no such means of ingratiating himself, and existence in Geneva would have palled on him as swiftly as those damp and chilly winds which so often sweep the city from across the Lake. Prison and/or fine for failing to doff a respectful beaver to John Calvin passing in the street, for singing or dancing at a wedding party, for being caught with playing-cards, for locking house-doors at night against inquisitors empowered to swoop for inspection at any hour, for (if a woman) infringing Calvin's hairdressing regulation; prison likewise for any public expression of deviation from or doubts concerning Calvinistic dogma, and in extreme cases, like that of Michel Servetus, liability to be burned for heresy; prison also, and extensively, for any discovered activities connected with Geneva's considerable underground movement . . . such a régime would lack attraction for Friar François Rabelais. The Lutheran districts in Germany offered little better; the language-difficulty, the eternal brawling of the rival sectaries, the rowdy bacchanalia, the suicidal gloom, and the striking brutality of German manners even among the intelligentsia would soon, I fancy, be enough for him.

He suppressed wanderlust for once, and he was wise.

---

[1] "Love, thou hast been my master; I have served thee above all the gods." (*De Soy-Mesme.*) Marot managed nevertheless to write one of the most charming of Christmas carols.

7

The next best thing was exchange to some more congenial *milieu* within the monastic family, and Rabelais had not far to look for one. The Order of St. Benedict, most venerable of all, beckoned him with obvious invitation.

For well nigh a thousand years before his time the Benedictines had been specialising in scholarship and education. To them alone is due the survival of Western civilisation during the long night of the Dark Ages, their roll of alumni is impressive, and the proverbial *travail de bénédictin* still continues a valid tribute to solid intellectual labour. To men of letters and artists, as Huysmans discovered, their Rule offers an ideal synthesis of spiritual, intellectual, and aesthetic aspiration in perfect proportion. As a Benedictine novice to begin with, Rabelais might well have settled down to a placid and erudite existence, one is sometimes tempted to think, though it may be doubted if St. Benedict's insistence on the priority of the *Opus Dei*, the daily performance of the complete Roman Liturgy in all its dignity and beauty, could ever have evoked much enthusiasm in him; nor, somehow, can one imagine him even as a full-blown doctor of medicine recognising Christ in every one of his sick. Once more the question of discipline arises. Serene, discreet, and liberal as he made it, St. Benedict's Rule is an ordered code of law demanding obedience like any other.

However, it was to the Benedictine Congregation that Friar François' fancy now turned. If not himself aware from the dawn of this decision of the difficulties attending its consummation, he would be speedily put "in the picture" by his Father Guardian on first broaching the matter. A personal petition to the Holy See was essential, and it would need influential backing. Fully-professed religious, Rabelais' superior must have acidly reminded his troublesome friar, are supposed to know their own minds and not rove like butterflies. In the light of subsequent events it is clear that Rabelais solved his problem by an appeal to his diocesan, Geoffroy d'Estissac, Bishop of Maillezais, whether with or without permission is not ascertainable. His Father Guardian may have been as ready to rid the community of an obvious *agité* as Friar François was to go.

Bishop d'Estissac proved flatteringly responsive. He knew and esteemed Rabelais already, and he had known Amy for some time. A theory, based on some tradition or other, that he and Rabelais had been fellow-novices at La Baumette is highly improbable. The bishop at this moment was forty-seven years old and had occupied the see of Maillezais since 1518. A keen humanist and a frequent visitor to the Tiraqueau circle, he entertained one or two of its members occasionally at his château of L'Herminault and his priory of Ligugé and might therefore be regarded as their patron. A travelling bookseller's receipt dated June 1519 shows Amy paying in his behalf for a Homer, an Aristotle, a Cicero, an Erasmus, and other books *vendus cejourd'huy à Monsr. l'evesque de Maillezais.* D'Estissac was, in fact, a man of some quality and presence, a scholar-prelate on the Italian Renaissance model, energetic, affable, and hospitable. Though he owed his bishopric, a royal appointment under Leo X's concordat with François I, to his soldier-brother Bertrand's services in the Italian campaigns of Charles VIII and Louis XII, his character was unexceptionable and he ruled his diocese with strict efficiency. Some pedestrian verse in a subsequent letter to Rabelais from Jean Bouchet of Poitiers, lawyer and humanist, seems not to exaggerate unduly when it commends

> . . . la bonté du reverend evesque
> De Maillezays, seigneur de ce beau lieu,
> Partout aymé des hommes et de Dieu,
> Prelat devot, de bonne conscience,
> Et fort sçavant en divine science,
> En canonicque, et en humanité . . .[1]

Such an amiable prelate could naturally be summoned without much difficulty to the aid of a friar of a type rare in his remote diocese, and induced to assist him to the limit of what Canon Law permitted. Of the late trouble at Fontenay d'Estissac was, of course, fully aware; indeed, as bishop of the diocese he must have settled it.

Bishop d'Estissac, then, took up Friar Rabelais' case with

[1] ". . . the kindness of the reverend Bishop of Maillezais, lord of this pleasant place and loved alike by men and by God; a devout prelate of high integrity, most learned in theology, Canon Law, and the Humanities."

characteristic vigour. Any difficulties with the Franciscan authorities were smoothed out and Friar François Rabelais' humble petition, endorsed by his diocesan and not, perhaps, without a compliment or two on the Ciceronian elegance of its Latin, was forwarded to Rome. Clement VII's brief, or indult, of authorization was received at Maillezais not long afterwards. It contains an interesting phrase, repeated in the subsequent indult of Paul III (1535) granting Rabelais' *supplicatio pro apostasia* after his later exchange, without permission, to the secular priesthood. "In altaris ministerio saepius ministraveras," says the indult—"You have diligently performed the service of the altar." In other words François Rabelais, O.F.M., priest, addressed by formal papal courtesy as "Our beloved son", has carried out his principal sacerdotal duty at Fontenay-le-Comte in a regular and conscientious manner, and is accordingly granted the desired permission *propria virtutum merita.*

Such a phrase as "*In altaris*", etc., originally embodied in Rabelais' petition, cannot have been submitted to Rome without the knowledge and concurrence of his Father Guardian. As already observed, it is more than likely that pressure, in our bland modern phrase, had been brought to bear by Bishop d'Estissac in the matter of the Greek ban. It might equally be that the Guardian of Fontenay, who had he chosen could have made an issue of *l'affaire Rabelais* with some much higher authority, does not entirely deserve the shrill scoldings he receives from all progressive thinkers as a bigoted medieval tyrant, obstructionist, and enemy of polite letters. Having tempered discipline with patience, with two tough cases on his hands, he is herewith awarded, so far as I can judge for the first time in four hundred years, a tentative good mark.

III

Black Monk

I

IT MUST HAVE BEEN TOWARDS THE AUTUMN OF 1524 THAT FRIAR François Rabelais doffed the grey-brown habit of Francis for the black of Benedict and swore allegiance in the abbey church of Maillezais to his new superior, Geoffroy d'Estissac, bishop and abbot. He rose from his knees nevertheless no rank-and-file Benedictine monk. One or two privileges attached to this formality testify illuminatingly to his prestige in the eyes of his bishop, to whose recommendations to Rome they were due.

Patient scrutiny of the recent papal indult, a composition, rehearsing that of Clement VII, in the style favoured at this period by the secretariat of the Roman Curia and employing three words for one in the best manner of the late Middle Ages and modern Big Business (the Counter-Reform was to tighten up their Latin), discloses that Dom François Rabelais, for so he may now be formally addressed, is authorised to hold one or more benefices and/or one secular cure "in the due form of law", and is dispensed from the monastic vows of poverty and obedience. This was, technically speaking, an abuse, fairly common and dating from the late fourteenth century. It made hay of the Rule of St. Benedict, and, like other abuses, had not much longer to run. Meanwhile it exempted Dom François from all monastic obligations. Like Fray Carillo in the old Spanish song, he may henceforth be looked for anywhere but in his cell, Bishop d'Estissac having taken him forthwith into his household as private secretary. One may see the complacent glow on his features from here.

There was going to be no mistake about the *agréments* of this latest turn in Rabelais' affairs. The life of Riley, I think Dom

François would have agreed, roaring with laughter at the homely idiom. In the bishop's service no bells drove him frantic by ordering his movements from dawn to dark, and no ever-looming authority frowned on recurrent Hellenistic dithyrambs. A wealthy, agreeable and highly-cultivated patron shared his tastes and entertained much polite company: nor was what the new secretary would call the belly-furniture of the episcopal table to be despised. Whether Rabelais was required, as has been surmised, to tutor the bishop's nephew and ward, Louis d'Estissac, seems uncertain. According to Jean Bouchet of Poitiers, the youth was a horsy type,

> . . . chevalier très hardy,
> De corps, de bras et jambes bien ourdy[1]

though apparently intelligent and well-mannered. In any case Rabelais' secretarial duties would keep him sufficiently occupied. Eminently satisfying to a man of his temperament were Bishop d'Estissac's tireless visitations of a diocese, formerly part of the Diocese of Poitiers and since reabsorbed, covering a large slice of Poitou and the Vendée and embracing 228 parishes, with 146 religious houses. Before the end of his employment with d'Estissac Rabelais will know nearly every nook and corner of it. Some fifty rural place-names stud the First Book alone, with enough local colour to furnish out a novel.

The Poitevin countryside is still a pleasant one, in its unexciting way; verdant, wooded, valleyed, undulating, well-watered, with a soil "soft as silk", as I have heard it described at a farmers' "ordinary". In the forest of Moulières, just north of Poitiers and the only notable one in the province, wolves were numerous down to the beginning of the twentieth century; elsewhere no more disturbing local fauna than innkeepers, lawyers, and a possible brigand or two awaited the traveller in Rabelais' day. The nearest vineyards of any consequence are those of Anjou and the Loire, and though Mr. Justice Bridlegoose of the Third Book refers to *le bon vin de Ligugé* it may be more judiciously said, adopting the current argot of connoisseurship once more, that if the little wines of Poitou have not a great

---

[1] "A most dashing horseman, well equipped in arms, legs, and frame."

deal to say, they are at any rate devoid of insolence. Regional dishes likewise are not showy. *Poulet poitevin*, the principal local contribution to French cookery nowadays, unless one can add *jambon cru de Poitou*, may have been so equally in Rabelais' time. Another local dish seems to have been among the five hundred or so served at Gargantua's supper-party to celebrate the defeat of King Picrochole, but Rabelais does not say how the *chappons de Loudunois* were treated. He loved his food, but he would not have qualified for the Home Page of the *Daily Snoop*.

In Poitiers, the old Roman capital of the province, Bishop d'Estissac had one of his numerous houses. The city was the third most important in France, with a strong University, founded by Charles VII in the previous century, and many Gothic and Romanesque buildings of distinction like the Cathedral, the Law Courts, the Hôtel de Ville, and the tall churches of Notre-Dame-la-Grande and St. Hilaire-le-Grand. Some eight miles outside the walls the elaborate château of Bonnivet, newly erected in the Franco-Italian style for Guillaume de Gouffier, Admiral of France, was due to survive for posterity in Rabelais' pages, after being destroyed in the eighteenth century, as the inspiration and, more or less, the model for the Abbey of Thélème. A passage in *Pantagruel* has led to a surmise that Rabelais may have entered himself in the Faculty of Law, for which the University of Poitiers was noted, during his three years' employment with Geoffroy d'Estissac. In another passage, describing a great stone upheaved by Pantagruel from a ledge of rock outside the city and called the *Pierre Levée*, on which students carved their names, he seems familiar with local undergraduate ritual:

> In remembrance whereof there is none entered into the Register and matricular Book of the said University, or accounted capable of taking any Degree therein, till he have first drunk in the Cabbaline fountain of Croustelles, passed at Passelourdin, and got up on the Lifted Stone.

He retails stories of every other University town he visits with the same air of intimacy, so this evidence may not amount to much, and the registers of Poitiers University covering this time have vanished. The *Pierre Levée* may still be viewed at Poitiers; a kind of rough dolmen-stone of disappointing size, cracked in halves. If we are to regard Mr. Justice Bridlegoose, doyen of comic lawyers, as a typical product of its Faculty of Law, and proud of it, Rabelais' opinion of the legal horde infesting the city would seem to have been low; his view of the contemporary judicial system as a whole, to be noted in its place, likewise.

He certainly esteemed the life of the Poitevin countryside. To and fro against a bustling rural scene the black habit of Dom François Rabelais, O.S.B., may be viewed flitting constantly for the next three years, whether at leisure or in the bishop's service, noting, listening, appreciating, haunting fairs, pilgrimages, and festas, chatting interminably with the yokels, almost certainly filling a notebook. Why he is always assumed to have carried a great mass of detailed observation in his head for at least ten years I cannot say. The patois of Poitou would be to a Tourangeau, till he mastered it, about as intelligible as the Cornish to a foreigner from adjacent Devon in this same period, and the wealth of Poitevin locutions scattered through the First Book alone seems to me to argue that our scholar drew up a glossary for use in a systematic manner, though he will not always bother to share it with his public. ("What is a *hutaudeau*?", one may hear his Parisian readers crying fretfully, "and how the devil does one *chalupper*?"[1]) But they could not complain that their author was merely hurling a mass of guide-book material at them. An example of his method is his somewhat un-Barriesque handling of the Fairy Mélusine. From this diaphanous portent, a considerable figure in Poitevin folklore and of Celtic origin, the great crusading Lusignans, once Kings of Cyprus and Jerusalem—their last known descendant, an aged governess, died in poverty in a dim London suburb some years ago—claimed descent, being a trifle more modest in this way than the ducal house of Lévy-Mirepoix, which at this time, as I think Proust recalls, claimed collateral descent from the Mother of God. The Fairy Mélusine was given to bathing at dusk in the Font de Cé at Lusignan and to building castles in the neighbourhood. To two of these, Tiffauges and Pouzauges, attached a horrid local reputation deriving from the black-magic orgies of Gilles de Raiz, Marshal of France, in the previous century, and it is curious that Rabelais never mentions this fantastic ogre. However, having jotted down the

---

[1] The first being a young capon, the other meaning "to shell nuts".

Mélusine legend he will use the fairy as a peg for a very raw joke in the chapter on the Nature of Chitterlings in the Fourth Book. The Doctor wasted very little.

In the intervals of exploring Poitou he was making, as was his habit, new friends, of whom the lawyer-humanist Jean Bouchet was the first. Something of a personage in Poitiers, where he practised as a *procureur*, a solicitor to the Courts, and the most worthy, amiable, obliging, pedantic, and genuinely cultivated of lawyers, ever conscious of having a large family to support, Bouchet was patronised by numbers of Poitevin magnates and was a frequent guest of Bishop d'Estissac; also, which is even more interesting, of Messire Loys de Ronsard, father of the poet, at Couture-sur-Loir in Anjou. Bouchet could very easily have made his friend a welcome guest at the Ronsard manor, one imagines, but this, disappointingly enough, he never did. Doubtless François Rabelais and Pierre de Ronsard would not have had a great deal to say to each other at the end of this particular year, 1524, Ronsard having been born in the previous September, and half a dozen years later, when Bouchet had begun to help tutor the boy during his longer stays under M. de Ronsard's roof, their contact would still be limited. A well-bred sixteenth-century child knew his place and did not aspire to his elders' company, let alone to contradict or insult them as modern self-expressionism requires. At the age of ten Ronsard went up to the Collège de Navarre, proceeding shortly afterwards, as a page in Queen Madeleine's suite, to Scotland. Before this time Rabelais had quitted Poitou for good. They could often have encountered each other in Paris in later years, but seemingly did not, and a seventeenth-century story, embroidered by Michelet, about their hobnobbing at Rabelais' presbytery at Meudon in the early 1550's has been proved a myth. One may pause to reflect again on the curious fact that the orbits of the two greatest literary figures of the French Renaissance, frequently so very close, seem never to have touched at any point.[1] The epitaph which Ronsard will dedicate in 1554 to a Rabelais portrayed as a glorious tosspot is

[1] As already noted, they were both present (with a few hundred others) at Guillaume de Bellay's funeral in Le Mans Cathedral on March 3, 1543. Here if anywhere, since Loys de Ronsard was one of the pall-bearers and Rabelais one of Du Bellay's chief protégés, the future poet might have had a word or a nod from the Doctor. But nothing is known.

merely a *jeu d'esprit* based on legend and gossip—or is it? The Pomme de Pin tavern in Paris, like the Mermaid in London, was a Café Royal of the period, a literary and artistic exchange and rendezvous. Both men were on the fringe of the Court, moreover, for some time. How could they not have met? Conjecture remains, grimacing vexedly.

A jocular letter in French, and in verse, from Rabelais to Jean Bouchet, written in bed and dated September 6, year unstated but probably 1525, gives us the next news of him. He is staying with Bishop Geoffroy d'Estissac at the Benedictine priory of St. Martin at Ligugé, a village seven miles from Poitiers. Bouchet, lately the bishop's guest, has returned to his solicitor's office at Poitiers. The bishop's secretary writes to inform him that everyone at Ligugé, His Lordship included, wants that *faconde et eloquente bouche* back at table again.

> A Ligugé, ce matin de septembre,
> Sixième jour, en ma petite chambre,
> Que de mon lict je me renouvellais,
> Ton serviteur et amy, Rabellays.[1]

Ligugé today is doubly a place of "atmosphere" and recollection. The monks are back again, after many vicissitudes ("Chants grégoriens à 10h. et 18.30," notes the serviceable *Guide Michelin*, current edition, for the benefit of visitors to Poitiers), and another distinguished Benedictine and literary shade now flits around sharing the village with Rabelais—or more likely, avoiding all contact with shudders. How violently Huysmans, who became an oblate at St. Martin's Abbey in March 1901, just before the expulsion of the monastic Orders from France under the Combes Laws, would have disliked (and vice-versa) any monk at Ligugé in his time even remotely resembling a Dom François Rabelais may easily be imagined. If stone and mortar retain any influences from past occupants there must stretch between the surviving tower of the original priory called the *tour de Rabelais*, where tradition places the Doctor's "little room", and the Maison Notre-Dame, the villa built by Huysmans not far away, and so long afterwards, a sea of antipathy wide as the Pacific.

---

[1] "At Ligugé, this morning of September 6, in my little room and in bed, from which I once more declare myself your servant and friend, Rabelais."

Regretfully unable to return to Ligugé, since he had a living to earn, Bouchet acknowledged Rabelais' compliment in verse characteristic of a lawyer nicknamed by his friends *le grand rhétoriqueur*, stuffed with classical allusions and chiefly interesting for a reference to Bishop d'Estissac's passion for gardening. Not sharing the Baconian predilection for alleys of sweet-smelling flowers and herbs, including "those which perfume the Air most delightfully, being trodden upon and crushed", d'Estissac planted (or caused his gardeners to plant) exotics like ebony and pistachio with fruit-trees of many kinds, set out, in the fashion of the time, amid formal box-bordered flowerbeds and arches of trellis. His kitchen-garden interested him equally. From Rome in 1535 and 1536 Rabelais will send him, with letters retailing the latest Roman gossip, packets of seeds for raising salads, such as *graines de Naples*, "of the kind grown in the Pope's gardens at Belvedere", and roots of flowers new to the bishop, such as "Alexandrine carnations" and a species of violet called *viole matronale*; adding at least once, after directions for cultivation according to the best Italian methods, an apologetic reminder of his being short of money, to which his patron was doubtless responsive. They were on the best of terms.

To complete the pleasures of his present employment Dom François had by the bishop's introduction been admitted to a select circle of virtuosi meeting at the Benedictine abbey of Fontaine-le-Comte, near Ligugé, under the aegis of Abbot Antoine Ardillon—*le noble Ardillon*, on whom Pantagruel will pay a courtesy-call in the Second Book, as on *le docte Tiraqueau* at Fontenay. The Ardillon group was composed of scholars, dons, lawyers, and professional theologians of three Orders, Benedictine, Augustinian, and Franciscan, mostly connected with the University and the Diocese of Poitiers. Bouchet mentions a few—Jacques Prévost, doctor and professor of theology, Nicolas Petit of the Faculty of Law, Canon Jacques de Puytesson of Ménigoute, and

> Ce Rabelay, sans oublier Quentin,
> Trojan, Petit, tous divers en vesture
> Et d'ung vouloir en humaine escriture . . . [1]

---

[1] "Our Rabelais—not to forget Quentin, Trojan, and Petit; all differently habited, but all one in their zest for humane letters."

Bouchet is sighing in the stuffy lawcourts of Poitiers for the Attic zephyrs of Abbot Ardillon's garden. Though his fellow-members were all provincials, some of the company had travelled in Italy and some corresponded with French fellow-humanists. All but, apparently, two of them were free-spoken Catholics holding a midway position between the Old Guard of the Sorbonne and the "Evangelicals" flirting with Geneva, and as such represented the overwhelming majority of Catholics in Christendom. Aware as anyone else of the urgency of reforms and looking impatiently to Rome for action, they were to be satisfied at length by the vigour of the Council of Trent. M. Plattard's research has discovered that only one of Ardillon's group left the Church: the Jean Trojan of Bouchet's lines, a Franciscan, who ultimately withdrew to become a Calvinist pastor elsewhere in France.

To the conversation of such a group it seems to me that Rabelais must have listened much as a crypto-Communist would listen to a gathering of orthodox Socialists, with ill-concealed impatience and secret contempt, although those grave and reputable clerics and lawyers, and the Abbot of Fontaine-le-Comte himself, could undoubtedly approve and supplement stock Rabelaisian tirades now familiar to us, since none of these attacked any essential doctrine of the Catholic Church. One may be permitted a momentary pause to marvel politely (*saepe miratus*) at the many quaint conceptions of this fundamental matter of doctrine aired by numbers of Rabelaisian commentators in modern times, some of them deriving plainly from the fogs of Cloud-Cuckoo Land. A fairly recent study of Rabelais lies before me, bearing the imprimatur of a great British university. Explaining that an "integral part" of the teaching of the Medieval Church was belief in succubi, witchcraft, and the Loup-Garou (which is amusing enough to begin with), it proceeds to establish the Doctor's final position as "almost as hostile to the doctrines of the Church as he was an avowed critic and enemy of Calvinism". There is in existence, as it happens, a contemporary corrective of such a notion.

Before rising in 1563 the Council of Trent issued a concise official summary of Catholic doctrine, past and present, commonly known as the Creed of Pius IV, regularly reprinted, and used today in the reception of all converts. Perusal of this Tridentine document, which takes about three minutes, shows the judgment on Rabelais quoted above to be fantasy. No essential of the Catholic belief as defined by Trent a few years after his death, is anywhere attacked by Dr. Rabelais; hence, no doubt, his benign treatment by Paul III and his absence from the Index. And hence, one feels, he would be justified in accusing wishful thinkers from his present place, whether in Purgatory or (one trusts) Paradise, of trying to make him look a fool. *Hors d'icy, caphards! de par le diable, hay!* But perhaps the Doctor has by now ceased to bellow.

Between what he wrote and what he said in the give-and-take of easy conversation with his peers may be a difference, naturally. That restless mocking tongue must have run away with him frequently at Fontaine-le-Comte as elsewhere; not invariably without protest, challenge, or contradiction. The Sorbonne, for example, was fair game, but only up to a point. Again, Pope Julius III's use of papal troops against Parma in the Emperor's behalf could be reasonably denounced—and, God knows, was, and by better poets on the Catholic side than Jean Bouchet of Poitiers, himself outspoken enough:

> Las! Faut-il voir la chaire de saint Pierre
> Teincte de sang? Quel horrible tonnerre!
> O quelle éclipse et scandalle en l'Eglise![1]

Ronsard on the contemporary Papacy is far more powerful. There is nevertheless a limit here also, and no true Catholic will overstep it. That the conversation of Abbot Ardillon's circle had a palpably Gallican tinge would be normal enough, Gallicanism in some degree having been a "positive" in the French Catholic bloodstream from the baptism of King Clovis down to the Vatican Council of 1870, which finally disposed of it. Except that the new chauvinist nationalism was now exacerbating it, resistance to recurrent demands by the Holy See in the sphere of jurisdiction, appointments, and dues coexisting with unimpaired spiritual allegiance to the Vicar of Christ was one of the routine commonplaces in the history of the West, as a sequence of bans, interdicts, Pragmatic Sanctions, and Concordats proclaims. As

---

[1] "Alas, are we to see St. Peter's Chair stained with blood? How horrible this thunder! What an eclipse, what a scandal for the Church!"

men are made, such clashes were, in a united Christendom, inevitable. The distinction is sufficiently demonstrated by Dante, in whose irascible bonnet Boniface VIII, as no lover of the *Divine Comedy* need be reminded, is an outstanding bee; yet of the abhorred Boniface, consigned by the poet to deepest hell, Hugues Capet is permitted to say in the *Purgatorio*: "I see the Fleur-de-Lis enter Anagni, and in his Vicar Christ made captive." Thus also did Abbot Antoine Ardillon's Gallicans distinguish, and thus in the Fourth Book, though sailing very near the wind, does even the careless and boisterous Rabelais, the king's propagandist; a magnifying-glass being admittedly required to see the dividing-line at times. Molière's case inevitably occurs as a parallel. Some of the barbs loosed off at the arch-hypocrite in *Tartufe* whizz dangerously near, if they do not actually wound, the devout. This fact Louis XIV's intelligent queen at once perceived, though the king—and, oddly enough, the papal nuncio—did not. To some extent in each case, no doubt, the blame attaches to the too-excitable Muse. Mightier than the sword, the pen is frequently less under control. It may be that the poets were rightly excluded from the Platonic State.

Contemplating Abbot Ardillon's circle in conclave and striving to distinguish the voice of Rabelais, the truly cautious will be on their guard against assuming that his position is finally definable now or at any time. In this aspect he is assuredly an enigma to which there is no key. For a time he appears to be a confirmed crypto-Calvinist, only to enrage Calvin by turning to blast Geneva and all it implies. Thenceforward, he is successively, or alternately, a Platonist, an anti-Platonist, an indifferentist, a Deist, and what seems a vague sceptic and materialist. Would any of these positions be the basic one? Consulting a surviving specimen of those annual almanacs he published at one period, as a sideline, we find the texts and teachings of any Catholic pulpit cropping up amid the ritual buffooneries. "Salut et paix en Jésus le Christ", begins the *Pantagrueline Prognostication pour l'An Perpetuel* (1532). Further on "Monseigneur Sainct Paul" is twice quoted in all earnestness, and the reader is reminded that neither Saturn, Mars, Jupiter, nor any other planet, and neither angels, saints, devils, nor men can exercise any influence over him *si Dieu de son bon plaisir ne le donne.*

In this passage, one may pause to remark, some have detected an echo of Rabelais' "evangelical" phase. The Reform having commandeered St. Paul, despite his teachings on the Mass, the Rabelaisian suffix of *trompette evangelicque* may seem to support this view. On the other hand the Reform strictly avoided any salute of the Apostle in the old idolatrous way, either as "Monseigneur" or "Saint", its claim to a monopoly of publishing the Gospels in the vernacular was quite unjustified (I have in my possession a beautiful little Catholic pocket-Testament in French, printed at Lyons in 1548), and the Doctor's "evangelicque" may, therefore, be as unreformed as Thomas à Kempis. And lest we should imagine him capable of keeping up any kind of gravity long, ensuing passages of the *Prognostication* return us, with him, to normality. Especially the final one:

Winter

In Winter, according to my tiny understanding, only those will be wise who sell their furs to buy wood. Thus do not the Antipodeans, according to Avenzouar [an Arabian sage]. If it should rain, be not melancholy; it is so much less dust on the roads. Keep yourselves warm. Beware of catarrhs. Drink of the best, till the rest is better, and do not s—— so much henceforth in your beds. Oho, chickens! Do you make your nests so high?

With one more unanswered question we may end the series. Those recurring sallies at Catholic theologians and practices, the monastic system, the temporal power of the Holy See, and one or two Popes in person—how do these chime, one asks oneself yet again, with such a testimonial from the Supreme Pontiff as the brief of 1536? What is one to think? Where did the Doctor stand? What did he believe? Did he know himself? Was he a Pirandello character, with half a dozen different egos functioning in turn? The mystery might be finally disposed of if we had any first-hand account of Rabelais' deathbed, but there is none. What evidence survives is posthumous and contradictory. The Enigma remains.

With which we may return to the year 1525.

It was a black year for France; opening with the news of Pavia, which must have shattered the serenity of Abbot Ardillon's

conversaziones like a bomb and interrupted even Dom François'
dalliance with the classical Muses for a time. A French campaign
for the domination of Italy, waged by François I against the
considerable forces of the Emperor—at this moment assisted,
not noticeably, by Henry VIII, not in person, and backed by
Leo X—had begun badly in 1521, when the French, let down
by their Swiss mercenaries, lost Milan, Parma, and Piacenza.
In 1524 the exiled rebel Constable of Bourbon, failing to take
Marseilles, was driven back over the Alps and Milan was re-
captured. Then came disaster. Besieging Pavia early in 1525,
and taking the advice of Bonnivet, his chief of staff, a general
given to misjudgments more than is normal, François launched
a strong attack with artillery preparation. The Imperials fell
back but swiftly rallied, the Swiss in François' pay let him down
again and ran, a sortie from the city took the French in the rear,
and the day, February 24, was lost. Fighting like a lion, horsed
and unhorsed, François barely escaped death in a hot mêlée before
he was taken prisoner. His generals Bonnivet, La Palisse, and
François of Lorraine were killed and his army decimated, with
half the fighting nobility of France dead or captured. "Nothing
is left me now," wrote the King to his mother that night, before
starting for Madrid and imprisonment, "but honour and life."
One may well conjecture that any decent French incarnation of
Browning's Renaissance grammarian on receiving this news would
cease temporarily to worry over settling the business of *Hoti*,
properly basing *Oun*, and proclaiming the doctrine of the en-
clitic *De*.

No doubt Ardillon's group had returned to their normal interests long before 1527, when the news of Bourbon's sack of
Rome would shock them—one member perhaps excepted—even
more thoroughly. Towards the end of that year Dom François
Rabelais was no longer among them, and had quitted Poitou
for good.

2

For the next three years his history is a blank, and only conjecture drawn from the Four Books has ever filled it.

Why Rabelais left the employment of the Bishop of Maillezais,
with all its delightful amenities, may not be so entire a mystery,

fundamentally speaking, as some of the learned make it.[1] The
Doctor was, as we shall soon perceive, something of a gypsy.
It seems to me that the simplest clue to his present disappearance
(and one or two others) is boredom. After three years or so of
the same group-contacts he was quite likely as ready for a new
deal as that member of one of Dr. Johnson's clubs who roused
the lion to a roar by suggesting that everyone in it had now
sufficiently travelled over everyone else's mind. ("Sir, you have
not travelled over *my* mind, I promise you!"—the two Doctors
should have met.) *Erupit, evasit;* Rabelais departed, therefore,
in seemly-wise, and by leave of his amiable patron. Or so one
might judge from those long, regular letters Rabelais will write
to the Bishop from Rome a few years hence, showing them to be
on the old terms, and himself still on the bishop's gratuity-list.

He left Maillezais, then, with the bishop's blessing—or did he?
In the petition of 1536 to Paul III begging absolution for another
offence he admits to quitting the abbey of Maillezais, to which
he was formally attached, without his superior's permission,
absque licencia sui superioris; which may refer to either the prior
in charge or the bishop-abbot himself. Can this mean that he
simply took French leave? Genial a prelate as was Geoffroy
d'Estissac, highly as he esteemed his brilliant secretary, was he
the type to condone a simultaneous breach of Canon Law,
discipline, and ordinary manners and to continue, as Rabelais
styles him in a letter to Tiraqueau some seven years later, *Mae-
cenatem meum benignissimum*, "my most generous benefactor"?
Would such a ripe canonist as d'Estissac be the man to connive
at the self-excommunication of a monk in his jurisdiction?

Adding one more insoluble mystery to the others, we plunge
further into fog. Where Rabelais went from Poitou, or what he
did for the next three years at least, is mostly undiscoverable.
When light breaks again he is signing the matriculation-register
of the Faculty of Medicine of Montpellier University on September 17, 1530, having decided long since for what Ronsard's
sardonic parent called the moneyed (*argenteuse*) science.

There is nothing very mysterious in this choice. Medicine
fascinated large numbers of the contemporary intelligentsia,

[1] M. Clouzot observes that if Rabelais had been tutoring the bishop's nephew
Louis, his duties would have ceased by 1527, when the young man married.

clerical and lay; a couple of immediately recurring illustrations
are the extremely eminent English clerico-medico-humanist
Thomas Linacre, one time parish priest of Wigan in Lancashire,
later physician to Henry VII, and his favourite French correspondent Guillaume Budé. Numbers of the secular clergy and
one or two of the Orders, especially the Benedictines, practised
medicine at this period, and it is hard to say whether they or
their rivals of the Faculty aroused more vomiting ecstasies of
fury and contempt in the redoubtable Paracelsus, who had incidentally included Montpellier University in his "Great Pere-
grination" a few years before Rabelais' entry. To the pragmatical
mind of Dom François Rabelais medicine would have appealed
ever since his Fontenay days; it was one of the topics of the
Tiraqueau circle. Since then, we gather from a Latin tribute by
the poet Salmon Macrin, he had specialised in the medical
theory of Hippocrates and Galen, adding to this a mass of knowledge in such more or less allied fields as botany, physics, mathe-
matics, and astronomy.

We may lawfully recognise the Doctor's commonsense. Paying
due lip-service to one of the most vainglorious bats in the Renaissance belfry, the cultus of encyclopaedic learning—"Let me see
thee an Abyss and bottomless Pit of Knowledge," writes Gargantua to his huge son in Paris—he is not among those of its
victims driven to a smattering of as many unrelated subjects
as possible, and a corresponding diffusion and waste of effort,
not to speak of premature old age and dumpish death.

> "Let me know all! Prate not of most or least,
>   Painful or easy!
> Even to the crumbs I'd fain eat up the feast,
>   Ay, nor feel queasy."
>
> Back to his book then; deeper drooped his head;
>   *Calculus* racked him;
> Leaden before, his eyes grew dross of lead;
>   *Tussis* attacked him . . .

Not such a fool as Browning's pedant, whom one suspects of
being a vegetarian, a water-drinker, and the dustiest of owls,
is our Doctor, who will at length cast up at the celebrated medical

D

schools of Montpellier in 1530 as fond of wine, laughter, and good company as any Falstaff. His wanderings in the interval seem to have been considerable.

Following in Pantagruel's wake through the opening chapters of the Second Book (and however meagre the clues, there are practically no other), one may assume his creator's present itinerary to have covered the seven University towns of Bordeaux, Montpellier, Valence, Angers, Bourges, Orleans, and Paris, in that order. Such a programme would be, for him, both pleasant and economical. However Dom François Rabelais travelled between given points, whether on foot or by mule, horse, waggon, or barge, alone or in company, he could rely for bed and board, if he could find no friend to lodge him, on any house of his Order in the vicinity. Nor could this particular Benedictine be mistaken by any kind of provost, as he paced the highway, discreet, observant, and quizzical, for the kind of monastic *gyrovagus* who was often as great a nuisance on the roads of the Dark and early Middle Ages as some of the Mendicants were to become later. Common prudence, though not one of his main traits, had surely ensured the inclusion among his papers of his dispensation, a very necessary passport. Indiscreet at times, he was not the man deliberately to court trouble, and decorum in public is his unvarying use. The Roystering Buffoon legend so firmly attached to his name has no foundation. Even when "between two wines", in the graceful French phrase, in agreeably learned company, the scholar would continue to merit that respect from men of position and worth with which we find him constantly regarded, whatever his relaxations with boon-companions. Any visions of wayside-tavern orgies, brawlings, masquerades, horseplay, thefts, fights, seductions, and general Rabelaisian whoobub and skulduggery at this or any time may, therefore, be dismissed as fantasy. Such pastimes Rabelais reserved for his romances, as all his acquaintance were aware.

Not so the Man in the Street, who declined long before the Doctor's death to make any such distinction. So the Legend grew, lewd, enormous, and naïve, merging creator with creation in the popular manner and eventually covering practically the whole of Rabelais' life down to his last dying gasp. Thus even at studious Fontenay he is alleged to have played a number of clownish tricks on his fellow-friars; doping wine, planting booby-traps, posing as the statue of St. Francis in the friary church. There is no truth in such inventions, which were given a fair impetus by the attack of Gabriel de Puits-Herbault, monk of Fontevrault, who returned as good blows for his cloth as Rabelais ever gave. The Doctor had certainly, as we say, asked for it. In Puits-Herbault's *Theotimus* (1549), he certainly received it.

Round about 1590 the Legend burst into vigorous new blossom. By that time the Rabelais family had quitted the house in the Rue de la Lamproie, which under new ownership became, as the historian De Thou records, a boisterous inn called The Lamprey, remaining so for nearly a century before transference further down the street. To this may be traced the libel on Maître Antoine Rabelais, who never tapped a cask in his life. Some years beforehand yellow journalism was already at work, as may be perceived from a fantastic note at the end of my 1588 Lyons edition. Professing to clear up one or two obscurities in the text, Jean Martin's anonymous editor remarks:

He makes a great issue of the Painted Cellar and the shop of Innocent the pastrycook. This was Rabelais' own house, and to my own knowledge belonged still to his son. To go from this house into the Painted Cellar one must—instead of descending, as is usual with cellars—go up as many steps as there are days in the year, since it is much higher than the house itself, and in fact stands as high as the Chateau, which dominates the town.

Plainly the honest fellow had never set foot in Chinon, merely passing on a picturesque story in the best manner of the Sunday Press, though the reference to "his son" is accurate enough, as will be perceived in due course. Of the rest of the surviving Rabelaisian Apocrypha it may be said, as is said of the Lowland gossip's recital in *Catriona*, that some of it is dull, some awful, and some both dull and awful. One anecdote which happens to be free alike from obscenity and blasphemy may be cited as conveying the mountebank atmosphere of all.

The time is May or June 1536, the place Lyons. Arriving from Rome on the way to Paris and finding himself penniless, Rabelais stuffs his travelling-bag with rags and other rubbish from the nearest dump and seeks a comfortable inn. Here, addressing the hostess with the air of a man of means, he demands a good room, a good dinner, and, beforehand, a smart boy to write from dictation. Once in his room he swiftly makes several paper packets of soot and ashes scraped from the chimney. On these packets he orders his hostess's young son, who appears at length with pen and inkhorn, to write distinctly "*Poison for the King*", "*Poison for the Queen*", "*Poison for M. le Dauphin*", and so on down the whole royal family. He then stows the packets carefully away in his bag, and whispering: "Boy! Both our lives are at stake! Not a word to your mother!" dismisses the lad and goes serenely to dinner. Very shortly, as might be expected, the Provost's police are on the scene, and Rabelais is arrested and conveyed under guard to Paris, free of charge, protesting on arrival that he has an urgent message for the king in person. Taken ultimately into the royal presence, amid the laughter of the king and the whole Court he unfolds his stratagem.

Such is the story, and it bulges with nonsense. In Lyons of all cities Rabelais need never go short of money, having a dozen intimate friends there, not to speak of three prosperous publishers, François Juste, Claude Nourry, and Pierre de Sainte-Lucie; men not merely of that high integrity and benevolent impulse traditional in the publishing world but doing remarkably well out of Rabelais' first two best-sellers, of which, as the trade-custom then was, they pocketed the entire profits, less a *douceur* vouchsafed the author on publication. And again, no chief of police in his senses would have Rabelais conveyed with an escort four hundred miles to Paris at the Crown's expense on the evidence before him; such a suspect would be clapped into the nearest prison till the Provost could examine his case at leisure, with unpredictable consequences. And again, the Dauphin happened to be gravely ill at this time, dying shortly afterwards; the Doctor's jape would therefore have been most untimely, and indeed dangerous. And in June 1536, finally, the king left Paris to deal with Charles V's invasion of Provence.

The rest of the Legend is equally baseless. Before bidding it farewell one may note that the most popular of the witticisms it puts into the mouth of the dying Rabelais, still accepted in some quarters as a typical piece of sceptical persiflage, has been shown by Étienne Gilson to be a common metaphor of the

contemporary Franciscan pulpit. "The farce is played . . ."
With which we may now catch up with Dom François as he
enters the gates of Bordeaux.

He may, as M. Plattard observes, have visited Bordeaux
before. Bishop d'Estissac had a château at Cahuzac, in Périgord,
and an abbey, to which a pilgrimage was attached, at Cadouin,
near Bergerac. From either place his secretary could easily
travel the few miles west to Bordeaux. He has little to say about
the city in the Second Book. The University is dismissed in
six words—"where he found no great exercise"—and nothing
else in Bordeaux claims Pantagruel's attention except "some
Marriners or Lightermen a-wrestling on the Key or Strand, by
the river side". Bordeaux University at this time was, in fact,
declining and in difficulties. Having a friend in the city, Rabelais
nevertheless—here we come on firmer ground—lingered some
time. His host was a cultured magistrate named Briand Vallée
du Douhet, formerly president of the *siège-royal* at Saintes in
Saintonge, where Rabelais had met him with Pierre Amy in his
Fontenay days. Something of an epicurean and a *bon vivant*,
which would do his reputation no great harm in his guest's eyes,
Vallée will earn a compliment in the Fourth Book—"that good,
learned, and just President"—which points to an agreeable stay.
It is during this Bordeaux period that Rabelais may be seen
at the medical school at Agen, twenty miles up the Garonne,
run by a celebrated and notorious friend of Vallée's, Julius
Caesar (or Giulio Cesare) Scaliger, mentioned by Rabelais in
his one and only letter to Erasmus, and in tactful Greek, as
"well-known to me . . . a thoroughgoing atheist". The waspish
and erudite Italian, who styled himself an Averroist of the School
of Padua, had left his native Verona in 1528 as physician to the
Bishop of Agen and settled in that town to practise and teach
medicine with considerable success, despite excessively venomous
gifts of tongue and pen. Like every other Left Wing Renaissance
savant of note attracting a modern biographer, he is, I have
gathered, the greatest man of his time. From the evidence of a
brace of insulting epigrams of 1557 aimed at Dr. François
Rabelais, then dead, in which our Doctor is himself branded an
atheist, not to mention a glutton, it would appear that he had

once had the misfortune, like Erasmus and many others, to disagree with Dr. Scaliger. Possibly the burden of fifteen children added to Scaliger's normal irritability. Perhaps a brush with the Inquisitor of Toulouse, which might have developed into something disagreeable but for the timely intervention of Briand Vallée, had not sweetened his temper either.

Quitting Bordeaux at length, Rabelais may be presumed to have made for Toulouse, where he acquired two new learned acquaintances, Jean de Pins and his ex-pupil, Georges d'Armagnac, now Bishop of Rodez. Pantagruel seems to have exhausted the interest of this city after learning to use the two-handed sword, "as the fashion of the Scholars of the said University is to bestir themselves in Games, whereof they may have their hands full". Of Toulouse University itself, plainly a progressive one, no word, barring a *boutade* on its custom of burning its tutors "like red herring". And Pantagruel travels on to Montpellier, where the Faculty of Medicine was celebrated throughout Europe. Even so, even though Rabelais will himself qualify and lecture here a few years hence, Pantagruel cannot be allowed to survey the dispensers of what Jules Romains' cynical Dr. Knock calls *la lumière médicale* without scoffing. "He thought to have set himself to the study of Physick, but he considered that calling was too troublesome and melancholick, and that Physicians did smell of glisters like old Devils." Thence he passes, by way of Avignon, with a passing fling at the women of that city, who "take great delight in playing at the close-buttock game, because it is Papal ground", to Valence, where "he saw no great matter of recreation, only that the Lubbards of the Town did beat the Scholars"; resenting which insolence Pantagruel instigates a gown-and-town battle and nearly drowns the louts en masse in the Rhône.

News of the rest of Pantagruel's road to Paris is scanty and a trifle dull, and may be briefly dismissed. Driven after a short stay by the plague from Angers, "where he found himself very well", he proceeds to Bourges, where he reads for some time in the Faculty of Law and finds the Civil Code "like unto a wonderfully precious, royal, and triumphant robe of cloth of Gold, edged with dirt"; wherein are denounced the medieval glosses of the learned Accursius, which in the Doctor's opinion make

French law "so scurvie, vile, base, and unsavourie, that it is
nothing but filthiness and villany". At Orleans, his next stop,
Pantagruel learns to play tennis, their principal occupation, with
the "swaggering Scholars", acquires thereby a licence in law,
and frequents the principal "Cupid's houses of Commerce".
Otherwise not a word is said about the University of Orleans, at
this period vigorous and prominent under the rule of Pierre
d'Estoille, tutor of Calvin and Béza and a jurist of European
reputation. No word, either, of a greater figure than he. Less
than a century beforehand St. Joan of Arc's rehabilitation-
process had linked her glory with the civic pride of Orleans for
evermore. Rabelais does not mention his country's saviour anywhere. She is a medieval barbarian and not even a comic one,
like the goose-footed Queen Pédauque of Toulouse, a considerable figure in southern French folklore whose alleged tomb was
still shown in Rabelais' time in the cemetery of Notre-Dame de la
Daurade in that city. Such an epitome of the ridiculous Gothic
Age his sparkling eye could scarcely overlook, nor did it. She is
duly glimpsed in the Fourth Book. The Midi was full of the
Regina Pedauca's story and pictures; round, astonished eyes, large
webbed feet, golden crown, a nursery heroine of the quaintest.
For some reason unknown no don has yet included her legend in
the "integral Church teaching" of the Middle Ages.

And so Rabelais comes at last to Paris.

3

As our provincial monk enters the capital from the Orleans
high road and strides under the vault of the Porte St. Jacques
into the reverberating main artery of the University quarter we
may pause a moment to survey him as he passes, perhaps a trifle
dizzied by the *ramage de la Ville*, down the long Rue St. Jacques
in the direction of what is now the Quai des Grands-Augustins.
Here, on the corner of the Rue St. André-des-Arcs, not far from
the Augustinian abbey dominating the left bank, the Benedictines
maintained a considerable house of studies called the Hostel St.
Denis. It depended on the Abbey of St. Denis-en-France, whose
present abbot was a brother of Admiral Bonnivet of Poitiers, and
it will be Pantagruel's headquarters in Paris. There seems no

reason against assuming that it was his creator's likewise; at least for a time.

Research has sufficiently established that Rabelais' first visit to Paris could have occurred at no other period in his career than this; whether he is still in his Benedictine habit is another matter. I am apt to conclude, for reasons set forth elsewhere, that he is.[1] Several respectable authorities, however, conjecture that he has already flouted Canon Law by assuming without permission the habit of a secular priest, a move which will afford him periodical tremors culminating some six years hence in a humble *supplicatio* to Rome. To the time of this exchange there is actually no clue.

Dom François Rabelais is at this moment round about thirty years old. Of his size and shape nothing is known. One imagines him as above average height, ruddy, robust, vigorous, and in short, as he describes himself in the Prologue to the Fourth Book, "hale, and cheery, as sound as a Bell, and ready to drink if you will". His face we know. Its arresting features are a pair of dark, shrewd, vigilant, questing, sardonic eyes; thin brows, seeming continually about to be arched in amusement, mockery, or wrath; an aggressive nose; a firm, imperious, impatient mouth. Since Benedictine monks went, and go, clean-shaved like the majority of clerics, the fringe of beard and the moustache decorating Rabelais' only known portrait will be assumed later, with the medical biretta. Fresh to the capital from nearly half a lifetime in the remote provinces, this monk does not seem to me the kind of bumpkin out of whom any jaunty *parigot* can take a rise. His eyes can blaze, his tongue can wound, and his command of Billingsgate in three or four languages can strike to admiring dumbness any saucy fishwife of the Petit-Pont or porter of the Halles. But such surprises must be very rare. A Roman *gravitas*, suitable to a man conscious of his powers and welcome in any civilised company, stamps Dom François' deportment normally, however much his eyes may twinkle, dance, or glitter. The attitude towards him of so many of the learned of his time affords sufficient testimony to this.

So he strides down the Rue St. Jacques towards the river, with a glint of derision at the tall, twin-towered Gothic pile of the Sorbonne on his left hand; scanning the elaborate multi-coloured signboards creaking from every gable, halting every

[1] See Appendix A: The Exchange of Habits.

few yards at another bookshop, printer's, or binder's, sniffing
fragrant wafts from a score of taverns and cookshops, dodging
splashes from a muddy kennel, sizing up passing dons and tutors
at a glance, wincing at the sudden clangour of the midday or
evening Angelus from a hundred bells, ignoring beggars and
ballad-mongers, kicking aside stray dogs, thumbing the grubby
pages of a second-hand Aldine or Plantin plucked haphazard
from a stall, elbowing through straggling vociferous groups of
academic youth, throwing an interested glance, undoubtedly,
at the long-since-vanished cloister of St. Benoît-le-Bétourné on
the corner of the Rue St. Jean de Latran, formerly the home of
the eminent François Villon, *poëte parisien* (to whose later years
is attached a bloodthirsty and totally apocryphal adventure detailed at length in the *Fourth Book of Pantagruel*), and generally
beginning to absorb and digest the sights, sounds, and smells of
a capital whose population the Doctor will in due course sum up,
a trifle arbitrarily, as *sot par nature, par bequarre et par bemol*; fools
by nature, by B-flat and B-sharp.

The University quarter was hardly changed from the time of
Villon, for whom Rabelais displays such a curious esteem, given
his opinion of the Medievals, that Gautier's theory that he used
him to a large extent for the portrait of Panurge seems plausible
enough. Clustering round and climbing the steep, winding Hill
of St. Geneviève, with its network of alleys, courts, and byways,
was the same Gothic forest of spires and belfries springing above
a conglomeration of fifty or sixty colleges, with their chapels,
schools, lecture-halls, hostels, and official residences. Crowning
the hill, the imposing Collège de Navarre doubtless preserved
in the bursar's quarters, and still in use, the stout iron-bound oak
chest which was robbed of five hundred gold crowns by Villon
and a couple of fellow-crooks at Christmas, 1456. In the great
hall of Navarre Panurge will rout the English scholar Thaumaste
in the fantastic dumbshow-debate of the Second Book. It may
be inferred that Rabelais looked over this important college,
where a dozen years later he might (had Jean Bouchet of Poitiers
done his duty) have clapped an avuncular hand on the shoulder
of Villon's coming successor to the throne of French poetry, the
undergraduate Pierre de Ronsard, aged ten.

Recalling the sufferings of his adored Erasmus, I see him

bestowing a dirty look *en passant* on the Collège de Montaigu, noting that this illustrious doghole stood, appropriately, in the Rue des Chiens. None of the half-dozen colleges founded since Villon's time, such as Sainte-Barbe, La Merci, and Le Mans, was of sufficient importance to detain his eye, and he would be far too well-informed to waste time looking for the site of the most sensational academic foundation, so far, of the Renaissance —the Collège de France, established by François I in this year 1530 at the instigation of Guillaume Budé and Jean du Bellay, Bishop of Paris, the Doctor's future patron, though not on the scale either of them had dreamed, and the first in Europe to dethrone the Queen of Sciences in favour of the Humanities exclusively. The Collège de France was to have no home of its own for some time, being in fact a roving body of professors called *Lecteurs Royaux*, designed to perform in any college in the Quarter which would receive them. Not till Henri II's reign would they find temporary anchorage in the colleges of Cambrai and Tréguier, and not till the time of Louis XIII, ninety years ahead, would the foundation-stone of their own establishment be laid at last on the site of the demolished Collège de Cambrai. One may well imagine Dr. Rabelais aglow with exhilarating reflections on the king's contribution to progress, the talk of every learned circle in France for some time, as he climbs the sacred Hill. During his later stays in Paris, a city he came to know as intimately as Rome, he must have become well aware of one other new foundation in the Quarter no less significant in French history. In 1540, and in the teeth of furious Gallican opposition from the Parlement of Paris, the Sorbonne, and the whole jealous academic horde—"The learned advocates and professors of Paris," observes René Fülop-Miller, "displayed more bitterness, tireless energy, and persistence than all the spies and informers in England put together"—the recently-mobilised Society of Jesus began demonstrating the New Pedagogy at the Collège du Trésorier, moving in due course to make the Collège de Clermont celebrated throughout the scholastic world. But Dr. Rabelais never once mentions the Jesuits, surely a target of targets. Did not a number of highly-respectable citizens of Breslau testify on oath about this time that they had with their own eyes seen a Jesuit preacher carried away by the devil in mid-sermon at the

Cathedral? The Doctor could have embroidered a story like that quite marvellously.

Meanwhile he was immersing himself very pleasurably, as three of the four books of Pantagruel testify, in the bustle of the University. In the Schools of the Four Nations in the Rue du Fouarre were held, as in Villon's time, the final disputations for the Arts degree; at the Sorbonne every divinity-student in the University still had to pass for licence and doctorate. Lusty black-gowned youth from all over Europe shouted and sang in the Mule, the Magdaleine, the Fir-Cone, the Striped Ass, the Trou-Perrette, and other taverns Villon knew, played ball-games, brawled, and fought in the Pré-aux-Clercs, devised those unseemly practical jokes on professors, dons, beadles, and the long-suffering city night-watch in which Panurge will all too energetically specialise, rioted in picnics at Gentilly, Boulogne, or St. Cloud, and slid away from under proctorial eyes to visit the *meretricules amicabilissimes* in the brothels of Champgaillard and the Cul-de-Sac. One can very well see Dom François Rabelais adding to a fresh notebook in a corner of some reputable tavern of the Quarter. Some *capette* from Montaigu, so called from his distinctive short cape, would embellish the horrors of his college's régime with gusto for a visiting provincial's benefit, and in their favourite rendezvous of the moment he must have surveyed and listened to members of the highbrow "pindarizing" set so well represented by the undergraduate from the Limousin who has an unfortunate brush with Pantagruel in the Second Book.

He poses very clearly in Rabelais' pages: "young and spruce-like", a precious, finicking youth, disguising native rusti-city—the Limousins were stock hayseeds and metropolitan butts of the period, alleged to live on turnips—under a mincing Parisian gait and accent. Every university knows the type. Meeting and greeting Pantagruel and his entourage one summer evening of vacation outside the gates of Orleans, and being asked whence he comes, the young man lisps: "From the alme, inclyte, and celebrate Academie which is vocitated Lutetia." And Pantagruel knits his brows.

What is the meaning of this? (said Pantagruel to one of his men). It is (answered he) from Paris. Thou comest from Paris, then (said

Pantagruel), and how do you spend your time there, you my Masters the Students of Paris? The Scholar answered, We transfretate the Sequane at the dilulcul and crespuscul; we deambulate the compites and quadrives of the Urb; we despumate the Latin verbocination; and like verisimilarie amorabons, we captat the benevolence of the omnijugal, omniform, and omnigenal foeminine sexe. Upon certain diecules we invisat the Lupanares, and in a venerian extase [etc., etc.].

It was a style favoured by a precious literary clique at this time, and Rabelais, who indulges himself frequently in much the same eccentricity, was the last man entitled to mock. What is chiefly interesting is the reaction of the enormous Pantagruel, elsewhere depicted invariably as a figure of slightly prosy rectitude, benevolence, and judiciousness, "the best little great good Man that ever girded a sword to his side", one who "never vexed nor disquieted himself with the least pretence of Dislike to any thing". Having frowningly listened for a space to the Limousin's prattle, the giant suddenly grips him by the throat and nearly chokes the life out of him. "Thou flayest the Latine! By St. John I will make thee flay the foxe!" Gasping for mercy in his native brogue—"*Vée dicou! Ho, Sainct Marsault! adiouda my!*"—the poor young man is finally released, and after surviving a few years in appalled recollection of Pantagruel's rage, dies of thirst. "A work of Divine vengeance," comments the Doctor genially, "shewing us that which saith the Philosopher [Aristotle] and Aulus Gellius, that it behoveth us to speak according to the common Language." There seems no valid reason for an outburst of savagery which the most bloody-minded of philologists must deprecate. It would be interesting to know what, if anything, lies behind this incident. Could some indiscreet member of the Pindarites, flushed with insolence and wine, have attempted to guy Dr. Rabelais one evening in their favourite tavern, for example?

Outside the University Quarter there was plenty to attract and divert the newcomer. The air of Paris was full of sparkle and animation. With Braun's beautiful map of the city (1530) before one it is possible to share some of its impact on Dr. Rabelais' eyes, ears, and nose, an organ less allergic to rich complicated stinks than our own, as may well be assumed. It was, as MM.

Dupech and D'Espezel remark in their admirable history of Paris, a sunny period; a period of prosperity and of artistic and intellectual stimulus on which a later generation of Parisians embroiled in civil war would look back with nostalgia, a period of elaborate public festivities, especially those connected with royal receptions and progresses, native and foreign. From under a great simultaneous wave of reconstruction a new Paris was steadily emerging. A contemporary official survey computes the number of the city's private houses at ten thousand, together with five bridges, fourteen gates, eleven public markets, and ten *faubourgs*, five on either bank. With the normal metropolitan uproar and perpetual bell-music now mingled a regular symphony of pick and shovel. In once-fashionable quarters round the Bastille and elsewhere the elaborate Gothic mansions of princes of the Blood, Burgundy, Flanders, Artois, and a dozen more, now reverted to the Crown, were being demolished to make way for new buildings and broader streets, and Pierre Lescot's workmen were battering away at the medieval Louvre; the massive donjon came down in 1528. The Italianate face of the new Paris was already displayed on the Pont Notre-Dame, which had collapsed in the floods of 1499 and been completely rebuilt. It carried sixty-eight tall, matched, comely houses in two rows, all of brick with stone facings and decorative swags, wreaths, and loops, *style renaissance*. Like their predecessors these houses were numbered; beneath them on road-level was a piazza with shops. Royal planning-schemes here as elsewhere invited the Municipality to conform in rebuilding to scale and pattern, and Rabelais must have seen the site being finally cleared for the new Hôtel de Ville by Domenico di Cortona, better known as Boccador. Of this stately monument François I personally passed the plans; till the Commune of 1871 destroyed it Paris had few finer jewels. The crumbling and "competently scurvie" twelfth-century ramparts of Philippe-Auguste on the left bank, out of which the city was long since bursting, certainly engaged the Doctor's attention. Panurge has a rebuilding scheme for these fortifications in the Second Book. Of the kind called "typically Rabelaisian", it bears no resemblance to Charles IX's solution later in the century. Discussing the new building-schemes at large with some complacent chance-met burgess, the Doctor would, doubtless, have learned the fact, interesting to him, perhaps, as to us, that contrary to provincial belief King François I did not rule Paris, and was indeed scrupulously careful to avoid any kind of interference with the affairs of a Municipality which, though unable to refuse him recurring loans during a long, expensive struggle with the Emperor, stood jealously foursquare on its civic rights and was hence "invited" to conform with the new plans, not "ordered". Within a reign or two this protocol would be one more loss on which Parisians looked back with a nostalgic sigh.

Of the pastimes of Renaissance Paris—tennis, the *jeu de paume*, was becoming the rage about this time, and tourneys were frequent—the Doctor records nothing, oddly enough, considering the space he devotes to the games and sports of Gargantua and Pantagruel; and if he ever witnessed one of the periodical hangings at Montfaucon, the Tyburn of Paris, he does not bring this great gallows, with its Villonesque memories, into the excursus on hemp in the Third Book. One may, I think, deduce that, apart from one singular escapade, to be noted shortly, he took little interest in the Paris outside the University, his spiritual home. *Aquí està encerrada el alma del licenciado.* At some time or other before the early autumn of 1530, at any rate, his first visit—a longish one, possibly of a year at least—came to an end, and we find him again in the south. During his wanderings in the provinces he had, we may recall, visited the formidable Scaliger's medical school at Agen near Bordeaux. Here he met, and as usual impressed, a professor of the Faculty of Medicine at Montpellier, Dr. Jean Schyron, one of Scaliger's ex-pupils, later chancellor of his university. To this meeting we owe our next sight of Dom François. He is at Montpellier, signing the matriculation register of the Faculty, having taken Schyron for his sponsor, *pater*, in the customary form.

The entry, written with a thin quill in Latin, in a legal hand, goes thus:

> I, François Rabelais of Chinon in the diocese of Tours, present myself here for the purpose of studying medicine, taking for my sponsor the eminent Master Jean Schyron, doctor and professor in this bountiful University. I undertake to observe all the statutes

of the Faculty of Medicine aforesaid as they are customarily obeyed by all inscribing their names in good faith and on oath, as usage prescribes. I accordingly sign my name in my own hand this seventeenth day of September, in the year of our Lord 1530.

He signs himself, *Rabelaesus*, with a flourish. And since a monk of St. Benedict would normally signify this condition in official documents, one may surmise that he is now wearing the habit of a secular priest, for his own convenience and in defiance of the regulations.

IV

Enter the Comic Muse

I

"Follow me, Avicenna, Galen, Rhasia, Montagnana, Mesus! Follow you me, not I you—you from Paris, from Montpellier, from Wirtemberg, from Meissen, from Cologne, from Vienna, from the Danube, the Rhine, and the Islands of the Sea, from Italy, Dalmatia, Sarmatia, and Athens—Greek, Arab, Israelite, follow you me, not I you! Of you not one will survive, even in the most distant corner! I shall be the Monarch! Mine will be the Monarchy!"

Thus Dr. Bombast von Hohenheim, the Great Paracelsus, in one of his politer manifestos to the medical universe, and one could wish with fervour that his irruption into Montpellier University had coincided with Rabelais' entry some fifteen years after him. How gloriously they would have clashed may well be imagined—every Faculty of Medicine in Europe being in Dr. Paracelsus' judgment a nest of fools, rogues, and assassins, with his choicest execrations reserved for the "medical priest-crew", who not only poisoned and maimed their victims but—this would hardly include Dr. Rabelais—added prayers to the bill. Moreover the German bully had results to show now, let alone a few years later, when he would flourish a flattering testimonial from Erasmus, whom he treated successfully for stone and kidney-trouble at Bâle. A sizeable jewel from the Markgrave of Baden, whose chronic dysentery yielded to a prescription involving "trochisks" of powdered bloodstone, coral, spodium, and tanacetum, would speak for itself likewise.

How long and in what fashion the professors at Montpellier coped with Paracelsus is not known. Medical brawling has become so genteel down the ages that even the historic riposte of Dr. Woodward to his enemy Dr. Mead after being disarmed in a brisk rapier-duel two hundred years ago is rarely quoted, still less commended, in textbooks of medical practice and etiquette nowadays.

> "Beg for your life!"
> "Never, till I'm your patient!"

Pondering these things, one may be permitted again bitterly to regret the short gap in time and space which deprives lovers of medicine and gaiety of a collision at Montpellier University between Dom François Rabelais of (still) the Order of St. Benedict and the "Prince of Spagyrists and Trismegistus of the Mechanical Arcana"—Dr. Paracelsus had a nice range of self-awarded honorifics—which must inevitably have blossomed into a shindy, with a rollicking chapter of *Pantagruel* to immortalise it. Whether Rabelais ever acquired sufficient Hebrew to master the Cabbala, the study of which Gargantua recommends, in his airy way, to his student-son in the Second Book, is not apparent. These sixty famed manuscripts, containing the secrets of all knowledge and alleged to be the work of the Prophet Esdras, fascinated not a few of the Renaissance intelligentsia; even a genius like Pico della Mirandola had been fooled by them. Dr. von Hohenheim had their mystical jargon constantly on his tongue, and such of his pet whimsies as the infallibility of the Blessed Balsam of the Heavenly Stars, which restores youth to the aged dying, and the powers of the Magical Hat of Moses and the Hidden Word *Schemhemphorasch*, by which anyone possessed of the Great Secret can re-create Heaven and earth, obviously cry aloud for a little Pantagruelist treatment. But Rabelais leaves this rich lode untapped. His arrival at Montpellier fifteen years late robs us thereby not only of an episode in medical history more diverting than the Mead-Woodward duel, but of a chapter of the Third Book in which Panurge, pursuing his quest for palatable advice on marriage, should have gone on from the astrologer-cuckold Her Trippa to a Cabbalist of super-Paracelsian lunacy. He does not, and what Béroald de Verville calls *les tristes enfumez*, the melancholy smoke-begrimed alchemist horde brooding over their aludels, crucibles, and alembics, stock figures of fun for every satirist from the dawn of the Middle Ages down to Rare Ben Jonson's day at least—all these indomitable optimists go scot-free. Even if modern science, by proving transmutation practicable, has shown the alchemists to be not the fools they seemed, their absence from the Four Books is deplorable.

On research in fields less esoteric than astro-alchemy—in which branch alone Montpellier's most notable pioneers, including such encyclopaedic masters as Ramón Lull and Arnaud de Villeneuve, were all β-minus morons to Dr. Paracelsus, the only adept in the world to carry a piece of the veritable Philosopher's Stone in his sword-pommel—was based the European reputation of the Montpellier Faculty, second only to that of Salerno all through the Middle Ages. Its prestige had declined somewhat by the sixteenth century, though it is said to have enjoyed a brief St. Martin's summer round about the period of Rabelais' stay, and Montpellier now was well behind the times. "While the schools of Italy hummed with the disputations of the new scholarship," observes a British medical historian, "Montpellier and Oxford slept and Avicenna ruled"; to which the majority of illustrious names in Renaissance medicine, Fracastoro, Capri, Matteoli, Acquapendente, Fallopio, Cesalpino, will testify. With such figures there was none comparable on Montpellier's staff, more than half of whom, at a period when every scholar in Europe interested in the subject was damning the medical science of Arabia as the spawn of corrupted Greek texts, continued to extol the Arab masters in the traditional manner, with Avicenna still their guide and lodestar. Even those progressives who had gone over to the Greeks lectured from Latin versions of dubious accuracy.

Might a violent Hellenist like Dom François Rabelais have been expected to choose a less notoriously conservative university? One suspects the choice was not entirely his. Somebody, doubt- less his generous patron the Bishop of Maillezais, must have guaranteed his board and fees, the total of which at Montpellier over a five-year course could be estimated, in the 1530's as today, at some hundreds of pounds sterling. Ruled by a chancellor, a dean, and two procurators, the Faculty supported four full-time professorial chairs, embracing a couple of subjects at least in which Dr. François Rabelais is awarded a good mark in most histories of Renaissance medicine. Botany had been his darling hobby for years. In anatomy, for which demonstrators at Mont- pellier were furnished with human skeletons and, at intervals, a whole criminal corpse for dissection, he will make a considerable name. And if the principal medical preoccupation of the period involved one of his most consecrated jokes, it is permissible to visualise him bent over a recent textbook in Virgilian hexameters entitled *Syphilis, vel Morbus Gallicus,* published by the master Girolamo Fracastoro of Verona in 1530, to become immediately a European classic—

> What varied fortunes and what germinations have produced a fierce and rare disease which has ravaged all Europe . . . all this I shall tell in my song.
> And I shall tell of new treatments . . .

—with a countenance as drained of hilarity for once as those of the new scourge's most stricken victims. I fancy Fracastoro's treatise would provide a few choice Rabelaisian japes for the common-room notwithstanding. That fundamental gaiety must swiftly have made the new arrival popular with even those shellbacks of the Old Guard who continued to combine Arabian medicine with astrology, horoscopy, and the ritual uroscopy, for their addiction to which an old gibe is hurled at them in the Third Book:

> Stercus et urina medici sunt prandia prima . . .[1]

Some of the Old Guard's research-chemists, had their activities attracted him, could probably have inspired him to even more derision, seeing that a century after them the most-eminent Van Helmont will be recommending a simple experiment to prove spontaneous generation, namely the sealing of a foul shirt in a glass vessel with a quantity of selected grain at a given temperature; which fermenting compost will in a month or two generate live mice. Yet, on second thoughts, would such fantasies necessarily divert a Rabelais? Numbers of Science's modern sceptics trust in the amulets and ju-jus of the African Bush, as is well known. The aggressive new Bachelor may have cherished an amiable superstition or two likewise.

For a Bachelor of Medicine by examination Rabelais had become six weeks after arrival, as the Montpellier registers show,

[1] A medical joke.

thanks to outstanding brilliance and the influence of Dr. Jean Schyron, the normal qualification-period being two years; and already he was blowing a loud trumpet for the Greeks. Having elected to read Hippocrates and Galen once more for the three-months' course known as the "Little Ordinary", he was soon impressing his tutors by correcting the Faculty's textbooks from a Greek manuscript of his own, how acquired is not known. Though not so extensively as Italy, France at this time was a haven for refugees from Byzantium, and an occasional manu-script, authentic or otherwise, could be picked up, for example in the Midi, very cheaply.

Bachelors of Medicine at Montpellier might be called on at intervals to lecture. Rabelais was duly invited to address the Faculty on his burning theme. Recalling this occasion in the preface to his edition of Hippocrates and Galen published at Lyons in 1532 he observes with pardonable satisfaction that the Great Hall was full. Doubtless the new man showed off his paces to some effect, amid the customary pooh-poohs and Oh-my-Gods of the Old Guard, who, according to one or two medical authorities, had heard it all before. Rabelais will deal briefly with these reactionaries in the First Book. Figuring in Urquhart's translation as "a rabble of loggerhead Physicians nuzzled in the brabling-shop of Sophisters", they are not so recognisable as in the original *tas de badaux medecins herselés en l'officine des Arabes*. Such a view would naturally not have been aired by the lecturer in those words, since Dr. Rabelais never forgot himself in public. As for his propaganda for the Greeks, which he repeated apparently more than once, it turned out to have no great effect. Avicenna continued to rule Montpellier for at least half a century more.

Once more inevitable qualification imposes itself. It is on record that Dr. Rabelais—as we may permissibly henceforth style him, as he does himself, though he will not take his final degree, a formality in any case, for some years yet—actually did play the fool in public at Montpellier; on a special occasion, however, and *en famille*. Like lawyers, whose Christmas gambols at the Inns of Court in London all through the Middle Ages and down to the Georgian era make such incredible reading, doctors were merrier fellows then than now, relaxing in a body at intervals like schoolboys and continuing to welcome the chief festivals of the Church with traditional whoops and junketings. At Montpellier University they made a feature of celebrating Epiphany, Twelfth Night, in the customary way with feasting, dancing, moralities, and farces. In one of these latter productions Dr. Rabelais is perceived taking a leading part. Its title, slightly compressed, is *The Dumb Wife*, and the piece is plainly inspired to some extent by the evergreen medieval farce of *Maistre Pierre Pathelin*; very likely he wrote it himself. "I never in my Lifetime laughed so much as at the acting of that Buffoonry [*pathelinage*]," says Carpalim to Pantagruel in the Third Book, recalling the rompings of Dr. François Rabelais, named with seven of his brethren, Doctors Anthony Saporta, Guy Bourguier, Balthazar Boyer, Tolet, Jean Quentin, François Robinet, and Jean Perdrier; nearly all professors and officially grave and dignified persons, whom we must strive to see roaring and bouncing about the stage of the Great Hall and whacking each other vigorously to the delight of an audience of dons, tutors, students, and servants of the Faculty.

In many ways *The Dumb Wife* may have lacked alike the construction of a Sardou and the epigrammatical finesse of a Wilde. His speechless bride having been successfully operated on, her husband finds himself swiftly driven half crazy by continuous nagging. For this disaster the two doctors concerned can suggest no remedy but to render him stone-deaf "by Vertue of some Drugs, Charms, or Enchantments". This they do, the result being to drive the wife into a frenzy in her turn. So we work up to the dénouement, from which Molière stole a little for his *Médecin Malgré Luy*.

> Some time after, the Doctor asked for his Fee of the Husband; who answered, that he truly was deaf, and so was not able to understand what the tenure of his Demand might be. Whereupon the Leech bedusted him with a little, I know not what, sort of Powder, which rendered him a Fool immediately; so great was the stiltificating Vertue of that strange kind of pulverized Dose. Then did this Fool of a Husband and his mad Wife joyn together, falling on the Doctor and the Surgeon, and did so scratch, bethwack, and bang them, that they were left half dead upon the Place, so furious were the Blows which they received.

Good hearty red-nosed stuff, reminiscent more than once of the parent-farce, in which the shepherd Thibault's great line, when pressed for payment by cunning Maître Pathelin, his lawyer, is a repeated "Baa, baa!", as taught him before the lawsuit. Doubtless a wealth of clinical and intramural jokes supplied *The Dumb Wife* with many lines such an audience would appreciate, and eight doctors playing a piece written for four characters certainly added to the fun. Two of them at least were, like Rabelais, men of future distinction. Saporta, in due course chancellor of his university, was later appointed physician to the King of Navarre; Tolet is hailed by André Tiraqueau in his treatise *De Nobilitate* as an honour to French medicine. And if the profession itself took a few gay knocks throughout the piece, the spectacle was not offered to patients.

Thus did Rabelais hurl himself as wholeheartedly into play as he undoubtedly did into his work, which will furnish such a wealth of allusions in the Fourth Book of medical, physiological, botanical, zoological, anatomical, and other scientific import, not to speak of numerous citations of Galen, not a few of Hippocrates and Aristotle, and the long lyrical oration of Panurge in the Third Book in praise of the Microcosm, as the human body was called by medieval medicine, for which it illustrated on a tiny scale the harmonies of the Macrocosm, or universe. As Panurge waxes in enthusiasm we see the bodily organs functioning all together neatly like the working model of an engine under glass in some scientific museum. "*Vertuguoy!* I sink, I drown, I perish, I wander astray and quite fly out of my self when I enter into the consideration of the profound Abyss of this [physiological] world!" And Panurge proceeds to extol above all that system of demand-and-supply whereby is ensured "the future Conservation and perpetuating of Human Kind". From this ecstatic tribute to Nature's efficiency Dr. Rondibilis, cross-examined later by Panurge, will dissent. In the case of womankind, Rondibilis thinks, Nature has gone somewhat astray; in fashioning such an imperfect sex she seems to favour "the social delectation of the Man" rather than "the perfect'on and accomplishment of the individual Womanishness, or muliebrity". From this debate will emerge the fact that Dr. Rabelais is not invariably the derisive gynophobe he seems. As the discussion on marriage in the Third

Book proceeds he will change his tune, *pro tem.*, remarkably, as we shall perceive. Women as a sex will cease for a moment or two to be a ribald joke. A few of them will actually be praised for virtue. It may or may not be of significance that this surprise follows a period during which Dr. Rabelais has stooped to collaborate with at least two of the species in that "perpetuating" process Panurge so admires (he would). Truly *amor vincit omnia*, though whether the lover ousted the physiologist we shall, alas, never know.

So much must he have continued to enjoy the academic round at Montpellier that it is with something of a mild shock that we find this agreeable existence coming abruptly to an end within less than two years. In the spring of 1532 he is found living in Lyons, working for a bookseller. There is no available explanation, saving the conjecture that whoever might be paying his terms at the University must have ceased doing so. If this benefactor were indeed Geoffroy d'Estissac the mystery merely deepens, since the bishop will continue to assist his ex-secretary at intervals until his death. But the wealthy are notoriously wayward. It might even be that they had quarrelled.

Whatever had happened—to get back to firm ground—the Bachelor of Medicine was thrown for a time on his own resources, and a move was imperative.

2

Next to Paris, Lyons was the obvious goal for any French Renaissance scholar in urgent need of employment. Standing then as now (to echo a Victorian guide-book on the Pyramids) at the confluence of the great rivers Rhône and Sâone, this opulent city, the half-way halt for traffic each way between Paris and Rome, was notable for its quarterly international fairs, its money market, with resident Italian bankers, its printing-houses and a dozen other flourishing industries, its export trade West and East, its close commercial and cultural contacts with Italy, the civic pride of its wealthy bourgeoisie, and the splendour of the Cathedral canons, all of noble birth and, in choir, mitred.

Inhaling the mingled river-fogs with the bustling dour-faced Lyonnais citizenry at this time was a fairly considerable colony, native and foreign, of the sectaries of whom Lyons has ever since sheltered an assortment; the most interesting specimen in recent times must be the mystic, slightly sinister Vintras conventicle of the 1880's with which Huysmans became temporarily entangled. In the world of letters the city was particularly esteemed in Rabelais' day for its neo-Platonic intelligentsia, as impressive a cenacle of humanists, philologists, grammarians, bibliophiles, and other cultured types as any French city could show, Paris alone excepted. There was also a rising Lyons School of verse, ruled by the poets Maurice and Guillaume Scève, and specialising in obscurely-precious languors and mopings, often of oddly Yellow Book flavour. A decade or so hence a sprinkling of women poets will lend the Lyons School a peculiar *cachet* in advanced Parisian literary circles. Most famous of these ladies in posterity's judgment is the formidable bluestocking Louise Labé, said to have fought in male armour at the siege of Perpignan as *le Capitaine Loys*; a poet of excessively weepy and cloying femininity.

> Quand vous lirez, ô Dames Lyonnoises,
> Ces miens escrits pleins d'amoureuses noises . . .[1]

And in even more lachrymose condition:

> Ne reprenez, Dames, si j'ay aymé;
> Si j'ay senti miles torches ardantes;
> Mile travaus, mile douleurs mordantes;
> Si en pleurant j'ay mon tems consumé . . .[2]

The fair Labé was a child of six or seven when Dr. Rabelais arrived in her native city. They might quite conceivably have encountered and disliked each other in some Lyons *salon* before his final departure ten years later. Her sister-poet Jeanne Gaillarde was another bright young star in the galaxy clustering round the Scèves and Antoine Héroet, whose celebrated manual of Platonic Love in decasyllabic verse, *La Parfaicte Amye*, perfectly exhibits the kind of pallid, finicking mysticocardery which in some

---

[1] "Ladies of Lyons, when you read these verses of mine, so filled with amorous plaints . . ."

[2] "Blame me not, ladies, if I have loved, if I have known the flame of a thousand blazing torches, a thousand labours, a thousand cruel pangs, if I have consumed my days in weeping . . ."

quarters offset the crudeness of Renaissance sensualism. Since a master-poet like Pierre de Ronsard did not much care for the muses of Lyons one may well assume that Dr. François Rabelais, fixing women in general with a humorous and clinical eye, would steer clear of this portentous clique. He found sufficiently congenial company among the main body of literati, calling themselves the *Sodalitium Lugdunense*. Among these, Étienne Dolet and his ally Bonaventure des Périers, the bibliophile Guillaume de Choul, the Latin poet Gilbert Ducher, who eulogised Rabelais in verse, the lawyer-humanist Jean Voulté, who did the same and was a few years hence to become concerned for Rabelais' soul (a rare happening), and Jean de Boyssonné, yet another learned poet, will be among his intimates almost from the beginning. Having a living to earn, it is possible that the Doctor did not see as much of these kindred spirits for a time as he would have liked. His days were now spent in hacking for one of the city's leading booksellers, at this period publishers as well. The well-known Sébastien Gryphe, or Gryphius, had been sufficiently impressed by Rabelais' Montpellier notebooks to find him a place among the needy back-room erudite who edited and annotated new publications, drew up prefaces and dedications, corrected proofs, compiled catalogues, collated manuscripts, and received and forwarded those lengthy epistles in Greek and Latin with which savants all over Europe so liberally bombarded one another, with their booksellers' assistance.

Over and above literary and learned conversaziones mitigated, doubtless, by not a few convivial evenings with Dolet, a noted tosspot, and his immediate cronies, the city of Lyons (less grim a citadel of Mammon in the 1530–40's than the Manchester of France we know today) was to furnish Dr. Rabelais with relaxation of a special kind. Now or later during his stay, and following the example of some of the highest Roman hierarchy till the arrival of the Counter-Reform, he acquired a mistress, name unknown, by whom he had a son, christened Théodule, who died at the age of two. This adventure, which causes some of the Doctor's devotees such embarrassment that one of them dismisses Canon Law and describes it as a "marriage", has been accepted by the learned since the earliest dawn of Rabelaisian exegesis as the Doctor's one and only *affaire de coeur*. It would still be so accepted but for a document discovered by M. J. Lesellier in the Vatican archives and published in the Parisian quarterly review *Humanisme et Renaissance* in 1938. Celibacy evidently bored Dr. Rabelais at times as thoroughly as Lent. Little Théodule Rabelais, we learn, had an elder half-brother and sister, both alive at his birth and surviving him for years.

A formal certificate of full legitimisation of birth granted by Paul III on January 9, 1540 on behalf of one François, a school-boy, and his younger sister Junie, both of the diocese of Paris and the offspring of "François Rabelais, priest", and a widow unnamed attests the facts. Hacking his way with scholarly doggedness through the jungle of perplexities and conjecture enveloping this as so many other Rabelaisian exercises, M. Lesellier establishes beyond doubt that these children must have been born during and after Rabelais' first visit to Paris in 1529–30, and that on quitting the capital for Montpellier he apparently took no further interest in them or their mother, by whom the legitimisation petition—she was intending little François for the Church, it seems—was presented. A few technical and other issues involved in this direct papal grant, a rare one in the cir-cumstances, are discussed at length by Lesellier, but need not concern us.[1] A certain blithe Rabelaisian verve is perceptible in the setting up of another irregular and fruitful *ménage* so soon. On the other hand, it is possible that the Doctor continued to support his Parisian offspring, voluntarily or otherwise, even if he never set eyes on them or their mother again. The really remarkable thing is that his enemies never exploited either lapse.

It may well be, as M. Lesellier suggests, that lack of paternal authority accounts for both Rabelais' elder children turning out so unsatisfactorily. François frustrated maternal hopes, went to the bad, and was ordered by a court of the Parlement of Paris in 1558, some five years after his father's death, to be fined forty sols Parisis and flogged for his share with two other toughs in a theft with violence. Junie in her later years, if we are to believe Béroalde de Verville's mention of "the author's daughter", con-tributed some raw stories attributed to Rabelais to the *Moyen*

---

[1] Reg. Suppl. 2/405/f.232. The document is signed by an episcopal official, "C. Cesenatensis". Only six legitimisations were granted during the fifteen years of Paul III's pontificate, according to Lesellier's research.

de Parvenir; but De Verville is the least trustworthy of witnesses, drunk or sober. Of their mother nothing is known.

Thus the Vatican document affords no edifying glimpse of the great censor of monasticism. Little Théodule, had he been abandoned likewise, might have disappointed his father's adulators equally. One more Rabelais, Charles by name, was seeking benefices at Rome in 1551. Whether he was a nephew or the offspring of yet another liaison M. Lesellier does not venture to decide. And if the clemency of Paul III seems remarkable, we may recall that the Doctor had recently received absolution and now had, canonically speaking and *pro tem.*, a clean sheet. What was past was past, and to legitimatise his children was pure charity.

The liaison at Lyons, at any rate, failed to shock his friends. The Sixth—in some Reformed circles already altered to the Seventh—Commandment was somewhat languidly observed at this time in ecclesiastical circles, and not exclusively on one side; Calvin's chief lieutenant Théodore de Béza, for example, kept a mistress and ultimately married her. With Abraham the convert Jew in the Decameron every devout Catholic of the period could realise, with very mixed feelings, that only an institution directed and protected by the Holy Ghost could survive such scandals as many of its clergy provided. Some of these were being severely dealt with even now by prelates conscious of their responsibilities. The Counter-Reform would restore complete order ere long.

Striving for a glimpse of Dr. François Rabelais in the process of conducting his second (known) amorous intrigue, all heedless of a lately-deserted hearth in Paris, it occurs to one, watching him vanish discreetly into some house in a quiet Lyons by-street—possibly in the old St. Jean quarter surviving by the Sâone —that so far as he was ever capable of love he may have been experiencing it now. A relative matter, obviously. From end to end of the huge unwieldy Rabelaisian masterpiece there is only one fleeting reference to human love, though there is plenty and to spare about the sexual act, evoking the crudest japes of the medical students' common-room. On this evergreen topic the Doctor remains the complete *carabin*, the total Bob Sawyer whom Dickens never dared to draw. Normally, love is to him no more

than it was to be, two centuries later, to the cynical Chamfort—
"l'échange de deux fantaisies, le contact de deux épidermes"—and
he will have no truck with the Platonic worship of women preached
by Héroet of the Lyons School and his flock, a gospel immensely
fashionable in highbrow circles. But if it is almost as difficult to
imagine a Rabelais in love, properly speaking, as it is a Stendhal,
who published a treatise on the subject, there is no doubt at all
about the actuality of the Doctor's liaison. It emerges into daylight at two-year-old Théodule's death, when some Latin verse-
tributes from Jean de Boyssonné, to be quoted in their place,
will offer the child's father the respectful sympathy of all his
learned friends.

And that, unfortunately for amateurs of the bizarre, is all. A
vanished Lyons alcove has taken its secrets with it. A Rabelais
tender, a Rabelais passionate, a Rabelais transfigured, a Rabelais
subdued and captive, a Rabelais possibly outdoing Dante and
Petrarch in pure transcendental love, above all a Rabelais mild,
purring, and mellowed by paternity—what a loss to posterity
that the Doctor's anonymous flame and her Parisian predecessor
failed to publish their memoirs, as they would certainly not fail
to do today.

The first fruits of many working hours in the pay of Sébastien
Gryphe appeared in 1532, in the shape of an edition of the
second volume of the Latin letters of Dr. Giovanni Manardi of
Ferrara, dedicated to Maître André Tiraqueau of Fontenay-le-
Comte. Of the critical edition of Hippocrates and Galen which
shortly followed it M. Plattard remarks that Rabelais' performance is not invariably impressive or of much philological
value. "Several of his corrections are quite insignificant. He
seems often to have given way to the pleasure of confronting a
hackneyed text with his own manuscript." He likewise, apparently, overdid his notes and comments, later pruned.

What Gryphe paid him for this and other work is not known.
He was soon on the lookout for something more, and a precious
marginal entry of January 15, 1532, in the account-books of
the principal hospital of Lyons, the Great Hospital (Hostel-
Dieu) of Our Lady of Pity of the Rhône Bridge, shows that he
cannot greatly have added to his income by a new occupation:

Physician's wages: A new physician in the place of M. Pierre Roland, named Françoys Rabellet.

The forty-livres annual salary attached to this post was practically nominal, the chief medical officer being presumed to offer his services to the poor as an act of charity.[1] From a description, dated 1539, of this long-vanished hospital it seems that in *décor* if not in organisation it closely resembled the superbly surviving Hôtel-Dieu at Beaune. It was staffed by a doctor, a barber-surgeon, an apothecary, a chaplain, an almoner, two head nurses, sixteen "reformed Magdalen" nurses, five servants, male and female, a gardener, and a porter. The doctor made his daily round with the barber-surgeon, who took notes and wrote down prescriptions; he also daily inspected the staff and supervised all surgical and other work. He was responsible to a board of governors called "consuls-rectors", drawn from the merchant princes of Lyons.

With between one hundred and fifty and two hundred patients on his hands, all of the poorer class, Dr. Rabelais would not have overmuch leisure for literary work. That he flung himself into his hospital duties with enthusiasm is deducible from the discovery of Dr. Drivon of Lyons in the 1900's that during the Rabelaisian régime the death-rate decreased by two to three per cent.

Except that the Hôtel-Dieu at Beaune today is staffed by a nursing Order of nuns it must present almost exactly to the casual eye the appearance of the chief Lyons hospital under Dr. Rabelais' ordinance, with its spacious, sunny principal ward opening from the chapel where Mass is said every morning, its long row of capacious wooden beds on either side—in Rabelais' day men lay on one side and women on the other, and a bed might hold two or three patients if judged advisable—and its atmosphere of solid serenity. It is during his off-duty time here, in December 1532, that *Franciscus Rabelaesus, medicus*, will address the hero-worshipping letter to Erasmus mentioned in an earlier page. The circumstances well illustrate the scholarly spirit of service of this period.

---

[1] The silver-value of the *livre tournois* varied considerably and is difficult to fix at this or any other period. It seems to have been roughly equivalent in the 1530's to four pre-1914 English shillings. For modern purchasing-power multiply by thirty (Thorold Rogers, *History of Agriculture and Prices*, 1902). Today, no doubt, by fifty.

Erasmus desired to make a Latin version of the Jewish chronicles of Flavius Josephus. Lacking a trustworthy Greek manuscript, he applied to the humanist Jean de Pins, Bishop of Rieux, whom Rabelais had met at Toulouse. Owning no such text, De Pins wrote to Georges d'Armagnac, Bishop of Rodez, whom Rabelais had also met, and D'Armagnac, happening to possess a suitable MS., responded gladly. From one of Erasmus' ex-secretaries Rabelais had heard of the master's need, and it was to him that D'Armagnac sent the manuscript; an eagerly-begged excuse for a covering letter to his idol, to whom Rabelais duly forwarded the package, sufficiently explains this. As already observed, it is not known if Erasmus replied to Rabelais' panegyric. He must have thanked D'Armagnac.

To eke out his income Dr. Rabelais found time before long to edit another work for Sébastien Gryphe, a supposedly-authentic Latin will, *Lucii Cuspidii Testamentum*, discovered fifty years later to be a forgery by our old acquaintance Pomponius Laetus of the toga. A Latin contract-of-sale attached to it turned out to be a forgery by another Roman humanist, signing himself Jovianus Pontanus. Why these two learned playboys went to the trouble of faking such unprofitable documents is a mystery unexplained, unless they did it to fool a colleague or two. They certainly fooled Dr. Rabelais, though he did not live to experience a useful corrective to intellectual pride.

Money-worries continued to perturb him, for not otherwise is his next literary impulse explicable. One day in 1532, in some Lyons bookshop of the humbler kind or perhaps at a fair, he must have picked up a modest little book of fun in clumsy Gothic type, newly published, without author's or publisher's name, designed to divert the least exacting of publics, and called *The Great and Inestimable Chronicles of the Great and Enormous Giant Gargantua*. Or in its actual form, which, seeing to what it led, seems worth giving:

> Les grandes et ‖ inestimables Chronicques: du grant et en ‖ orme geant Gargantua: Contenant sa genealogie, ‖ La grandeur et force de son corps. Aussi les merueil ‖ leux faicts darmes quil fist pour le Roy Artus, com ‖ me verrez cy aprez. Imprime nouuellement. 1532

And on the last page:

Cy finissent les cronicques. Nouuellement Imprimées A Lyon, 1532, pet. in-4.

From this humble little rustic fantasy about giants and fairies will spring the Four Books of Pantagruel, a perpetual glory to French literature. In the meantime it will suggest to Dr. Rabelais a good, easy, and pleasant way of making a little more money.

3

"Children," pronounced Dr. Johnson, laying down the law for all time, "like stories of giants and castles, and of somewhat which can stretch and stimulate their little minds." The *Gargantua* chapbook which caught Dr. Rabelais' eye that day at Lyons owed its success to captivating the huge public catered for nowadays by its derivative, the Tabloid Press, with almost this same formula.

It may be briefly scanned. By art-magic the Enchanter Merlin, of Round Table celebrity, creates two enormous giants to defend King Arthur—Grantgosier and Gargamelle, his wife, together with a great mare to carry them. From their mating is born the giant Gargantua. Catching a fever in Brittany, the parent-giants die of a purgative and young Gargantua goes to Paris. After astonishing the citizens with many wondrous feats and abstracting the bells of Notre-Dame (one of a dozen episodes which Dr. Rabelais will annex with no compunction whatsoever), he returns to Brittany, whence Merlin conveys him on a cloud to England. Here with his great club he helps Arthur to rout the Gos and Magos, and is duly feasted on a gigantic scale and arrayed in splendour. In Arthur's behalf he routs a Dutch and Irish horde in a subsequent battle, taking prisoner their king and fifty of the nobility and packing them all in a hollow tooth. Having performed many other extraordinary exercises and served Arthur two hundred years, three months, and four days, he is transported to Fairyland by Morgan le Fay and Mélusine, and the story ends.

Long and painfully have the best modern authorities toiled to trace this artless romance to its source. Even M. Abel Lefranc has not been able to do so. The Arthurian Cycle gave birth to a myriad folk-tales, told and retold in chimney-corners long before printing was invented. The name "Gargantua" has not been discovered earlier than 1470. Rabelais will derive it from Grangousier's admiring cry at the infant's first yell for drink: "Que-grand-tu-as le gosier!"—"What a big gullet you have!" Dull enough for mid-Victorian *Punch*? Let such things not dishearten men of goodwill. The hand of genius and a fantastically rich comic imagination will transform the majority of the Doctor's lootings from the beginning. Having supplied what Henry James calls "the prick of the needle", his rustic predecessor is swiftly outdistanced and discarded.

Rabelais' initial embroideries on a simple theme were published by Claude Nourry of Lyons towards the end of 1532, at about the time Sébastien Gryphe was publishing the bogus will of Lucius Cupidius. The Doctor's lighter work was called *The Horrible and Frightful Acts and Prowesses of the Very Renowned Pantagruel, King of the Dipsodes, son of the great Giant Gargantua, composed newly by Master Alcofrybas Nasier*. In the original:

Pantagruel. || Les horribles et espouenta || bles faictz et prouesses du tresrenomme || Pantagruel, Roy des Dipsodes || filz du grand geant Gargan || tua, Composez nouuelle || ment par maistre || Alcofrybas || Nasier.—*On les vend à Lyon, en la maison* || *de Claude Nourry, dict le Prince* || *pres nostre Dame de Confort.*[1]

"Alcofrybas Nasier", an anagram of "Françoys Rabelais", will soon become popular. And it may be noted that with typical Rabelaisian *je-m'en-fichisme* the first volume published is actually the Second Book in proper sequence, dealing with Gargantua's son. The First Book, *Gargantua*, will issue from Rabelais' same publisher three years hence.[2] One may note also that *Pantagruel* obviously took this hardworking medical man not very long to write. It has been surmised that like most scribblers he had a drawerful of odds and ends—notes, drafts, sketches, beginnings, middles, endings—mostly unfinished, hard to throw away, "bound to come in useful some time".

If so, they certainly did. Something new had burst upon the

[1] A second edition published at Lyons by François Juste very early in the following year has a striking addition to the title: "Pantagruel. Jésus Maria. Les horribles," etc., etc. The invocation, evidently interpolated by Juste, is never repeated.
[2] See Appendix B: The Gargantua Puzzle.

world of letters. Something like a whirlwind had hit them, the Doctor's first readers delightedly and gaspingly realised on coming to the end of the Prologue and finding themselves addressed as no Gentle Reader has ever been addressed by a fawning author before or since.

And therefore, to make an end of this Prologue, even as I give my selfe to an hundred Pannier-fulls of faire devils, body and soul, tripes and guts, in case that I lie so much as one single word in this History, after the like manner St. Anthonies fire burn you, Mahoom's disease whirle you, the squinance with a stitch in your side and the Wolfe in your stomack trusse you, the bloody Flux seize upon you, the curst sharp inflammations of wilde fire, as slender and thin as Cowes haire, strengthened with quick silver, enter into your Fundament, and like those of Sodom and Gomorrha, may you fall into sulphur, fire and bottomless pits in case you do not firmly beleeve all that I shall relate unto you in this present Chronicle.

Thence we plunge straight into the genealogy of "the noble Pantagruel, my Master", son of Gargantua; a piece of breathless and bawdy bravura with which Sir Thomas Urquhart deals very capably, in his carefree manner. Having saddled himself with the *motif gigantesque* taken over from his humble predecessor, the Doctor proceeds to develop it into a symphony of fantastic and logical absurdity with which he doubtless grew bored long before the majority of his public. Soon after birth the infant Pantagruel is requiring the milk of 4,600 cows at every meal. He tears a great bear in pieces "like a pullet" with his baby hands and eats him raw for breakfast. But Pantagruel will shrink to more or less the size of his companions as his grown-up adventures proceed, or at any rate his gigantism will be no more remarked after the first two books, still less his original trick—derived from a minor devil named Pantagruel in a fifteenth-century mystery-play by Simon Gréban, whose lifework is the throwing of salt into sleeping drunkards' mouths—of engendering violent thirst in anyone to whom he takes a dislike.

Tossing inexhaustible supplies of tripe-and-onions to the vulgar, Dr. Rabelais has plenty of caviare for the sophisticated simultaneously up his capacious sleeve. Very decidedly the Giant Pantagruel is an intellectual. As early as the fifth chapter he is

E

visiting the six leading provincial universities of France. In the
seventh he is discovered in residence at the Benedictine *studium*
in the University quarter of Paris, at grips with the Seven Liberal
Arts and reading in the famous library of the Abbey of St. Victor,
on the site of the present Halle-aux-Vins. Parodying the Library's
catalogue affords Dr. Rabelais his first burst of top-flight clowning, though a half of it must have been unintelligible to seventy-
five per cent of his original readers. It is unfortunate that our
merry Urquhart fails to do so many of these comic titles justice,
apart from indulging himself a trifle frequently in whimsy (for
example, "The Invention of the Holy Crosse, personated by six
wilie Priests", conveys a different idea from that of the title of
the Passion-play listed by Rabelais: "L'Invention Saincte Croix
à six personnages, jouée par les clercs de finesse."[1]). However,
some of the Scotsman's renderings are near enough. Specimen
titles of the type devised to arride the commonalty:

The Pomegranate of Vice.
The Duster or Foxtail-Flap of Preachers, composed by Turlupin.
The Mustard-Pot of Penance.
The Flimflams of the Law.
The Bagpipe of the Prelates.
Of Pease and Bacon, *cum commento*.
The Teeth-Chatter or Gum-Didder of Lubberly Lusks.
A Perpetual Almanack for those that have the Gowt and the Pox.
The Fat Belly of the Presidents.
The Kissebreech of Chirurgerie [etc., etc., etc.].

Plain sailing enough and good fun, but some of the Doctor's
"precious pockified Blades" may well have consigned him to a
fate worse than theirs on finding these pleasing japes, all saucy
and many raw, mixed with a dozen or more such recondite
puzzles as:

Ars honestè petandi in societate, per Marcum Corvinum.
Quaestio subtilissima, utrum Chimaera in vacuo bombinans posset comedere
*   secundas intentiones?*
Decretrum Universitatis Parisiensis super gorgiasitatem Muliercularum ad
*   placitum.*

---

[1] *Inventio*, meaning "finding", and referring to St. Helena's discovery of the True
Cross at Jerusalem, *circa* A.D. 324, has often been deliberately misconstrued.

De Brodiarum Usu et honestate Chopinandi, per Silvestrem Prieratem, Jacopinum.
Chaultcouillonis, De Magistronostrandorum Magistronostratorumque Beu-vetis, lib. octo galantissimi [etc., etc.].

If this seemed far from fair, a worse trick was to be played on the Blades immediately in the shape of the long epistle received by Pantagruel from his father Gargantua in the chapter ensuing. Quite suddenly and without warning the four-hundred-and-eighty-four-year-old giant of the two opening chapters, the great ribald tosspot, weeping like a cow and laughing like a calf, has turned into a grave Renaissance savant-philosopher in the furred gown and earflaps of an Erasmus, counselling the diligent study of Greek ("without which a man may be ashamed to account himself a Scholar"), together with that of Latin, Hebrew, Arabic, and Chaldean, and proceeding to a sermon of the most unexceptionable and least expected kind.

Suspect the abuses of the World; set not thy heart upon vanity; for this life is transitory, but the Word of the Lord endureth for ever. Be serviceable to thy Neighbours and love them as thy self; reverence thy Praeceptors; shun the conversation of those whom thou desirest not to resemble . . .

"Whom thou desirest not——" In the very next chapter Panurge leaps on the scene like Harlequin: Panurge the impossible and the irrepressible; bibber, lecher, knave, roysterer, deviser of lewd practical jokes, braggart, mocker, coward, comedian; Panurge the "natural man". And Pantagruel joyfully clasps him to his heart, and they will never leave each other more. Thus does the jovial Doctor lead his readers to and fro like a jack-o'-lantern, even so early, and they never know where they may find themselves next.

As one of the three leading personages in the Pantagruelian Comedy, his creator's especial darling and most vital, dominant, and entertaining of the trio, with the Third Book almost exclusively his own, Panurge may lawfully pluck us by the sleeve a moment.

Mention has already been made of Théophile Gautier's interesting theory, *circa* 1832, that Rabelais drew the portrait of
Panurge largely from what he knew of the personality and appearance of the poet François Villon. This cannot have been very
much. None of the original documents concerning Villon was
unearthed, unless I err, before Vitu and Longnon began their
researches in the 1870's. Far more clearly—and so far as I can
discover, this has not occurred to anyone before—I see Panurge
stepping straight out of the *Commedia dell' Arte*, brought into France
from Italy by Catherine de Médicis in the 1560's.

At least five or six characters of the *Commedia* may be instantly
descried in the personality of Panurge. He is the spitten image,
tout craché, of Arlecchino. He is twin-brother likewise to the rascal
Brighella and the playfully-sadistic Pulcinella, first cousin in
moments of glory and terror to one of the swaggering Capitans
(Escobombardon, say, or Sangre y Fuente), and in knockabout
humour a very close relation to the flour-faced, gambolling Zanies
whose *lazzi* so diverted the stout and masterful Queen-Mother
of France, herself alleged to have once played Colombina in a
Court performance, if that is believable.

Summoning the other stock figures of the *Commedia*—how
brightly the gay heartless creatures flit across the stage, the lovers
Isabella and Leandro, Colombina and Flavio, the old fool
Pantaleone, the ridiculous Doctor of Medicine from Bologna,
the firebreathing and cowardly Capitan, the Soubrette, the
dancing Zanies!—I see Panurge as their natural playmate.
Before 1530 at least one troop of the Italian Comedians had
played in Germany, England, and elsewhere in Europe. How
could Dr. Rabelais not have heard of them? Lyons during his
long stay was a clearing-house for all the latest Italian news and
gossip. Returning virtuosi would be full of talk about a contribution to Renaissance Art as important in its way as Michael-
angelo's. Outside the Papal States, where the ban was permanent,
the Comedians were welcome at all the Italian courts. One of
their most benevolent patrons a little after the Doctor's time,
approving and even improving their scenarios in his own hand,
would be the great Archbishop of Milan, St. Charles Borromeo,
and their most famous of leading ladies, Isabella Andreini, the
theme of sonnets by Ariosto and Tasso and the rage of Paris,

would be given a splendid public funeral by the Municipality of Lyons. How could the Doctor help knowing all about them even in the 1530's? He had some practical experience of the theatre, we may recall. Almost certainly the script of *The Dumb Wife*, in which he played at Montpellier—quite likely the leading part—on Twelfth Night, 1531, was his. It would not surprise me if a man of such Dickensian gusto and vitality had produced the piece as well, performing the duties of prompter, stage-manager, scenic director, costumier, make-up artist, and call-boy in addition. And nobody, subject to correction, seems to have noticed that more than half the Panurge-Trouillogan scene of the Third Book, written entirely in dialogue, is a comic cross-talk act almost ready for the stage. With a little necessary polish and change of idiom and a proper climax it might be used in revue today, at least in France.

PANURGE: Well, then. If I marry I shall be a cuckold?
TROUILLOGAN: One might say so.
PANURGE: But if my wife turns out to be chaste I shall not?
TROUILLOGAN: I think that's right.
PANURGE: Listen——
TROUILLOGAN: As long as you like.
PANURGE: *Will* she be chaste? That's all I want to know.
TROUILLOGAN: I doubt it.
PANURGE: You never saw her?
TROUILLOGAN: Not that I know of.
PANURGE: Then why doubt what you don't know?
TROUILLOGAN: Because.
PANURGE: And suppose you did know her?
TROUILLOGAN: Much more.

Molière wrote worse. It is good "theatre", postulating at least an interest. Hence, even though Dr. Rabelais created Panurge a year or so before his first visit to Italy, and even though it was not until some ten years after the presumed date of his death that the Queen-Mother summoned the first company of the Italian Comedians to Paris, it seems to me more than likely that by 1532 the prehensile Rabelaisian mind had stored up enough information about Harlequin and his confederates, the *improvisatori*, and the Comedy's stage-business generally, to give

birth to a composite Panurge, and that in three visits to Italy
the ever-inquisitive Rabelaisian nose must have led him to a
performance or two—at Florence, say, or Ferrara, or some other
halt on the road. The absurd Bolognese medico alone would
fascinate him as the absurd "B.B." in *The Doctor's Dilemma* fascinated Harley Street. And he would highly approve the scenarios,
I think. The *Commedia dell' Arte* is the essence of Pantagruelism
in terms of the theatre. So and thus, unless I miserably delude
myself, may Panurge have blossomed in the three succeeding
Books into the great comic figure he is.

Gautier's theory need not be discarded nevertheless. It blends
sweetly enough with Panurge's putative Italian birth. Extremely
little, it may be repeated, was known of François Villon—himself
a *Commedia* character—in Rabelais' time apart from the one or
two fleeting autobiographical hints in the *Testaments* and a vague
deposit of Parisian underworld legend. Panurge's resemblance
to him must perforce be dim, especially as regards Villon's
physique, of which we know no more today than Rabelais did.
On this point the Doctor in his cheery way metagrabolises us
almost immediately. Having introduced Panurge in the ninth
chapter of *Pantagruel* as "a young Man of very Comely Stature,
and surpassing handsome in all his Lineaments", if a trifle
battered after recent experiences in Turkey, he has forgotten
this by the time he comes to Chapter XIV, from which emerges
a figure much less reminiscent of a *Saturday Evening Post* cover
glorifying Young America:

> Poor Panurge bibb'd and bows'd most villainously, for he was as
> dry as a Red-Herring, as lean as a Rake, and like a poor lank
> slender Cat, walked gingerly as if he had trod upon Egges.

This might be a faint echo from the *Petit Testament*, perhaps:

> Sec et noir comme escouvillon . . .[1]

And possibly of the Rondeau in the *Grant Testament*:

> Il fut rez, chief, barbe, et sourcil,
> Comme ung navet qu'on ret ou pelle. . . .[2]

[1] "Dried-up and dark as a baker's mop."
[2] "As deprived of hair—head, beard, and eyebrows—as a turnip peeled and pared."

On arrival at Chapter XVI Dr. Rabelais decides on what is practically a full-length portrait. Here a little more of Villon may, with some effort, be discerned—in his purely raffish aspects, naturally, since neither Villon's penitence nor his deep devotion could be expected to appeal to the Doctor:

> Panurge was of middle Stature, not too high nor too low, and had something of an Aquiline Nose, made like the handle of a Rasor; he was at that time five and thirty years old or thereabouts, fine to gild like a leaden Dagger; for he was a notable Cheater and Cony-catcher. He was a very gallant and proper Man of his Person, only that he was a little leacherous, and naturally subject to a kinde of Disease, which at that time they called lack of Money: it is an incomparable Grief. Yet notwithstanding he had three-score and three Trickes to come by it at his Need, of which the most honourable and most ordinary was in the manner of Thieving, secret Purloining and Filching; for he was a wicked lewd Rogue, a Cosener, Drinker, Royster, Rover, and a very dissolute and debauch'd Fellow, if there were any in Paris; otherwise, and in all Matters else, the best and most vertuous Man in the World; and he was still contriving some Plot, and devising Mischief against the Serjeants and the Watch.

One or two brief strokes are added later. Panurge is a master-spendthrift. Panurge is "naturally fearful" of blows, taking swiftly to his heels whenever these are imminent. Panurge is subject now and again to sudden fits of dumb melancholia—and the portrait is finished. Note, drinkers (as the Doctor would cry), that this hero of a thousand tricks and dashing stratagems is well past his youth. Thirty-five in the sixteenth century was sober middle-age. Yet so indefatigably does Panurge prance about the stage that we forget all his Renaissance coevals, for the most part grave and solid personages in furred gowns with gold chains round their necks, each with a paunch, a family, and perhaps a trifle of gout or stone thrown in. I do not recall this interesting matter of Panurge's age being raised or discussed in any disquisition known to me, still less any attempt to attach significance or symbolism to it. Might it be that thirty-five happened to be the first age that came into the Doctor's head, being round about his own at the time?

Since *Pantagruel* (to resume) has no plot whatsoever in any sane sense, being merely a sequence of hilarious episodes slung together as the Doctor's fancy, flying zigzag and woodcock-fashion, may take him, it is only possible to mention one or two of the admittedly most pleasing. The lawsuit between the Seigneurs of Kissebreech and Suckfist, on which Pantagruel delivers judgment in the presence of "foure of the greatest and most learned Parliaments of France, together with the Great Council and all the principal Regents of the Universities, not only of France but of England also and Italy", seems to me the best sustained piece of lunacy ever set down by mortal pen, wilder than Lear at his wildest. It is assumed by many authorities that in these long gibberish-speeches Rabelais is trailing a naughty coat before the ever-watchful censors of the Sorbonne, which may well be. All of them are pure moon-talk, as an extract from Kissebreech's opening may illustrate, with no reasonable beginning, middle, or end.

Car le temps estoit quelque peu dangereux de la foire, dont plusieurs francs archiers avoient esté refusés à la monstre, non obstant que les cheminées fussent assez haultes, selon la proportion du javart et des malandres de l'ami Baudichon. Et, par ce moyen, fut grande année de cacquerolles en tout le pays d'Artoys, qui ne fut petit amendement pour messieurs les porteurs de coustrets, quand on mangeoit sans desguainer coquecigrues à ventre deboutonné. Et, à la mienne volunté, que chascun eust aussi belle voix, l'on en jouait beaucoup mieux à la paulme.

Which Urquhart renders:

And indeed the time was very dangerous in coming from the Faire, in so farre that many trained bowe-men were cast at the muster, and quite rejected, although the chimney-tops were high enough, according to the proportion of the windgalls in the legs of the horses, or of the Malaunders. And by this means there was that yeare great abundance throughout all the country of Artois of tawny buzzing-beetles, to the no small profit of the Gentlemen-great-stick-faggot-carriers when they did eate without disdaining the Cocklicranes till their belly was like to crack with it again; as for my own part, such is my Christian charity that I could wish from my heart every one had as good a voice, it would make us play the better at the Tennis.

Brief extract from the speech for the defence by Suckfist, exposing arguments equally lucid and cogent:

Very true it is, that the foure Oxen which are in debate and whereof mention was made were somewhat short in memory; nevertheless, to understand the *gamme* aright, they feared neither the Cormorant nor Mallard of Savoy; which put the good People of my countrey in great hope that their children sometime should become very skilful in Algorisme. But the great Devil did envy it, and by that means put the High-Dutch farre behind, who played the devils in swilling down and tipling at the good Liquour, *trink meen Herr, trink, trink.* By two of my table-men in the corner-point I have gained the Lurch; for it is not probable, nor is there any appearance of truth in this saying, that at Paris upon a little Bridge the Hen is proportionable.

In the same fantastic mood the Doctor creates and develops the great dumbshow debate in the packed hall of the Collège of Navarre, in which Panurge by signs alone makes a fool of "a great Scholar of England", Thaumaste by name. Against "Thaumaste" in my cherished Lyons edition of 1588, written in ink still black and in a contemporary hand, is the marginal note *Thomas Morus*; but I doubt very much if More is Rabelais' target here. The fact, which had shocked Europe, that the ex-Chancellor of England had died under the axe for upholding the supremacy of the Holy See quite recently, just before the publication of *Gargantua*, was due to shock the Doctor not at all; but More had been Erasmus' dearest friend, and any man Erasmus loved and revered as he did More (his acceptance of Cromwell's gold to keep his mouth shut notwithstanding), would, I think, have been *ipso facto* immune. My distant predecessor in ownership of these two little volumes was fond of guessing. On a flyleaf, and written in a bolder hand, is one of those "keys" to the Four Books to which many of his contemporaries were addicted. Grangousier, for instance, is Louis XII. Gargantua is François I, though François was not Louis' son. Pantagruel is Henri II. Panurge and Friar John, whom we shall soon

encounter, are the Cardinals of Amboise and Lorraine respectively.
Utopie is France, Dipsodie is Lorraine, and, most ungallantly,
Gargantua's great mare, who in the First Book deforests the
entire Beauce with one sweep of her tail, is François' costly
mistress Madame d'Étampes. To such guesswork clings a faint
fragrance of orris-root and pomander. It represents, as one may
oneself conjecture, the essence of the drawing-room chatter of
many and many a château of the sixteenth century, and it is in
its way diverting, though less diverting than Voltaire's personal
discovery nearly two centuries later, with the usual cockatoo-
like screeches, of much the same Rabelaisian "key", with a few
added revelations not without value; for example, the chapters
on Gargantua's education are a satire on the contemporary
education of princes, and it is impossible not to recognise Charles
V in King Picrochole. Most amusing, had one the strength to
cope with it, must be the early nineteenth-century "Variorum"
edition of Rabelais by Esmengart and Johanneau mentioned
by Plattard, who observes: "There is not a single paragraph,
however clear it may be, which is not a cryptogram for these
editors, in which they discover allusions to either political affairs
or to Court scandals." And not once, perhaps, did this brace of
master-pedants perceive hovering over them, during their molish
labours on his *roman à clef*, a mighty shade convulsed with extremely rude mirth . . .

What is actually interesting in the Panurge-Thaumaste episode
is its freedom from the anglophobia then as always recurrent.
The Frenchman having demonstrated his superior intellectual
powers and the Englishman having acknowledged them in a
graceful speech, Thaumaste is the guest of honour at the ensuing
dinner, presided over by Pantagruel, towards the end of which
"they neither knew where they were, nor whence they came".
And the liturgical Rabelaisian refrain is heard once more:

> Blessed Lady! how they did carouse it and pluck (as we say) at the
> kid's leather; and flaggons to trot, and they to toote, Draw, give
> (page) some wine here, reach hither, fill, with a devil, so! . . .
> For the Weather was hot, and besides, they were very dry.

The Doctor proceeds to revel in one or two more of the monkey-
tricks of Panurge, already illustrated and mostly more dirty

than diverting. Panurge's attempt to seduce a virtuous "great lady of Paris", actually of the upper bourgeoisie, is of the crudest yahoo-kind, and his parting shot after repulse typical. "You do not deserve so much good, nor so much honour, but by G——! I will make the Dogs ride you"; after which Panurge takes to his heels "for feare of blowes". Next day, during the solemn public processions of Corpus Christi, he very nearly makes good his threat. Need one marvel that the Sorbonne took action?

After this improving episode we are ruthlessly whisked from Paris and reality back to the old rustic dreamland again. Gargantua has been "translated into the land of the Fairies" by Morgan le Fay, and the Dipsodes on learning of this have invaded Utopie and are besieging "the great City of the Amaurots". The punitive campaign of Pantagruel and his captains is not of the Doctor's best work. I suspect him of whipping up a temporarily-flagging fancy with a great deal of wine. Pantagruel eventually kills the Giant Loupgarou in a duel, and his lieutenant Epistemon, having lost his head in battle and being restored to life by a magic powder, reports the latest news from hell, where great men of history are all employed in menial or degrading tasks; six Popes among them, as against Dante's two, with an especial honourable mention for Sixtus IV, now "an anointer of those that have the Pox". At which point the Doctor pauses to savour an old familiar joke.

What (said Pantagruel) have they the Pox there too? Surely (said Epistemon), I never saw so many: there are there, I think, above a hundred millions; for believe, that those who have not had the pox in this world, must have it in the other. Cotsbody (said Panurge), then I am free; for I have been farre as the hole of Gibraltar, reached unto the outmost Bounds of Hercules, and gathered of the ripest.

With an account of how Pantagruel's digestive trouble was cured by swallowing seventeen hollow copper balls, each bigger than "that on the top of St. Peter's Needle at Rome", and each containing a trapdoor and a man with a basket and shovel, we reach the conclusion of *Pantagruel*. A few promises of, as the French say, mounts and marvels announce an imminent sequel.

Here will I make an end of the first Book; my head akes a little, and
I perceive that the Registers of my braine are somewhat jumbled
and disordered with this Septembral Juice. You shall have the
rest of the history at Franckfort Mart next coming, and there
you shall see how Panurge was married and made a Cuckold within
a month after his wedding; how Pantagruel found out the Philosopher's Stone, the manner how he found it, and the way how to
use it; how he past over the Caspian Sea, defeated the Cannibals,
and conquered the island of Perles; how he married the daughter
of the King of India, called Prestian, how he fought against the
Devil and burnt up five chambers of Hell, how [etc., etc., etc.].

Concluding with a visit to the Moon "to know whether indeed
the Moon were not entire and whole, or if the Women had
three-quarters of it in their heads". And having finally eased
himself with a great roar against monkish hypocrisy, the Doctor
flings down his quill. Nothing of what he promises will come to
pass.

What does come to pass, however, and speedily, is trouble.
That the *exalté* Doctor was expecting to get away, as we say, with
Pantagruel, which was selling vigorously by September 1533—it
is jotted down in that month in the book-list of a Parisian burgess
as a "must"—seems plain; having a professional career to think
of, having as yet no powerful patron, and being a lapsed cleric,
he would not deliberately court a clash with authority. However, he had misjudged. A letter from Calvin in October of this
year to a friend at Orleans, François Daniel, mentions in passing
that the censors of the Sorbonne have recently examined *Pantagruel*, together with a book called *La Forest d'Amours*, and censured
it—not, as one might expect, for irreverent jests and attacks on
Catholic theologians, but for obscenity. "Obscaenos illos Panta-
gruelem, Sylvam [Amorum] et ejus monetae," writes Calvin—
"obscenities like *Pantagruel*, *The Forest of Love*, and suchlike stuff"
—and dismisses the matter. Calvin is concerned with something
more sensational. Rumours were flying round Paris that a pious
work by the King's sister Marguerite called *Le Miroir de l'Ame
Pécheresse*—or in an English edition of 1548, *A Godly Medytacyon
of the Christen Sowle*—had been condemned by the Sorbonne
likewise, as Calvinist propaganda. These rumours, Calvin

assured his friend, were false. The Princess's book had been merely put aside for examination.

The sequel is interesting. Condemnation being duly, and not without courage, announced, the King in a fury ordered Nicolas Cop, the recently-appointed Rector Magnificus of the University of Paris, to annul the decree of his Faculty of Theology immediately; which was done, with a rider by Cop to the effect that the Faculty had been strictly within its legal rights. The book, a religious work published anonymously, had not been submitted to the censors beforehand, as ordered by a standing decree of the Parlement of Paris. So honours were even and the matter dropped. Yet how unpredictable are moves on the Renaissance chessboard! A month after this affair Cop, ex-Rector of the Collège Sainte-Barbe and son of an eminent French-Swiss physician, Guillaume Cop of Bâle, was himself in trouble with his Faculty of Theology. A speech delivered by him in November in defence of the Princess's book and strongly impregnated with Genevan essence turned out to be the work of Calvin, still a resident in Paris. Charged by the Parlement with heresy and granted on demand the privilege of trial by a tribunal of his University, Nicolas Cop lost his nerve, fled across the frontier to his native Bâle, and is no more heard of, having held his Rectorship barely twelve months. His ally Princess Marguerite, on the other hand, will a few years hence, being now Queen of Navarre, abjure her Calvinism with notable vigour and return to the Church to spend the rest of her life in austerest Catholic devotion. It is during this period that she is said to have tried to reconvert Calvin by correspondence.

Whether Dr. François Rabelais was very deeply perturbed by censure on *Pantagruel*[1] one may take leave to doubt. Obscenity, always relative, and in the Doctor's case no more morally noxious than a manure-heap on a farm, was not yet a criminal offence. Prudery had yet to be enthroned among the cardinal virtues. But even in that age, still healthily freespoken in the medieval tradition, there were limits, and Panurge all too blithely oversteps

---

[1] The Sorbonne's sentence may have embraced *Gargantua*, which was similarly censured round about this time, To Calvin, as to many others, *Pantagruel* stood for both books or either. The name was later attached to Rabelais himself by his Genevan enemies.

them; not merely passing from the lewd to the obscene but mingling a little light blasphemy with open caricature of Catholic devotion; for example in Chapter XVII, where his theft of alms from the "basins of the pardons", in itself sacrilege, is justified by text-twisting and the whole procedure turned into a cynical farce. A censure merely for obscenity let the Doctor off pretty lightly, it may be agreed. He himself seems not to have taken it seriously, and he will never trouble to purge his pages of what may be called good farmyard-muck. Nevertheless he is aware that the cold eye of the Sorbonne is henceforth upon him, and the editions of 1542 will show with what anxious care he has gone with a toothcomb through his first two volumes and removed really serious grounds for trouble, such as the gibes at the theologians—the word itself is replaced henceforth by "sophists"—and the more obvious japes parodying Holy Writ and other phrases bordering on the blasphemous. Such matters in his forthcoming *Gargantua* as attacking monasticism and pilgrimages and using some of the pietistic formulae of Geneva, he will allow to stand, depending on the favour of the king's sister and the growing power of the Calvinist element. And having thus backed the wrong horse, the Doctor will need still more protection before long, not to speak of a timely skip across the frontier. A deal of anxiety, in fact, awaits this wayward son of Holy Church.

In the meantime, having with his gifts and charm acquired a powerful and agreeable new patron, Dr. Rabelais is about to discard the drudgery of hospital routine, *pro tem.*, for a far pleasanter occupation, which will incidentally involve him, at least as a spectator, in the most doom-laden crisis in England's history.

4

A smile, a discreet *bon mot*, a reference to Touraine, an instantly-effective prescription—with such lawful exercise of the Hippocratic art may we visualise Dr. François Rabelais arresting the sympathies and capturing the esteem, in the early summer of 1533, of Jean du Bellay, Bishop of Paris, Envoy-Extraordinary to the Most Christian King of France, and the most important patient so far in the Doctor's case-book.

At Lyons in the May and June of that year public junketings

on a lavish and elaborate scale, with the king, the queen, and the entire court participating, were taking place to celebrate the Dauphin Henri's marriage to Catherine de Médicis. Of the guests Bishop du Bellay was possibly enjoying the revels least. What is popularly called a "veritable martyr" to sciatica, he was at this moment snatching brief respite from a diplomatic mission involving journeys between Paris, Rome, and London. Almost certainly it must have been at the suffering bishop's request that the chief medical officer of the leading hospital of Lyons, who would have his Court entrée with other notables of the city, and whose professional reputation was already more than local, was sooner or later presented to him; either by a fellow-physician, Dr. Hubert Sussanné, one of the bishop's protégés, or else by another recent acquaintance of the Doctor's, the neo-Latin poet Salmon Macrin, one of the episcopal secretaries. And it would seem that Dr. Rabelais brought professional skill and personal charm to bear on his exalted patient to such effect that some months after the Court's return to Paris Bishop Jean du Bellay was still remembering the cultured and agreeable provincial doctor with gratitude. In January 1534, accordingly, when the bishop halted at Lyons again on his way south, we find Dr. Rabelais granted two months' leave by his hospital board, together with twenty-seven *livres tournois*—about £250 in modern value, no doubt—of his salary, and travelling Romewards in the bishop's suite as his private physician.

Bearded, aquiline, cultured, perspicacious Jean du Bellay, who had arrived in Lyons from London by way of Paris, needed all the relief his new physician could afford him. Considerable diplomat as he was, his latest task was almost hopeless. His object was to delay, if possible, at the eleventh hour, the long-impending excommunication sentence reserved at Rome in July 1533 for Henry VIII of England, with whom François I had concluded a secret alliance against the Emperor a year previously. Sentence had been suspended by Clement VII till September to allow Henry a last opportunity, after three years of defiance and evasion, of taking back his noble and lawful wife, Catherine of Aragon, the Emperor's aunt, and dismissing the trollop to whom Cranmer, his Archbishop of Canterbury, had secretly married him in the previous January. For the Gospel-light, to echo the most deliciously satiric line in English verse, had shone from Boleyn's eyes. The woman whom gallant Will Somers, Henry's court fool, was to describe in full Court a year hence, with Canon and Civil Law alike behind him, as a whore and the mother of a bastard,[1] after which the too-daring clown had to fly for his life, was now proclaimed Queen of England, as she had intended. Whether she was her royal husband's illegitimate daughter as well as her brother's ex-paramour is still one of the many fascinating unanswered questions in our rough Island story.

With a terrified Parliament and Convocation at his feet, Henry was already half-invested with that title of "Supreme Head of the Church in England" which would shortly make him, in the classic phrase of the historian Stubbs, "the Pope, the whole Pope, and something more than the Pope", and the subsequent diversion to the royal treasury of all papal dues was a natural consequence.

It was in these dismal circumstances that Jean du Bellay was now on his way to Rome to make, by order of François I, a final appeal to Clement VII in Henry's behalf, Henry himself having refused to recognise the papal law courts and the accorded delay being long overpassed. Such gratifying anxiety on the part of the King of France to see his prodigal brother of England's return to the Fold was not wholly spiritual. Important French big-business interests would be in jeopardy if England, most Catholic of countries, known for centuries as Our Lady's Dowry, were suddenly cut off by a lustful monarch's intransigence from the unity of Christendom.

Like all travellers of the age, Bishop du Bellay, with Dr. Rabelais and a secretary in attendance and a squad of servants, would either take ship from Marseilles to Leghorn or Genoa, a crossing far from attractive in winter, or cross the Alps by the Mont Cenis, an alternative devilishly uncomfortable but involving fewer hours, or even days, of agony. One may sympathetically (assuming the latter) listen to the sciatic bishop's groan as he is hoisted into his *chaise à porteurs* and jogged down those icy steeps by four brawny and indifferent Swiss. In the first week of February the party reached Rome, where Du Bellay's host was

[1] July 1535; recorded by Chapuys, Imperial ambassador.

the Bishop of Faenza, and as swiftly as possible Jean du Bellay presented himself at the Vatican with the French Ambassador. By this time the Emperor's representative was daily at Clement VII's elbow, urging the promulgation of sentence against the Tudor apostate without further delay. Applying himself vigorously to the haranguing of Pope and Cardinals to the contrary, Du Bellay was able, before long, in the teeth of opposition from the majority of the Curia, to persuade Clement VII to sanction the despatch of a last-moment courier to London before the special Consistory called for March 23. The courier spurred north. A week passed. Two weeks passed. Three weeks passed. On the eve of the Consistory Du Bellay in desperation appealed for an extra week's grace, on the score—as we learn from his brother Martin's memoirs—of the roughness of the English Channel and some possible accident to his courier on the road. His appeal was rejected and the Consistory assembled.

Present among Jean du Bellay's suite that fateful day was Dr. François Rabelais, whose opinion of his patron's final effort to avert disaster is conveyed in his Latin dedication to Du Bellay of a forthcoming edition of Marliani's Roman antiquities.

> With what joy we were filled, what pride uplifted us, what affection animated us as we heard you speak, amid the admiration of the Sovereign Pontiff Clement and his illustrious cardinals, and the applause of all! What clarity in your arguments, what subtlety in your discussion, what dignity in your replies, what acuteness in your refutations, what ease shone forth in your delivery . . .

In vain. Not all Du Bellay's eloquence could avail in such a pass, much as Clement VII, patron of Michelangelo and Raphael, esteemed virtuosity in every medium. When the Consistory rose the validity of Queen Catherine's marriage to Henry VIII had been confirmed and her husband declared excommunicate. Two days later Du Bellay's courier galloped into Rome with a letter from Henry according Du Bellay full powers to act in his behalf. Astonished and aghast (to quote Martin du Bellay again), those cardinals who had helped to precipitate action by pressing for one single Consistory, instead of at least three, assembled more than once to endeavour to find some way out. But it may well be doubted if anything, humanly speaking, could have rectified the situation, given Henry's present frenzy. Jean du Bellay at any rate cherished no illusions. Ten days after the Consistory he left Rome with his suite for Paris.

Attendance on the bishop during these six agitated weeks left Dr. Rabelais plenty of leisure for a schedule drawn up, as he informs his patron in the dedication already quoted, in advance; but he had not achieved a great deal. Having no great ache to visit the Seven Basilicas and other major Roman shrines and sanctuaries, he wasted no time, apparently, on any of them, though he notes in passing that Michelangelo's vast new basilica of St. Peter, on which work had been suspended since Raphael's recent death, still lacks "a cover". What the Doctor wanted to do in Rome was to confer with some of the learned on certain unspecified problems then occupying him, to make notes on any discoverable plants and flowers unknown in France, and, of course, to scrutinise all visible remains of pagan Rome, which he intended to embody in a topographical plan. The first two of these schemes will not come to much. He meets no scholars of any note, unless the Greek humanist Lascaris was in Rome at this time, and he finds nothing new in the botanical way apart from one of the earliest plane-trees imported from Asia Minor, flourishing in a nobleman's park near Lake Nemi. While he is still pottering round the Forum, taking "lunars" in the Forsyte manner, copying inscriptions, and preparing an arduous topographical scheme with the assistance of a couple of fellow-members of Jean du Bellay's suite, Bartholomeo Marliani of Milan brings out his own *Topographia*; on which the Doctor, with an audible grunt of relief (. . ."ut valde ego ipsi gratuler"— "I heartily congratulate him"), drops the geodetics. He has at any rate acquired some new knowledge. Contact with Graeco-Roman architecture has furnished him with many a new technical term, to be duly paraded and explained in the Books.

Rome was not at its best during Dr. Rabelais' first visit. What Clement VII called "the lacerated Body" had only partly recovered from the disaster of 1527; the treasury was depleted, not all the ruins were cleared, the Curia still awaited reform. A general lassitude was in the Roman air, one gathers, so that the incurable playboyishness of a Benvenuto Cellini—who may

quite likely have half-murdered the notary Ser Benedetto in the
street and skipped to the country during Rabelais' stay—must
have seemed to most of his fellow-citizens a tiresome affectation.
The Doctor had, alas, no contact with this most rascally and
diverting of master-goldsmiths. His interest was fully engaged
elsewhere. He may be viewed at this period, in company with
his friends Nicolas Leroy and Claude Chapuis, both of the
cardinal's suite and ardent amateur archaeologists, as spending
most of his spare time in grubbing round the Forum or inspecting
the excavations in progress at a *vigna*, or estate on the outskirts of
Rome, recently acquired by his patron. Himself interested in
antiquities, and following the current vogue among Roman
cardinals, Jean du Bellay in his own leisure was supervising a
"dig" in the grounds of this villa, apparently with no success.
The big-scale European racket in patched-up "bustos" and
statuary, authentic or fake, which Joseph Nollekens, R.A., among
others, was to exploit so profitably two centuries later had still
to take shape in some fertile Italian brain, but there were already
the beginnings of a market.

It is a pity that the Doctor's nose was so firmly glued to Roman
remains during this stay that he has nothing vital to tell us about
contemporary Rome, barring a brief allusion to the number of
its citizens who get their living by stabbing and poisoning. Of
its beauty he notes nothing. From this, from a reference of guide-
book banality in the Third Book to the marvels of Florence, where
Du Bellay and his suite halted ·on the homeward journey, and
especially from the scoffs Rabelais puts into the mouth of a French
monk who would give all the palaces of Florence for the cookshops of Amiens, and all the Florentine porphyry and marble for
the cheesecakes of the same town, one is half led to suspect that
the Doctor is perhaps something of a philistine. Which is no
great crime in a man of science, though some of his commentators have been at pains to prove him a connoisseur in Italian art
as in everything else. And perhaps it was merely another excuse
for a crack at the monks.

Dr. Rabelais was back at his Lyons hospital early in May—
on the 18th of that month Bishop du Bellay arrived in Paris—
and writing hard in off-duty hours. On August 1 he received
twenty-five livres of salary, covering six and a half months,

though not entitled, a note in the treasurer's register records, to the full rate. In the autumn François Juste published *The Inestimable Life of the Great Gargantua, Father of Pantagruel, composed by the Abstractor of Quintessence ; a Book full of Pantagruelism.* The "abstractor" is Maître Alcofrybas Nasier, alias Dr. François Rabelais.

5

Gargantua is a vastly more entertaining book than *Pantagruel*. It may open with a few rather clumsy fooleries based still on the gigantesque, but in addition to boasting one short chapter of pure scatology—as one might say, "the old familiar faeces"—unsurpassed even by Ulrich von Hutten, it has a plan. When the Doctor unmasks his batteries one perceives that this time the Sorbonne is not to be his only target.

In Lyons, it may be recalled, there was at this period a colony of erudite sympathisers, in varying degree, with the work of Luther and Calvin. Rabelais' friend Pierre Amy had joined it in 1524. Not all its members went over finally. Extremely few humanists did. But whatever their shades of what was vaguely called "Evangelical" thought they all inclined—and God knows not without reason, while Rome still postponed a series of surgical operations for which all Christendom was crying—to look on the wreckers with indulgence. To this school *Gargantua* turned out to be a gift which may well have relaxed, for a moment, the grimness of the future Genevan dictator himself. For despite Calvin's contemptuous reference, noted already, to the censuring of *Pantagruel* "and such-like stuff", the coming anti-Rabelaisian outburst in his treatise *De Scandalis* will seem to indicate that he had been deceived in a possible new recruit of considerable value.

After a slow start (but that superb fugue the Discourse of the Drinkers at Gargantua's birth-feast remains a *morceau de choix* for every connoisseur, a rich and sprawling Flemish Old Master brought to life) *Gargantua* moves into the attack on the theologians with the beginning of the child Gargantua's education under Master Tubal Holofernes, the typical *sorbonicole, sorbillan, sorbonagre, sorbonigène*—all of which pleasing inventions will be struck out of every edition before long and replaced, alas, by something anodyne—as Rabelais loves to paint him; a reactionary fool and ignoramus and, more ignoble still, a scholastic, stuffing the child with all the pseudo-Scotist rubbish his creator remembers from La Baumette days. Six brief chapters later Gargantua will be handed over by his father to the enlightened Ponocrates, humanist and Evangelico-Platonist. Gargantua's day will now begin no longer with Mass but massage, alleviated by a simultaneous reading of Scripture, and as soon as he is dressed the ruthless Ponocrates plunges the adolescent neck-deep into a tumultuous daily course of secular studies, alternated by bursts of strenuous physical exercise and embracing dashes of everything from astronomy to practising the sackbut, with endless reference to the Greeks and Latins.

To compare such a hectic jumble even distantly with the co-educational system of the famous fifteenth-century master of pedagogy Vittorino da Feltre of the *Casa Giocosa*, the House of Joy at Mantua, seems to me quaint, but it has been done, though Da Feltre and the Doctor have nothing in common but love of the classics and recognition of the educational value of sport, and differ totally in fundamentals. Da Feltre's curriculum is essentially a Christian one. His pupils began the day with Mass and the recital with their devout preceptor of the Little Office of Our Lady, and religious instruction ranked high on the schedule, whereas apart from a modicum of devotions of the kind called today "free from outmoded dogma", and an occasional visit on rainy days to the pulpits of "evangelical" preachers, the new religion is noticeably shown its place by Dr. Rabelais. What Evangelism the Doctor displays at this period, the four Scriptural references in Chapter X notwithstanding, is pretty obviously skin-deep and vague, with a Deist tinge at that. His bias as it develops in *Gargantua* is sufficient nevertheless to lead those of the learned unfamiliar with such matters (they seem to be plentiful) to assume as axiomatic that he is attacking Catholic doctrine. The Doctor is, of course, doing no such thing, however near to it he may seem to an outside eye. Pilgrimages, for example, are not matters of faith, and nobody has more strongly denounced their abuse than a string of canonised saints. If Rabelais goes further and derides such pious practices in principle he is censurable but not excommunicable, especially as he defeats his own gaily mischievous ends by misrepresentations any instructed child could detect. When Grangousier asks the body of pilgrims of Chapter XLV where they are bound, one of them answers that they are returning from the shrine of Saint Sebastian near Nantes, where they had been to "offer up unto that Saint our vows against the Plague."

Ah, poor men (said Grangousier), do you think that the plague comes from St. Sebastian?

Yes, truly (answered Sweertogo), our Preachers tell us so indeed.

Which gives Grangousier his cue to denounce "abominable Imposters"; and had Sweertogo's answer been anything more than a little spurt of Rabelaisian malice, rightly. The Doctor's cynical twist shows how far he was ready to go at the moment to please the party of Marguerite de Valois, at whose cultured little court at Pau in the Béarnais every shade of anti-Roman expression was now or later represented from the Princess's three favourite preachers, Calvin, Roussel, and Lefèvre d'Étaples down to epicurean sceptics like Clément Marot and Claude Gruget and confirmed atheists, then called *libertins*, like Dolet and Bonaventure des Périers.

In *Gargantua* the Doctor goes, in fact, quite far. In the heat and enjoyment of caricaturing the Sorbonne in the person of the idiotic Master Janotus de Bragmardo he may even have raised a few critical eyebrows at Pau. "Reason?" says Master Janotus scornfully to his colleagues. "We use none of it here!" Had the Doctor forgotten that this was the pure essence of the Lutheran word? "Reason is the Devil's greatest whore! A noxious whore, a prostitute, the Devil's appointed whore, eaten up by scabs and leprosy"—perhaps Dr. Luther's celebrated exordium had not been brought to his notice by his friends of the Reform in Lyons. However, any slip here is amply compensated by the frontal attack on monasticism which begins with a broadside of the Doctor's heaviest guns in *Gargantua* and is continued at intervals through the Four Books. On monasticism, it will be observed, not simply on monks, whom any Catholic might criticise; on the system itself, established by St. Benedict, Patriarch of the West, at Monte Cassino Abbey in the sixth century A.D., and now being denounced by the new sectaries in chorus as a depraved invention.

"But they pray to God for us," says Grangousier, suddenly moved by compunction after some opening abuse of monks in Chapter XL. Gargantua grunts something about the "tingle-tangle jangling" of their bells. Eudemon then proceeds with the case for the prosecution in phrases made familiar by four centuries of repetition:

> They mumble out great store of Legends and Psalmes, by them not at all understood; they say many Patrenotres, interlarded with Ave-Maries, without thinking upon, or apprehending the meaning of what it is they say, which truly I call mocking of God, and not prayers. But so help them God as they pray for us, and not for being afraid to lose their victuals, their manchots, and good fat pottage. All true Christians, of all estates and conditions, in all places and at all times send up their prayers to God, and the Mediatour prayeth and intercedeth for them, and God is gracious to them. Now such a one is our good Friar John [etc., etc.].

This piece of homely polemic—there are far juicier specimens to follow—need not detain us. But the great swashbuckling figure of Frère Jean des Entommeures, Friar John of the Chops, or Slices, who comes banging on the scene in Chapter XXVII, demands respectful attention. For Friar John is not only to be one of the three leading actors in the Pantagruelist comedy but, as some hold, the essential third in what Rabelais intended to symbolise as the Platonic trinity of human nature; Pantagruel representing the rational man, Panurge the sensual, and Friar John the effective.[1]

If the Doctor cherished any such lofty conception, "smelling more of lamp-oil than wine", if one may echo a phrase of his own, he omitted to develop it to any extent; possibly because he grew bored with contemporary Platonists, at whom, after quitting Lyons, he will mock more than once. A simpler theory explaining

[1] A monk is not a friar, though *moine* is often loosely used for both. Since Urquhart makes no distinction it would seem pedantic to correct the Friar's traditional style to "Dom John". Urquhart likewise mistranslates his name as "Friar John of the Funnels". Moland's glossary derives "Entommeures" from *entommer*, a Tourangeau verb meaning to chop or slice (cp. Gk., εντομή).

Friar John occurs to one, namely that needing a monk *à sa façon*
to express his total opinion of the system, Dr. Rabelais drew on
his native countryside and created his ideal in a few vigorous
strokes: a tough, rollicking, hypothetical ex-member of the
Benedictine community of Seuilly, possessing, like himself, a
hatred of discipline and no spiritual leanings; a roaring, truculent
Rodomont whose principal interests are drinking, eating, forni-
cation, and fighting; a man of action full of oaths and anti-
monastic gibes, mingling claustral patter with near-blasphemies;
a swaggering pagan wholly of this earth, whose perpetual cry of
"Matière de bréviaire!" is a recurring slogan like the "Fen du
bruit!" of Tartarin's noisy soulmate at Tarascon. It is notable
that from beginning to end of the Four Books Friar John utters
only two brief phrases conformable to his monastic state, and they
ring curiously false, like an artistic flaw. More frequently than
either Pantagruel or Panurge he speaks with the veritable voice
of Rabelais. Full of gross courage, he makes a perfect foil to the
cowardly Panurge. He is a great standby in battle or storm, a
roistering table-companion, a leader in every adventure, better at
making snares and rabbit-traps than—as is once claimed for him,
rather half-heartedly—defending the oppressed or comforting
the afflicted, a duty which bothers him not at all. In a word,
Friar John has nothing of the monk about him but his habit,
which he continues to flaunt to the end.

With a delight perhaps mingled with reverential awe the
Doctor, having summoned this portent from the deeps, must have
found him immediately taking charge and rattling away almost
too lustily for pen to follow.

Diavolo, is there no more must? No more sweet wine? *Germinavit
radix Jesse, je renie ma vie, j'enrage de soif;* I renounce my life, I rage
with thirst. This wine is none of the worst; what wine drink you
at Paris? I give myself to the Devil if I did not once keep open
house at Paris for all comers six months together. Do you know
Friar Claud of the High Kilderkins? Oh, the good fellow that he is!
But I do not know what flie hath stung him of late, he is become so
hard a Student. For my part, I study not at all. In our Abbey
we never study for feare of the Mumps, which disease in horses is
called the mourning in the Chine. Our late Abbot was wont to
say that it is a monstrous thing to see a learned Monk, by G——!

Master, my friend, *magis magnos clericos non sunt magis magnos sapientes*. You never saw so many hares as there are this year. I could not anywhere come by a Gosse-hawk, or tassel of falcon. My Lord Beloniere promised me a Lanner, but he wrote to me not long ago that he was become pursie. . . .

Pausing for breath and a fresh supply of ink, Dr. Rabelais may well have heard a gratifying spirit-voice murmuring in his ear: "*Sursum corda!* Three or four hundred years hence this will be to grave and learned men a typical monastic conversation of your time." Hence, perhaps, the value Friar John sets on his habit; a symbolic, mystical, essential value attached to the debasing of St. Benedict's livery (incidentally his creator's own) which needs no footnote. Such habit-value is in fact established at the uproarious supper-party celebrating Friar John's arrival at Gargantua's headquarters about midway through the Picrocholian campaign:

> *Deposita cappa* (said Gymnast), let us pull off this frock. Ho, by G——! gentlemen (said the Monk), there is a chapter *in statutis ordinis* which opposeth my laying of it down. Pish (said Gymnast), a fig for your Chapter, this frock breaks both your shoulders, put it off. My friend (said the Monk), let me along with it; for by G——! I'le drink the better that it is on; it makes all my Body jocund; if I should lay it aside, the waggish Pages would cut themselves garters out of it, as I was once served at Coulaines; and, which is worse, I shall lose my appetite. But if in this habit I sit down at Table, I will drink, by G——! both to thee and to thy horse, and so courage, frolick, God save the company!

And so to the first of many ethical problems propounded by Friar John over the wine to his boon-companions, namely "the reason that the thighs of a Gentlewoman are always fresh and coole". In the eyes of some of Rabelais' commentators the Friar actually is, as Dr. Rabelais intends, a "typical monk of the period"; a somewhat severe reflection on the procession of monastic martyrs just beginning the march to a hideous death across the English Channel, not to speak of the Carmelite renaissance then in flower beyond the Pyrenees. Given this point of view it is not surprising that when the militant Gabriel Puits-Herbault,

monk of Fontevrault, rises up suddenly in 1549 and smites Dr.
Rabelais' hip and thigh in behalf of his brethren at large nobody
is more aghast or furious at such insolence than the main body
of the Doctor's learned henchmen, saving always the Doctor
himself. No prettier stroke of satiric comedy diversifies the Four
Books, as we shall perceive. It seems to me impossible to love
the Doctor completely without savouring the spectacle of the
great censor for once knocked unexpectedly off his lofty perch,
hopping mad and raising Cain.

So we may resume with *Gargantua* and the outbreak of the Picrocholian War. In this uproarious military farce, involving rivers
of bloodshed, the Doctor is simultaneously caricaturing the alleged
ambitions of Charles V, ruler of the Holy Roman Empire, and
rehashing an old legal squabble between his family and the Sainte-
Marthes, a clan of local squires. The hurly-burly develops swiftly
from a charming pastoral prelude:

> At that time, which was the season of Vintage, in the beginning
> of Harvest, when the country shepherds were set to keep the Vines
> and hinder the Starlings from eating up the Grapes; as some cake-
> bakers of Lerné happened to passe along the broad high-way,
> driving into the City ten or twelve horses loaded with Cakes, the
> said shepherds courteously intreated them to give them some for
> their Money, as the price then ruled in the Market. . . .

To this the truculent boors of Lerné return a rich sequence of
insults and abuse, expanded by our jovial Urquhart into nearly
double the original number, and often ("slabberdegullion Drug-
gels, scurvie Sneaksbies, ninnyhammer Flycatchers . . .") quite
admirably. Lerné lies in a fertile triangle between the rivers
Loire and Vienne, roughly speaking, peopled by rustics known
locally, from its principal village, as the Veronais. Sprung from
an eighth-century colony of Saracen refugees and inbred ever since,
they are notable still for uncouthness and differing even in
physique from the typical Tourangeau. To this tribe obviously
belong the men whose abuse of Gargantua's shepherds provokes
a retaliatory beating-up which develops swiftly into a great
war, ending with the rout by Pantagruel's army of the forces of
King Picrochole of Lerné, a world-conqueror *in posse* of the true
barnstorming Hitlerian breed. In the course of a campaign

conducted with rampaging strategy all over the Chinonnais countryside the Doctor's grave attention to detail on the smallest scale, successfully imitated by Swift, creates a pleasing kind of lunatic realism in the reader's mind. Of the flight and fate of the raving Picrochole no historian save Tacitus could have written with more marble restraint, tinged with a nobler pessimism.

> Picrochole thus in despaire fled towards the Bouchard Island, and in the way to Riveere his horse stumbled and fell down, whereat he on a sudden was so incensed, that he with his sword without more ado killed him in his choler; then not finding any that would remount him, he was about to have taken an Asse at the Mill that was thereby; but the Miller's men did so baste his bones and so soundly bethwack him, that they made him both black and blew with strokes; then, stripping him of all his clothes, gave him a scurvie old canvas Jacket wherewith to cover his nakednesse. Thus went along this poor Cholerick, who passing the water at Porthuaux, and relating his misadventurous disasters, was foretold by an old Lourpidon Hag that his kingdome should be restored to him at the coming of the Cocquecigrues. What is become of him since we cannot certainly tell; yet was I told that he is now a porter at Lyons, as testie and pettish in Humour as ever he was before, and would be alwayes with great lamentation enquiring at all strangers of the coming of the Cocquecigrues, expecting assuredly (according to the old Womans prophecie), that at their coming he shall be re-established in his Kingdom.

Ex-King Picrochole thereby misses Gargantua's address to the vanquished, for which purpose the giant *bon vivant* assumes all the gravity of a Platonic philosopher-king to deliver an allocution curiously dissimilar from one addressed a little previously by his father Grangousier to Picrochole's captain Touchfaucet after his capture in the field. To Touchfaucet, before releasing him, Grangousier speaks most excellent doctrine on the folly and wickedness of acquisitive war, quoting the Gospel of Christ also as commanding us (does it?) to "preserve, keep, rule, and govern every man his own countrey and lands, and not in a hostile manner to invade others". With the rest of Picrochole's staff in due course Gargantua takes a brisker line, proposing to treat the vanquished with the same clemency which yielded such admirable results in the case of Alphabal, King of Canarre, whose grateful subjects (he reminds his auditors) voluntarily paid Grangousier twice or thrice as much gold annually for years as could have been exacted by the harshest ransom. The inference was probably clear enough. It has been observed by the critical that the Doctor has shifted his ground somewhat on the ethics of war since he published *Pantagruel*. War was then the chief and natural preoccupation of a civilised prince. War can now be an evil. A few years hence it will be a blessing. In any case the conquered continue to be at the conqueror's complete disposition, and the Doctor will never arrive at any conclusion likely to please a modern pacifist.

And he is impatient, one suspects, long before the last echoes of the Picrocholian War have died away and Gargantua's captains are suitably rewarded, to get on with the building and endowment of that stupendous monument to natural virtue called the Abbey of Thélème, erected by Gargantua at the behest of Friar John. Nobly its six tall towers rise before us, with the double porphyry and marble staircases dividing them; its fair great libraries, painted galleries, and lofty marble halls; its nine thousand suites of handsome apartments, each hung with tapestries and equipped with embroidered beds and crystal mirrors framed in gold, before which these new-style monks and nuns with their rich and varied wardrobes must spend considerable time; its spacious pleasure-gardens opening into the park by the river, with labyrinth and tennis courts; its theatre and riding-school and swimming-baths; the magnificent alabaster Fountain of the Graces playing in the Inner Court; the stables, the archery-ground, the falconry, the quarter of the goldsmiths, jewellers, tailors and perfumers. To and fro across smooth lawns paces a high-born community of both sexes, flirting platonically and exchanging conversation of the most elevated kind, as we must believe. Here is the triumphal Rabelaisian retort to Western monasticism, past, present and future, and the apotheosis of Renaissance self-sufficiency; not to say snobbism, seeing that only men and women "that are free, well-born, well-bred, and conversant in honest companies, have naturally an instinct and spurre that prompeth them unto vertuous actions", no member of a mangy, pocky *canaille* (which embraces the religious orders) being permitted to set foot within the abbey precincts. The Doctor in his exaltation has overlooked nothing. There is even a private oratory for each suite where devotions of a presumably Platonic-Deist kind may be indulged in daily, engagements permitting. There are even—a distinctly belated concession to Geneva's friends—expounders of the Scriptures, new style, available for anyone wanting them.

A gorgeous dream, spread over seven lyrical chapters. And as so frequently happens where Dr. Rabelais is concerned, one or two teasing puzzles are attached. How, for instance, an uncouth *hurluberlu* like Friar John of the Chops was to rule this aristocratic, transcendental Thebaid is not easy to conjecture. As Abbot-elect of Thélème he approves the constitutions in advance but takes not the faintest interest in the place thenceforward. The great illusion on which the Abbey is founded has already been remarked. How long would this glittering community take to discover that it is quite impossible for men and women to live in amity together under the single commandment: "Do as thou wilt"? Voltaire, had it occurred to him, might have devised a pretty squib on the theme, ending with Thélème's swift and inevitable collapse in intrigues, quarrels, and dispersal. It may be justly argued that a dash of reality was not the Doctor's affair. Whether or not in sober moments he believed in the natural virtue of man as fervently as he proclaims in *Gargantua*, it was as fashionable a whimsy of the time as the co-existence of the West with armed and militant Marxism is in some cultured circles today. There may well have been bleak dawns in which it occurred to him to doubt whether Thélème was after all a rational challenge to St. Benedict. Whatever he may have felt about it later, the Doctor conserved his pipe-dream; yet it may be noted that having lavished so much ardent elaboration on this Utopia, forlorn today as the ruins of Palmyra, he passes on and will remember it only once; briefly, vaguely, at a long interval, and to no purpose.

> Here is no water but only rock,
> Rock and no water and the sandy road . . .

Alone among the Muses' favourites Swinburne was to perform a vigorous fandango before the remains of the Doctor's alabaster fountain, with its battered Graces and cornucopias, in later days:

But the laughter that rings from her cloisters that know not a bar
So kindles delight in desire that the souls of us deem
He erred not, the Seer who discerned on the seas as a star
                    Theleme.

Swinburne danced and beckoned in vain, alas. After a brief
and glassy stare the Victorians returned very wisely to their
ledgers, and the Laureateship went to a more sensible man.

So *Gargantua* ends, with a final piece of mystification in the
shape of a long rhymed "propheticall Riddle" of extreme obscurity, engraved on a bronze plate and discovered by the workmen laying the Abbey's foundations. Nobody can make head
or tail of it. At length Gargantua takes it to be a manifesto for
the Reform, urging "people called to the Faith of the Gospel"
to continue to the end "without being distracted or diverted by
carnal affections and depraved nature". At this interpretation
Friar John lets out a characteristic hoot of mirth. "Make upon
it as many grave Allegories and glosses as you will, and dote upon
it, you and the rest of the world, as long as you please; for my
part I can conceive no other meaning in it but a description of
a set at Tennis in dark and obscure Termes."

Here certainly whoops the wilful Doctor, to the approval of
Étienne Dolet and the confusion of some of his graver Lyons
friends, and so waves his public au revoir. He might, one feels,
have dwelt a little more on the mysterious "coming of the Cocqcigrues" foreshadowed by the hag of Porthuaux to King Picrochole. What are these fascinating dream-birds, presumably half-
cock, half-crane? Only once again will they flit across Rabelais'
pages, dimly and unexplained, and they haunt the memory
strangely. Doubtless the roosting-place of the Cocqcigrues is on
the Great Gromboolian Plain, near the Hills of the Chankly Bore.
Rabelais has quite a few such outbreaks of Learishness, and one
could sometimes wish he had been able to get the Renaissance
completely out of his system for a space and devote himself to
writing one of the world's great nonsense-books, full of those
creatures of pure lunar fantasy who bob up suddenly and vanish
from his pages all too soon. Such are the giants Hurtaly, "a fine
Soup-eater who reigned during the Flood" and Morgan, "the
first that ever played at Dice in Spectacles". Such are the monstrous Shrovetide, who fears "nothing but his own Shadow and

the cry of fat Kids", and amiable Gaffer Bringuenarilles of the Tohu-Bohu islands, who lives on windmills and at last, bereft of this wholesome diet, chokes to death after swallowing "a huge Lump of fresh Butter at the Mouth of a hot Oven, by advice of his Physicians", and a score more. If anything could enhance the fascination of such a volume as I venture to imagine, it would be the agony of not a few pedants who can never let the Doctor throw a single somersault without peering for the Platonic Idea behind it. *Arrière, cagotz!*

V

The Ring of Hippocrates

I

AT THE HOSPITAL OF OUR LADY OF PITY AT LYONS, THE YEAR
being 1535, the day late in February, there is excitement in the
air. Nods and winks and nudges among the staff; a suppressed
giggle or two from the "reformed Magdalen" nurses as they trot
to and fro; murmuring and grins from bed to bed; gesticulations
in the direction of the boardroom, where the "consuls-rectors",
governors of the hospital, are in conference—it takes no clair-
voyant to summon up the scene. Something must have disturbed
the placid daily round. Something indeed has. Dr. François
Rabelais, our genial and peremptory chief medical officer, is in
disgrace. Dr. Rabelais has not reported for duty recently on two
separate occasions. Dr. Rabelais is, in fact, still absent without
leave, apology, or explanation, and the governors have met at
length to deal with the situation.

Enough can be gleaned from the brief hospital records to enable
one or two of the voices in the boardroom to be overheard; the
rasp of one Master Pierre Durand in particular as he moves the
adjournment till Easter, having been informed that this fellow
Rabelais, *ledict Rabellays*, is in Grenoble, and may return. The
only visible trace of the Doctor is his just-published almanac
for 1535, signed with a flourish "docteur en médecine, et médecin
du grand hospital de Lyon". These almanacs of his, published
more or less annually since he took up his hospital post, I have
mentioned before. They are of that didactic type for mass-
consumption finally exploited by Benjamin Franklin, of no particular literary value, representing doubtless a useful addition
to Dr. Rabelais' income, and offering a mock-horoscopic forecast
for the year, a text or two from Aristotle, Plato, or Scripture, a

few moral apothegms, a few sound platitudes, and the inevitable sprinkling of puns and fooleries. There was a vogue for such productions in Renaissance France, and the Doctor had, in the literary phrase of today, cashed in on it. One may discern a copy of his latest effort lying on the governors' table. To all such rational men of affairs it would confirm previous impressions of their missing doctor's eccentricity and flightiness. These spare-time scribblers . . .

After interviewing three applicants for Dr. Rabelais' post, Dr. Pierre du Castel, Dr. Jean Canapé, and Dr. Charles des Marais, the board adjourned. Meeting again on March 5, there being still no word or sign from Dr. Rabelais, the governors formally struck him off the roll and appointed Dr. du Castel in his place, at the same time reducing the annual salary from forty livres to thirty. The secretary having recorded in the registers that Dr. François Rabelais had "absented himself and abandoned this Hospital without notice or leavetaking", the matter was closed.

Where was the Doctor?

Once more he has melted into space, leaving no clue. If he was really in Grenoble, as Master Durand assumed, no trace of him is perceptible there and he never mentions the town. Was he perhaps in Paris? Or the Chinonnais? Was he visiting his old patron at Maillezais? Was he even lying *perdu* in Lyons, to which city he had a special attachment, as already perceived? Wherever he was, this new disappearance has been traced not to normal restlessness but to *la frousse*, a fit of panic, not unreasonable at this moment.

The beginning of 1535 was no season for waggery at the expense of the Church. The Calvinist "Affair of the Placards" already noted, with its flagrant public insults to the Mass and to the king, had inflamed France with fury. Sanctions proper to that tough age were even now in progress. Burning at the stake was the final contemporary argument favoured by all sides. By poetic justice it might even happen, as in the case of Cranmer, Ridley, and Latimer in England, that the burners came themselves to be burned. Least of all men in the sixteenth century had Calvinists any reason to object in principle, since Calvin himself welcomed the stake for Dolet and made a bonfire of the luckless Servetus. In the early part of 1535 a score of France's most

F

militant sectaries paid the penalty in this way, a couple of hundred more were banished, and public anger was allayed. It may well have seemed prudent to the author of *Pantagruel* and *Gargantua*, a lapsed monk, to take cover till the storm had blown itself out, which it did very soon, by the end of spring, thanks partly to a stiff rebuke from the Holy See and partly to François I's latest change in foreign policy, which required an *entente* with the Lutherans. On February 13, at any rate, Dr. Rabelais drew thirteen livres of salary due to him and evaporated from the scene of his labours.

Since it is in Lyons, five months later, that we pick up the trail again, it might be that the Doctor had used a refuge in the city. On July 15 Bishop Jean du Bellay, newly raised to the Sacred College by Paul III and passing through Lyons on his way to Rome for the Hat, collected his esteemed physician as before, together with the Bishop of Maguelonne. So Dr. Rabelais was now safe.

This time Du Bellay and his party halted a few days on the journey south at the little ducal court of Ferrara, whose cultured French duchess, Renée, daughter of Louis XII, was apt to irritate her duke, history records, by her lavish hospitality to visiting fellow-countrymen, particularly to those of them sharing her leaning towards the Reform. A couple of temporary French exiles of mark were among the duchess's guests at this time: the poet Clément Marot, due before long to be expelled by Calvin from Geneva in disgrace for being unable to take Calvinism seriously, and Léon Jamet, late Clerk of the Finances, both of whom had prudently quitted France on the morrow of the Placards, in which affair Marot was named among seventy other ringleaders. With this considerable and charming poet, a sceptic and epicurean after his own heart, though inclined to use a dagger in religious dispute, Dr. Rabelais must have begun at Ferrara the friendship to which Marot's *Epigramme à François Rabelais* testifies. Though not of his best work, it is perceived to be that of a kindred spirit, echoing the "Fay ce que vouldras" ("Do-what-thou-wilt") slogan of Thélème.

> Librement vivre comme il faut vivre . . .[1]

[1] "Living at one's guise, the way one ought to live . . ."

On July 30 Cardinal du Bellay and his suite reached Rome. Here Dr. Rabelais will remain for the next nine months in attendance on his patron, despatching long regular news-letters, via the French Embassy bag and otherwise, to his old benefactor Geoffroy d'Estissac, Bishop of Maillezais, with whom he may after all have taken refuge during the late trouble. Three of these letters have survived. All are in French and rather disappointing. For the most part they equally lack the Rabelaisian verve and the kind of information one might expect from a cardinal diplomat's intimate, moving in or at least on the fringe of Curia and Embassy circles. As Louis Moland observes, the Doctor has very little news to impart which could not have been picked up by anybody, and is often far from well-informed. In a word (and if the thought be not uncharitable) "Our Rome Correspondent" to the life. Specimen passage, from the letter of December 30, 1535:

> A week ago the news arrived in this city, and the Holy Father received despatches to the effect from various quarters, of the defeat of the Turks by the Sophy, the King of Persia. Last evening arrived the nephew of M. de Vély, the King's [François I's] ambassador to the Emperor, who confirmed this to Cardinal du Bellay, adding that this is the greatest massacre which has happened for four hundred years in those parts, more than forty thousand Turkish horses having been killed. Imagine therefore the number of men-at-arms left on the field. Similarly on the Sophy's side. . .

The next letter (January 28, 1536) is much more interesting, affording a glimpse of Rome on the eve of the ceremonial entry of the Emperor Charles V, which prospect was causing the officials of the impoverished Papal Treasury acute anguish, the Imperial escort requiring, *inter alia*, three thousand mattress-beds and a stupendous provision of wine and food. Added to this was the expense of providing a triumphal road for the ruler of the Holy Roman Empire from the St. Sebastian Gate to the Castle of Sant' Angelo. Here the Doctor permits himself a chuckle while relating how the Emperor, now halted at Naples, has been prevailed upon by urgent papal envoys to delay his entry till the end of February.

> If I had as many gold crowns as the number of indulgence-days with which the Pope would like to reward *proprio motu, de plenitudine*

potestatis, anyone who could get it put off for five or six years, I
should be richer than Jacques Coeur [Charles VII's millionaire
banker] ever was.[1] They have started a lot of great schemes to receive him [the Emperor] in this city, including, by the Pope's order,
a new road for him to enter by, from the St. Sebastian Gate. . .
To construct and level this they have demolished and knocked
down more than two hundred houses and razed three or four
churches to the ground, which many people think is a bad omen. . .
It is a pity to see the ruins of the houses. No payment or com-
pensation has been made to any of the owners.

Such routine features of the Renaissance scene as a Medici
laying an ambush for a Strozzi, the daylight assassination of a
diplomat, and a vendetta and a stabbing or two the Doctor notes
as in duty bound ("these Italians! . . ."), though he could have
heard of much the same at intervals in Paris. Most vital of all
his news, especially to himself, is a passage in the third letter,
dated February 15, 1536, from which we perceive that he has
rid himself of his chief bugbear at last.

I have, thank God, concluded all my business, and it has cost me
nothing beyond the registration of the Bulls [*sic*]. The Holy Father
gave me the composition free at his own suggestion.

This was only relatively true. Having delved once more into
the Vatican archives, Lesellier finds that Dr. Rabelais was not
being quite honest with Bishop d'Estissac. Paul III had certainly
waived the usual legal costs of issuing a bull of the kind involved
in the Doctor's case, registration and one or two trifling fees to
minor *barbouilleurs de parchemin* or parchment-spoilers apart; but
this was no special concession to Dr. François Rabelais, as seems
to be implied. Every petitioner proposed by a member of the
Sacred College was equally privileged if his petition was granted.
Again, Dr. Rabelais' story that the advice, and as it happened,
wrong advice, given him on a short cut to his objective saving a
quantity of red tape came from the Pope in person ("Le Pape
estoit d'advis que je passasse . . .") is more than doubtful. And
finally the Doctor omits to mention that owing entirely to his
own fecklessness he was obliged to repeat the whole process with
a new petition at his own expense. Hence in his present need to

[1] The gold *écu* was equal at this period, seemingly, to two *livres tournois*.

dun D'Estissac again his simultaneous anxiety not to lose "face" with such a benefactor. Or so Lesellier surmises, and I think shrewdly.

The complications of this imbroglio with the Curia's lawyers need not concern us. In his haste Rabelais had omitted from his original *supplicatio* what he chiefly needed, next to absolution— namely a licence to practise medicine and the right to enjoy benefices. A brief embodying these essentials was issued to him at length on January 17, 1536. Opening with the formal greeting "Beloved Son, health and Apostolic benediction", and continuing in the customary way with a précis of Rabelais' *supplicatio*, it proceeds in a style which might seem faintly satiric were it not a formula of clemency recalling to a recipient of distinction already absolved his pledges for the future:

> Desiring therefore to show Our regard for the zeal for religion, science, and literature, the probity of life and morals, and all the merits and virtues which recommend you, and moved by your appeals, We absolve you [etc., etc.].

And Dr. Rabelais is granted everything. Having humbly confessed his nine years' vagabondage he has been given plenary absolution, doubtless with the usual penances, and permission to resume the Benedictine habit, to enter a house of that Order, and to practise medicine—including surgery within the limits then imposed on religious by Canon Law, that is to say so far as the application of knife and cautery, purely as an act of charity and without lucrative intent—with his future superior's consent. He is likewise qualified to receive benefices.

So the Doctor could be grateful to his patron Du Bellay, two of whose most influential friends, Cardinals Hieronimo Ghinucci, Judge of the Palace, and Simonetta, Auditor of the Apostolic Camera, had backed his petition. From whom he received the inefficient advice to take a short cut to the Camera bypassing the Court of Contradicts, a notion which the Curia's lawyers speedily corrected, is not known. His story to D'Estissac would hardly deceive anyone who knew Paul III, though we need not doubt that the return to the Fold of a strayed sheep of such quality had disposed the Holy Father to interest and benevolence.

Of Rome's generosity Dr. Rabelais would, one would imagine, have been sufficiently appreciative to temper his satiric flights henceforth to some little extent. He forbears to do anything of the sort, and in the Fourth Book, in fact, he will excel himself in Gallican sniping. One is forced regretfully to conclude that the Rabelaisian merits and virtues mentioned in the Papal Brief failed to neutralise a streak of that *méchanceté* in which, as not a few of his fellow-countrymen have admitted, the Gaul is apt to surpass all mankind. And again, perhaps, a long habit of scoffing is, like Cyrano's nose, not easy to discard.

> Puis on sourit, on dit: " Il va l'enlever" . . . Mais
> Monsieur de Bergerac ne l'enlève jamais.[1]

And once again, he would be at that future date, as Léon Daudet holds—and I think soundly—under orders.

Thanks chiefly to his muddled dealings with the papal lawyers, Dr. Rabelais was at this moment finding the cost of living in Rome a harassing problem. "I am constrained," he writes desperately to the Bishop of Maillezais on February 15, "to have recourse once more to your aims. The thirty crowns you were pleased to let me have are nearly at an end." He adds that he has certainly not been indulging in loose living, having his place either at Du Bellay's or the French Ambassador's table. The bishop's last gift has gone, he explains not quite fully, on the hire of furniture, the necessary upkeep of his wardrobe, and "little scribbles of despatches". His troubles were not unique. Everybody in Rome, apparently, was in the same state from the Pope down. Even Cardinal du Bellay was involved in one of those temporary financial crises from which the rich by God's mercy are no more exempt than the rest of us, and had recently pawned his silver plate. As for the Pope's Imperial guest-to-be, similarly afflicted, his vast commitments left him very often in this condition, and in fact his recurring inability to pay his thousands of mercenary troops had been primarily responsible for the sack of Rome. "The Emperor," Rabelais informs

---

[1] "One smiles; one says, 'It's coming off!' . . . However, Monsieur de Bergerac removes it never." (*Cyrano de Bergerac*, Act I.)

D'Estissac with another glint of amusement, "is short of money, looking for it everywhere, dunning everybody possible, borrowing in every nook and corner. Once arrived here he will certainly apply to the Pope for some, pointing out that he has waged all these wars with the Turk and Barbarossa for the security of Italy and the Papacy, and that a contribution is imperative. The said Pope will reply that he has no money at all and will show him obvious proofs. The Emperor will then demand the Duke of Ferrara's . . ." Ferrara had none to lend either.

A parting glimpse of the Roman scene ends Rabelais' third surviving letter. There must have been many such in those now lost, some of them diverting. The pre-Lenten Carnival, for example, was to the satisfaction of the populace revived in 1536. Though confined strictly within the bounds of propriety, unlike the Carnival of Venice, it embraced pageants, fireworks, tourneys, and races, and the Doctor's impressions would be interesting; likewise his comments on the effects of an edict of Paul III, issued this February of 1536, ordering those of the clergy who had discarded ecclesiastical dress off duty to put away their silks and satins and velvet boots and resume it permanently. Hitherto the spectacle of the Canons of St. Peter's halting in the atrium to doff cloaks and swords—worn at this period also by French Calvinist pastors, one may recall in passing—and assume their canonical habits before entering the basilica to recite the daily Office had been one of the sights of Rome which can hardly have eluded the Doctor's notice. However, he is absorbed in the topic of the hour. The Emperor, still at Naples, is expected in Rome within the fortnight, he reports. The City is all but ready, the triumphal road complete, the arches up. To pay for this and much more every Roman citizen is being taxed from *Messieurs les Cardinaulx* down to the watercarriers. Foreigners are swarming in. Among the latest distinguished arrivals the Doctor notes the Cardinal of Trent, a German prelate of some importance with an escort of more than a hundred in red-and-yellow livery. The cardinal's business in Rome, apart from greeting his Emperor, was to press for that General Council of the Church in which the greater part of the Christian world saw the only hope for the West. For this panacea the time was overripe, but not a few engineers of European intrigue were strongly opposing it, and the late Pope Clement VII, a Medici fatally absorbed in the affairs of his clan, had been noticeably lukewarm. Not so Paul III, who nine years hence will be able to summon the Council of Trent, nineteenth of its kind. When the Council rises in 1563 the Barque of Peter, repaired, refitted, and re-armed, all ship-shape and Bristol-fashion, will at last be ready to ride the storms of the centuries again.

Dr. Rabelais does not refer in any of these letters to a highly interesting acquisition to his stock of learning acquired in Rome during this stay. It is mentioned offhand in a glossary of learned or obscure words and phrases called the *Briefve Declaration*, which he considerately appends to the Fourth Book (and, it need hardly be added, not in alphabetical or any other order). Against the phrase *catadupes du Nil* the Doctor explains:

> A place in Ethiopia where the Nile falls from high mountains, with such a terrible noise that those living near the place are almost all deaf, as Claudius Galen affirms. The Bishop of Caramith, who was my tutor in Arabic at Rome, told me that the noise can be heard from the distance of a three-days' journey, which is as far as from Paris to Tours.

"My tutor in Arabic"—how much, one wonders idly, did Dr. Rabelais, who so despised Arabian medicine, acquire from this prelate *in partibus*? In the comprehensive Rabelaisian glossary attached to Moland's edition I find only about half a dozen Arabic words, most of them in traditional use in medical and allied circles. In the Doctor's own glossary appear none at all. Given his addiction to popping plums of Latin, Greek, and even Hebrew so lavishly into his literary pie, might one suspect that the airy reference to "my tutor" does not mean so much, perhaps, as the Doctor makes it convey? Might the whole business in fact have been merely a perfunctory gesture in the direction of that tyrannical Renaissance fetish of "universal knowledge" to which not a few strong and dogged scholars sacrificed sleep, nervous energy, prospects, friends, and occasionally reason, and which must have turned not a few addled pedant-brains to turnip-juice?

A great man nevertheless. Let us return his wink and pace on.

2

On February 29, 1536, Cardinal Jean du Bellay left Rome for Paris; discreetly, in haste and incognito, with a small escort, just before the entry of the Emperor Charles V, the last man the King of France's Envoy-Extraordinary could now desire to meet. His household, including Dr. Rabelais, he left behind, duly provided with safe-conducts. Not until early in May, it has been calculated, did the Doctor return to France. During his long stay he had considerably extended those observant strolls which made him at length, as he boasted, familiar with every byway and alley in Rome. His passion for Roman antiquities may have cooled. There is no mention of them in the three letters already quoted. Botanical research must have continued to absorb him; the letters are sprinkled with references to plants and flowers. He has likewise, as we observe, been toying with Arabic.

The sardonic Rabelaisian eye can hardly have failed to spy diversion in the expensive celebrations welcoming the Emperor's entry. Less amusing was Charles V's speech of reception at the Vatican on April 8, in the presence of Pope Paul III, the College of Cardinals, and all the Corps Diplomatique; for Charles on this occasion dropped all fine words and made no secret of his intention to teach the French a lesson. There is a story, barely credible, that almost instantly regretting this frankness he summoned the two French ambassadors, Mâcon and De Vély, and persuaded them to tone their despatches down. There is another story to the effect that Cardinal du Bellay was himself present at the Vatican reception incognito, and that on returning to his apartments he wrote down most of the Emperor's ominous words, aided by a mnemonic system of his own, and left for Paris the same night. Unable to reconcile this latter story with the date of Du Bellay's departure, though it certainly explains the Cardinal's disguise and hurry, I leave it and pass on.

War was certainly imminent, and the Emperor's case a strong one. In the confusing kaleidoscope of François I's policies and intrigues a few crude provocations are visible enough. His master-stroke of cynicism, the alliance with the Turk, now an ever-growing menace to Christendom, was the scandal of Europe. ("The Turks keep the Emperor occupied and are a surety for all princes", as François airily explained to the Venetians.) He had likewise allied himself with the Lutheran princes of Germany and the formidable Moslem pirates of Algiers, Charles V's next most indefatigable enemies; also with Henry VIII of England, who had publicly insulted and abandoned his wife, Charles' aunt, and cut England off from Catholic unity. He had at least twice sworn friendship to Charles, breaking faith almost immediately. Over and above all this, François had quite recently revived an old French claim to the Duchy of Milan, of which Charles was suzerain, and in April of this year a French force had occupied Turin to establish it. It was this act of aggression which finally decided Charles V. As he said in his Vatican speech: "If the King of France will not have peace I shall be forced to stake all for all, for the Turk will soon be master of Europe if Almighty God do not intervene." And having vainly offered to fight their quarrel out with François personally, sword to sword, he invaded Provence and Picardy in the June of 1536, an Imperial army of fifty thousand simultaneously crossing the Alps.

There was intense activity in France. Twenty thousand pioneers were set to work at speed on the fortifications of Paris and François I left immediately to set up his G.H.Q. at Avignon, entrusting Jean du Bellay with the defence of the capital and the north and east frontiers. However, Paris and the frontiers proved to be in no peril. Before long the invasion faltered and stopped, owing partly to famine and dysentery ravaging the Imperial troops, partly to French vigour and the blunders of Imperial generals. In June 1538 the Holy See intervened and a ten-year truce was signed at Nice.

Soon after the outbreak of war Dr. Rabelais was in Paris again waiting on his patron the Cardinal-Bishop, now neckdeep in national defence. During his leisure hours one may see the Doctor cocking an alert eye at the progress on the fortifications and asking a thousand questions. Some of the martial bustle echoes from the Prologue of the Third Book in a dissertation on the siege of Corinth by Philip of Macedon:

Others did fortifie and rampire their Walls, set up little Fortresses, Bastions, squared Ravelins, digged Trenches, cleansed Counter-mines, fenced themselves with Gabions, contrived Platforms, emptied

Casemates, barricado'd the false Brayes, erected the Cavalliers, repaired the Contrescarpes, plaister'd the Courtines, lengthned Ravelins, stopt Parapets, mortaised Barbicans, assured the Port-culleys, fastned the Herses, Sarasinesks, and Cataracks, placed their Centries, and doubled their Patrouille . . .

To a flush of patriotic gusto prompted by the reflection that before long the most noble Kingdom of France would have its frontiers "most magnifically enlarged" must be attributed the latest deviation in the Doctor's views on war. "Very little," he now cheerfully proclaims, "withholds me from the Opinion of good Heraclitus, which affirmeth War to be the Father of all good things." And again: "In War appeareth all that is good and graceful." Good and graceful!—"*Frisch und fröhlich!*" The shadow of a Crown Prince of Germany yet unborn flits with a guffaw across the Doctor's page. It will be very nearly three hundred and eighty years before the newest Rabelaisian judgment can be tested and confirmed on a truly Gargantuan scale.

Less exhilarating thoughts must have been occupying Dr. Rabelais as well. Writing from Rome on February 15, 1536, he had omitted to inform Geoffroy d'Estissac of a brief ceremony in the palace-chapel of Cardinal du Bellay four days earlier, when the Cardinal, officiating as Abbot of St. Maur-les-Fossés, a Benedictine house near Paris, formally admitted Dom François Rabelais, newly restored to the Order, into his community, though his recruit still owed allegiance to the Bishop-Abbot of Maillezais, from whose jurisdiction he had vanished in such mysterious circumstances years before. Sooner or later the bishop would have to be informed. Fortunately another complication obviated this awkwardness to some extent. By a bull of August 1536, in response to applications dating from 1533, the abbey of St. Maur-les-Fossés was turned into a collegiate church served by secular canons. A fresh *supplicatio* from the beneficiary had already prayed the Holy See to change his monastic status accordingly. To make doubly certain he followed this up with another, emphasising his scruples at taking advantage of the bull while still a regular. The papal reply has not survived, but was evidently acquiescent, since Rabelais took up residence at St. Maur as a secular canon forthwith.

Here the traditional story has been demolished by the research
of Lesellier at the Vatican. The resentment of Rabelais' eight
brother-canons at having the bishop's protégé foisted on them,
thus reducing their emoluments by one-ninth, their final appeal
to Rome in a body, and the interloper's resignation—all this is
seemingly a myth. The Doctor kept his three-hundred-livres-a-
year canonry, which was provided for, and may well have done
so to the end of his life. Why he sooner or later left St. Maur—
which retreat he describes in the Fourth Book as "a place (or
rather paradise) of salubrity, serenity, conveniency, and all desirable country pleasure"—is not known. He was not compelled to
residence, and it may be, I think, that he simply grew bored,
as was his way. How long could Canon Rabelais have lived in
amity with his new brethren? And even if he managed to love
and be loved by all of them, what of the old restless urge of the
Rabelaisian blood? Medicine was calling him again, in any case.
By the time of his departure from St. Maur-les-Fossés, which
seems to have been within six months of his entry, he must have
made up his mind, with Du Bellay's permission, to return to
Lyons and resume practice there; and it is permissible to admire
the bland insensitivity to public opinion displayed in such a
decision, considering the circumstances in which Dr. Rabelais
had severed his connection with the city's principal hospital just
over a year previously. Is this to be connected with that strong
streak of self-sufficiency with which we are now familiar? Or is it
merely one more indiscretion of a complex and impulsive temperament? At least he need worry no more over his position
under Canon Law. As with Erasmus, the secular habit to
which he is now entitled will be his wear for the rest of his
life.

Towards the end of February 1537 we get our next view of him.
He has apparently quitted St. Maur—though he will return
there more than once to attend his patron, Cardinal du Bellay,
whose favourite retreat it was—and is now in Paris and enjoying
himself at an agreeable supper-party, the guest of honour being
Étienne Dolet, that tough and—as Rabelais himself was to discover—unscrupulous literary character. Having had the misfortune to kill a boon-companion, his aggressor in a Lyons street-
fight on New Year's Eve, Dolet had just been granted a royal

pardon, thanks to the efforts of friends. A number of the intelligentsia gathered to congratulate him: Clément Marot, Salmon Macrin, Visagier, Bérault, Danès, and half a dozen more, headed by the aged, still illustrious Guillaume Budé. Did Dr. Rabelais greet his idol of Fontenay days this evening for the first, perhaps (Budé died in 1540) the only time? There is no evidence of any other meeting. One may well believe that the old scholar would be pleased to see his ex-protégé in his forties a savant of mark, receiving his due meed of the compliments ritual to agapes of this kind. Highly gratifying these must have been. In a Latin ode by Dolet, saluting his hosts and undoubtedly recited at table with clashing goblets in the Renaissance fashion, Dr. François Rabelais is lauded to the skies as the honour and glory of Medicine —nay, a genius who can raise the dead.

> Franciscus Rabelaesus, honos et gloria certa
> Artis Paeoniae, qui vel de limine Ditis
> Extinctos revocare potest et reddere luci . . .[1]

Which no doubt lent an extra bouquet to the Doctor's libations that night. It may likewise have reminded him that he still had to take his final degree. Six weeks later, at any rate, he is to be viewed at Montpellier, paying his licentiate's fees and (May 22) being admitted at last a Doctor of Medicine; a pure formality, the ceremony of reception taking place in the Great Hall.

Was one half-expecting some echo of the Walpurgis Night romp of surgeons, doctors, and apothecaries which ends *Le Malade Imaginaire*? Of what suggestions is the wicked Molière not capable! The etiquette at Montpellier, as in every other temple of the Hippocratic science, was calmer. Standing within a semicircle composed of the whole Faculty of Medicine in full academic robes, and facing a select audience, the doctor-elect was introduced with a eulogy by a sponsor, in Rabelais' case Dr. Antoine Griffy, after which he proceeded to expose a thesis, closing with a formula of thanks to the Faculty for the honour of his degree. He was then invested solemnly with the insignia proper to a Doctor of Medicine, namely a gold ring, a gilded belt, and a black cloth biretta with a crimson silk tassel, and finally

[1] François Rabelais, honour and undisputed glory of the healing art, who can even recall the dead from Pluto's threshold and restore them to the light . . .

handed the inevitable copy of Hippocrates. The proceedings ended with a Faculty dinner. An obligation to deliver one term's lectures came later.

From Montpellier Dr. Rabelais proceeded to Lyons, and apparently started in practice immediately, giving lectures on anatomy as well. Where these took place, especially when they embraced a dissection, is not known; nor is it possible to conjecture in what degree, if at all, his clash with the chief hospital of Lyons may have affected his prospects. The ebullient Dolet, who was to play his admired friend a shady trick before long, obliged around this time with a posy of Latin verse in praise of Dr. Rabelais' skill in dissection. The corpse of a lately-hanged criminal under the master's knife is warmly congratulated by the poet. What an honour for such a scallywag! Instead of being blown about at a rope's end and becoming food for the ravens, here he finds the most eminent of savants holding forth over his ignoble carcase for the benefit of a learned assembly. In a succeeding poem Dolet pictures by way of contrast a lesser practitioner at the same work, so nervous and bungling that his audience wonders which is the dumber, the corpse or the lecturer. And, Dolet might have added, holding its nose· meanwhile. Such demonstrations by a slow hand cannot have been an unmixed treat for the most enthusiastic audience. There was no "deep freeze" for cadavers in those days. It may be taken, I fancy, that while engaged in a public dissection an enemy of discomposure like Dr. Rabelais would waste little time in unnecessary rhetoric. From any history of medicine one may learn that dissections were infrequent in medical schools at this period and skilled operators correspondingly rare. Although Gargantua recommends "frequent anatomies" to his student-son as a means of acquiring knowledge of "that other world called the Microcosm, which is man", he does not indicate how the enormous youth is to go about it. Dexterity in this branch was now adding considerably to Dr. Rabelais' reputation.

A highly disturbing incident occurred about this time. Quite suddenly the Doctor found himself about to be thrust in prison for a breach of what is nowadays known as "security". A letter of his, discussing public affairs and addressed to "one of the worst blackguards [*paillards*] in Rome", had been stopped by the foreign correspondence censors of Cardinal de Tournon, newly-appointed Lieutenant-General for the South-West "to resist the Emperor's enterprises". The words above quoted are the redoubtable Cardinal's own, addressed to Chancellor du Bourg. Nothing is known of our imprudent Doctor's Roman correspondent. Having been officially warned not to leave Lyons till the Chancellor had come to a decision, he averted further trouble by hastily "acknowledging himself" to the King and the ever-sympathetic Queen of Navarre, which seems to mean a written apology and plea for pardon. The matter then dropped. By what means a recent British authority is enabled to state that Cardinal de Tournon "failed to convict his prisoner of heresy" is hard to discover, since Rabelais received no imprisonment and no question of heresy was involved. As the Cardinal had informed the Chancellor, his intention was to make an example of "Rabelezus" for the discouragement of all indiscreet babblers and *escripveurs de nouvelles*. It might be an incident of yesterday, or tomorrow.

This little trouble got over, Dr. Rabelais left for Montpellier to fulfil the obligations of his final degree. He was now, on entry into middle age, a man of increasing note in his profession and a rising figure in literature to boot.[1] Still making money for his publishers, his two comic works had appeared in new editions in 1533 from the presses of François Juste and Pierre de Sainte-Lucie, a new publisher, respectively. Let us hope that from each in turn the Doctor collected that variable *ex gratia* acknowledgment on publication which was in those days all the most successful author could hope for.

Arrived at Montpellier, where he now dined at high table, Dr. Rabelais assisted his brethren of the Faculty on September 27, the feast of Medicine's patron-saints Cosmas and Damian, in drawing up the lecture-schedule for the "Great Ordinary", a course extending from St. Luke's day, October 18, to the eve of Palm Sunday. On the appointed day he duly began his statutory course, planned to cover the whole term, his theme being Hippocrates' *Prognostics*, expounded as usual from the

---

[1] A few years after his death the *Chronologia Omnium Illustrium Medicorum*, a *Who's Who* of the medical élite of Europe published at Frankfort, fixes the beginning of Rabelais' reputation at the year 1534.

original text. He lectured publicly on anatomy in the Great Hall at least once, and apparently gave a certain amount of advice and treatment like any ordinary physician between times. It is at this period that he is said, on what authority I have not discovered, to have invented a new surgical instrument for use in throat-operations, called the *glottotomon*; presumably a less shuddersome piece of cutlery than some of the Renaissance exhibits illustrated in histories of the surgeon's art. As any nervous observer must constantly remind himself, this was a tough age.

Likewise attached to Rabelais' present engagement with the Faculty of Montpellier are a number of vague stories of rovings to and fro in the vicinity, for example to Narbonne, Castres, and other towns of the Midi; all doubtless true enough. "Paris, Narbonne, and the banks of the Aude," exclaims his friend Salmon Macrin in a subsequent Latin ode, "are witnesses to thy mirific cures, like the opulent city of Lyons, where are thy household gods and peaceful dwelling!"

A much more momentous, not to say surprising, glimpse of the Doctor, and this time an authentic one, is imminent. Having finished his lectures and left Montpellier for good, barring a brief return-visit in 1539 to sponsor a new entrant, he is discovered on July 14—a letter to Étienne Dolet from the Seneschal of Provence's lieutenant at Arles establishes it—at Aigues-Mortes in Provence, witnessing that most historic meeting between the Emperor Charles V and his enemy François I, which had with some difficulty been brought about by Pope Paul III in the hope of restoring European peace as a preliminary to the re-union of Western Christendom, if still possible, by a General Council.

What Dr. Rabelais was actually doing at Aigues-Mortes, near Marseilles, and in the Most Christian King of France's entourage, no less—in which exalted company he returned to Lyons a few days later—has never been satisfactorily explained, except for the obvious conclusion that Cardinal du Bellay had something to do with it. Whether or not the Doctor was acting as his patron's aide-de-camp and "observer", I incline to spy a plausible theory for his sudden hobnobbing with the Court, at least. Though some authorities for no very convincing reason postdate it half a dozen years, he must already have been nominated, at the cardinal's instigation, a Master of the King's Requests. This high-sounding honorific was a decoration at the royal disposal, reserved for suitably-recommended scholars, poets, savants, men of letters, and suchlike types. Involving no salary or duties, it carried admission to the entourage and, if so desired, leave to follow the Court at the applicant's expense. There were likewise professional Masters of Requests, hardworking salaried lawyers and royal officials functioning in Paris, but they had no connection with "the Bohemian element", as it is called by decent people. That Dr. François Rabelais, recently thus qualified, should be among those present at Aigues-Mortes, an occasion beckoning with obvious invitation to a man of his perpetual curiosity, becomes explicable, and the assumption seems to me to establish the date of his ascent into the royal orbit very comfortably.

The only mention of him as a Master of Requests, with four or five others, occurs in a poem of 1543 called *Le Discours de la Court*, by his friend Claude Chapuis of Cardinal du Bellay's household. There is no indication that this particular honours list of scholars and poets ("A pretty mixed bunch!"—one hears the familiar cry echoing down the centuries) is a new one and only two of the personages cited by Chapuis are of any consequence, the court poet Mélin de Saint-Gelais and Dr. François Rabelais. A patient of Jean du Bellay's standing may well have thanked his brilliant physician in this way on the return from Rome in 1536. Such a gesture would involve no more trouble, or awaken any more public comment, than the modern custom of rewarding British Cabinet Ministers with a peerage apiece for ignominious failure on the grand scale.

So the Doctor witnessed the temporary reconciliation of Emperor and King. The proceedings must have left a considerable impression on him. One can indeed see him looking a trifle shaken, for Europe's two principal antagonists had now pledged each other friendship and support in concerted action against those enemies of the Church who were fomenting public trouble in their respective dominions. They had likewise settled the course to be pursued. Friendly approach and persuasion to agreement and submission to authority first; if this was rejected, force.

Distasteful tidings for some of his Lyons cronies, as the Doctor would be well aware—particularly for such loudmouths among them as Dolet, Bonaventure des Périers, and Antoine de Gouvea, whose reputations were known far outside their circle. The case of Des Périers is edifying. Formerly a Calvinist of sorts, one-time *valet de chambre* to Marguerite de Valois, and author of the *Cymbalum Mundi*, a work declared pernicious and suppressed by decree of the Parlement of Paris[1] in the autumn of 1538, a whole edition being burned by the common hangman, he affords a handy illustration of the value of a patron. But for Marguerite's protection he would have met worse trouble on this occasion than his clandestine printer, one Jean Morin, *pauvre jeune garson*, *libraire de Paris*, who was clapped into the Conciergerie, threatened with criminal proceedings, and released only after abject and printed apology. Scanning the four dialogues which compose the *Cymbalum*, one cannot but conclude that the Princess's protégé got off very easily. Wholesale caricature and mockery of the Divine and repeated blasphemy, all disguised under the thinnest of veils, leap from every page. In the opening piece, featuring Christ Himself in the person of Mercury, the rascally messenger of the gods, divine pronouncements from the Gospels are parodied in tavern-talk, and the Incarnation and the Mass dismissed with ridicule. By the end of the second dialogue, described by La Monnoye as a *raillerie impie et outrée*, Des Périers in a kind of frenzy of derision has tossed the new Renaissance creeds into the same bag with the ancient Faith and booted them all away. In the third God the Father is an old babbler (*vieulx rassoté*). For the final dialogue, taking place between two dogs named Hylactor and Pamphagus, representing Luther and Calvin, the heat is turned on the Catholic religion exclusively, but the Reform gains little thereby; it merely represents the last dying gasp of Christianity, the new critico-destructive spirit having, we gather, whittled the Gospels away to nothing and made the worship of Christ impossible.

Des Périers committed suicide in 1544 by falling on his sword. Better men than he on both sides died a more complicated death in what I have seen called the "ideological dissonances of the

---

[1] The Parlements of France—one for each province under the presidency of Paris, established by St. Louis IX in the thirteenth century, abolished by the Revolution —·were legal tribunals. Parliament in the accepted sense was the States-General.

Renaissance". It is scarcely necessary to add that since then more than one strenuous effort has been made to prove the *Cymbalum Mundi* a piece of blameless fun, though large numbers of Des Périers' contemporaries of both religions agreed with Pasquier that the author deserved to be tossed into the fire with his book, described by Henri Estienne, a leading stalwart of the Reform, as "detestable". What is chiefly interesting about the argument over the *Cymbalum* in later days is that whereas Bayle in the seventeenth century oddly considers Des Périers Rabelais' equal as an imitator of Lucian, Prosper Marchand in the eighteenth even more oddly deems Des Périers the less outrageous of the two, lacking "the prodigious quantity of obscenities and that perpetual profanation [*sic*] of Holy Writ one finds everywhere in the works of Rabelais, though these are not labelled 'detestable' or consigned to the flames".

For all contemporary French specialists in anti-Catholic derision and abuse the red light went up soon after the king's return from Aigues-Mortes, when a royal edict extended the powers of examination and trial in such cases from the sovereign Courts to all provincial seneschals. Those of the Left intelligentsia who had been merely trotting after the bell-wethers of the flock in the traditional manner found no difficulty in executing a prompt about-turn; in many instances, perhaps, with relief. Such a possibility seems to occur to few or none of the learned. In the case of at least one member of the Lyons group, the young lawyer-humanist Jean Voulté, there is no doubt of it. Formerly a boon-companion of Rabelais, Dolet, and Des Périers, Voulté abandoned Lyons and its mephitic odours for Paris in 1538, returned with devotion to the religion from which he had lapsed, and addressed to Rabelais, whom he had not long previously hailed in Latin verse as a master-wit, a most moving, passionate, and unavailing appeal to drop his cynical persiflage while repentance was yet possible, reminding him of Doomsday Leet:

> Dices: Heu mihi, iam miser, miser sum,
> Erravi, fateor, Deum esse nosco;
> Vixi non homo sed canis . . .[1]

[1] "Then you will say: Alas for me now, I am a wretched, wretched creature; I have erred, I confess it, I perceive the reality of God, I have lived not like a man but a dog . . ." (*In Luciani Simium*, 1538).

Meanwhile those twin bashibazouks of the offensive, Dolet and Des Périers, lost no time in rushing into print an ode or two apiece in honour of the Immaculate Mother of God, no easy acrobatic feat for such as they. More embarrassing was the situation of another of the Lyons circle, Nicolas Bourbon, who had lately published a swingeing verse-diatribe against "the Hydra of the Triple Crown", hurriedly replaced in a fresh edition by yet another Marian ode. In other vocal anti-Catholic and libertine quarters much the same malaise and compromise was observable.

As noted already, only a handful of the main body of French humanists, when compelled to a decision, joined the enemies of Rome. To hint, as I have seen it hinted more than once, that a prevailing motive for the majority-choice may have been physical cowardice seems to me to illustrate one of the more ignoble impulses of donnish malice. Such an insult to a couple of hundred Frenchmen logically implies moreover a compliment to some thousands of contemporary Englishmen, faced with a similar choice, who chose the way of suffering—a compliment no "progressive" pedant would willingly let himself in for. However, finding Dr. François Rabelais among the majority is no surprise, as any faithful admirer must agree, and to assume that his decision involved any great spiritual struggle, the conquest of scepticism, caprice, and love of mischief, and emergence as an exemplary Catholic is certainly to misjudge our able Doctor, whose own change of tactics may be very easily accounted for. He was now, by Cardinal du Bellay's favour, attached to the fringes of the Court. Raillery of his favourite blend was therefore, at least for the time being, very definitely "out".

A change of occupation and prospects of more travel were to banish any depressions connected with Aigues-Mortes and restore Dr. Rabelais' normal buoyancy. In this year 1539 he left Lyons for Turin to take professional service with a new patron of eminence, Jean du Bellay's younger brother Guillaume, Seigneur de Langey, Viceroy of Piedmont, to whom the beneficent cardinal had just passed him on. Is it permissible to assume that Rabelais was affected by the recent death of his little son Théodule and parted from his mistress with pain? Speculation on his previous affair being open to all, one may reflect that the widow

in Paris may have been a slattern, a drunkard, a wanton, or a
scold, though she apparently did not discover that her paramour
was a lapsed monk dodging authority instead of the secular priest
he—judging by her petition to Rome—pretended to her to be.
His present inamorata had held the volatile Doctor much longer.
Whether, having abandoned two of his offspring, he was fond of
the child she had given him who can tell? It is possible. We
can judge only from half a dozen slightly extravagant Latin
verse-tributes by Jean de Boyssonné of the Lyons group, unearthed
at Toulouse some years ago and purporting to express what all
Dr. Rabelais' friends and admirers felt for him in his bereavement.

> In this tomb sleeps little Théodule, tiny in body but great by
> reason of his father, that personage of learning, skilled in every art
> appropriate to a man of piety and honour. Had little Théodule
> been permitted to live, he too would have acquired such learning
> and grown great in his turn.

Among Boyssonné's following threnodies and epitaphs one at
least is "contemporary" enough:

> Lyons is my birthplace, and my father Rabelais; who knows
> neither is ignorant of the two greatest things in this world.

> I, Théodule, sleeping in this narrow tomb, in life had Roman
> pontiffs for my servitors.[1]

Due allowance made for the wild poetic licence of the Renaissance, it may be inferred from this that Dr. Rabelais' current
breach of his clerical vow of chastity had been accepted and
waived with wellbred indulgence ("*Di niente ! Di niente ! . . .*")
by a Roman prelate or two passing through Lyons, quite possibly
of cardinalate rank; which, given the easy celibacy of some of the
Italian hierarchy at this period, would be likely enough and no
startling news to anyone. A few years hence a frail Dominican
ascetic nine years Rabelais' junior, Michele Ghislieri by name,
was to restore the Sixth Commandment permanently to the
Decalogue for the clergy's benefit with shocking vigour immediately on ascending to the throne of Peter as Pius V. By then the

[1] *Romanos habui pontifices famulos.*

liberal-minded had had a long and enjoyable run, ended just in time.

So, in the autumn of 1539, Dr. Rabelais takes the road to Turin with his newest patron and patient, Guillaume du Bellay, governor of that city and Viceroy of Piedmont, then an appanage of the French Crown.

Of all the distinguished Du Bellay clan, not excluding the fine poet Joachim, Guillaume is to me, as to his contemporaries, the most *sympathique*; a man of outstanding integrity and culture, the finest type of Renaissance aristocrat. The eyes of the strong, bearded face in the portrait at Versailles proclaim the steadfast goodness of heart which went with administrative and diplomatic talents and justifies all Dr. Rabelais' admiration. Governor Guillaume du Bellay was particularly loved by the Piedmontese for having in two successive famine-years, as we learn from his brother Martin's memoirs, bought large quantities of corn in Burgundy and had it transported at his own expense by river and sea to Savona, thence by road to Turin, after which it was distributed to the stricken areas at less than one-third of its original price. Having incurred many honourable debts of this kind, Guillaume du Bellay was to die in 1543 almost a bankrupt, most of his estate going to creditors. "I myself," says Martin du Bellay, "have since his death repaid a hundred thousand livres of his arrears to one single person. He never considered expense if it was in his Prince's service."

To his new physician Guillaume du Bellay will always stand for all that is most splendid in the human character. A contemporary Savoyard chronicler calls him "noble". His post was no sinecure. François I's recurring claim, inherited from Louis XII and deriving from Louis' Visconti grandmother, to the neighbouring Duchy of Milan, a fief of the Empire, made Piedmont the essential base for any French attempt to take the duchy by force, as had been tried in 1536, and the frontier fortresses of Moncalieri and Pignerol had been turned into effective strong-points by Du Bellay. He was now a sick man, racked by gout and a painful tumour which gave him fewer than four more years to live. Quite possibly he owed even this reprieve to Dr. Rabelais' skill.

Apart from anxiety for a patron he soon loved and admired almost to idolatry, the Doctor seems to have enjoyed his stay in Piedmont. He was swiftly adopted by a humanist circle, mostly legal, at Saint-Ayl, not far from Orleans, where he more than once enjoyed the extended hospitality of Étienne Lorens, commander of Turin Castle. From Saint-Ayl on March 1, the year being possibly 1541, goes a letter from the Doctor to Antoine Hullet, lawyer of Orleans, who has been visiting Paris, bidding him rejoin the jovial company for a Lenten dinner. It is the only letter extant in the Doctor's "pantagruelist" or whooping style, opening with a gibberish-line from the old farce of *Pathelin*.

To the Bailiff of the Bailiff of the Bailiffs, Monsieur Maître Antoine Hullet, Seigneur de la Court-Pompin, in Christendom, at Orleans :
    Hé, pater reverendissime, quomodo bruslis ? Quae nova ? Parisius non sunt ova ? These words, addressed to your Reverence and translated from the original Pathelinois into our vulgar Orleans tongue, are as much as to say: "Sir, you will be most welcome on your return from the junketings and revels of Paris" . . .

An outline of the fare awaiting Maître Antoine follows. The menu being composed of fish exclusively, the Doctor can hardly let this pass without a crack at the discipline of his Church. Hullet, he says, will dine according to the will of the great, good, and pitiful God, "who never created Lent, but certainly created salads, herrings, hake, carp, pike, dace, grayling, bleaks, etc., as well as good wine". And after a little further whimsicality, he signs himself: "Your humble wine-steward, servant, and friend, François Rabelais, doctor of medicine."

Another pastime very dear to him was soon affording Dr. Rabelais great content. The highly learned Guillaume Pellicier, Bishop of Montpellier, French Minister at Venice and a close friend of Governor du Bellay, was engaged in collecting Greek, Hebrew, and Oriental manuscripts for the Royal Library, and the Doctor was soon deep in correspondence and collaboration, apart from supplying choice roots for the Embassy gardens. It was unfortunate that in the midst of these innocent pleasures another little incident of the recent Lyons kind, though less disagreeable, should crop up, and again owing to Dr. Rabelais' indiscretion. In a letter to one Barnabé de Voré, Seigneur de la

Fosse, he apparently expressed himself far too warmly for De Voré, formerly a diplomatic agent of Governor du Bellay's in Germany, on the urgency of an *entente* with the Lutheran princes. De Voré, who had changed his views on this subject, showed Dr. Rabelais' letter to several people. Before long it had become a topic for Court gossip, with the result that De Voré and the Doctor duly received a rocket each from Guillaume du Bellay; Rabelais for dabbling in politics outside his competence and for not choosing his correspondents—since even in peacetime spies abound —more carefully, De Voré for betraying a friend's confidence. Whether there was any other trouble is not clear. De Boyssonné seems to hint in a letter at Rabelais' temporary suspension. The whole sequel is obscure. At least we observe again that Dr. Rabelais' pen is as apt to run away with him in private life as in his literary exercises. It may be noted, apropos this affair, that Guillaume du Bellay, who had ably carried out a series of diplomatic missions to the Lutheran princes at the moment when François I was angling for an alliance, had at the time favoured a "moderate" approach to the Reform's adherents, like his brother the bishop. Whether they still did so is not possible to judge.

In November 1541 Rabelais accompanied his employer on the road to Paris, remaining behind at Lyons to hand a Latin military treatise of the Governor's composition to Sébastien Gryphe for publication, and to look after important literary business of his own; for Juste was reprinting *Gargantua* and *Pantagruel*, and the revision and correction of not a few dangerous pages was urgent. Cutting and substituting very prudently (and, as it turned out, to no avail), the Doctor relaxed from his labours only to be stung to fury on discovering that his friend Étienne Dolet, who had a six-year royal licence to print, had just rushed out a pirated edition of both books in the unexpurgated text. Dolet had turned by this time into a detestable brute, increasingly violent and quarrelsome, and treacherous to the point of mania, and already dropped by nearly all his friends and acquaintances. A swashing "Notice to the Reader" by Dr. Rabelais[1] prefixed to the 1542 edition of *Gargantua* and *Pantagruel*, published at Lyons by Pierre de Tours, successor to François Juste, dealt faithfully alike with

---

[1] According to Brunet, Rabelais' own composition; according to most other authorities, "composed or inspired" by the Doctor. Brunet seems to me justified.

the piracy ("this bastard and adulterine production") and the pirate ("a plagiarist capable of any evil . . . a monster born to annoy and injure decent people") and ended their relations. At the beginning of May Guillaume du Bellay returned from Paris to Turin, where Rabelais, having passed some pleasant weeks at Saint-Ayl with the Lorens circle, rejoined him.

The Governor's end was near, as his physician and devout admirers must have perceived immediately on seeing him, with a shock of genuine pain. Towards the autumn Guillaume du Bellay took to his bed and began to prepare for death. His will, dictated on November 13, left fifty *livres tournois* a year to Dr. Rabelais until such time as the Church could provide him with a living at three hundred; unfortunately this bequest, with many others, was immediately swallowed by creditors. On January 9, 1543, having been borne across the Alps to end his days at home, Guillaume du Bellay expired at St. Symphorien-de-Laye, between Lyons and Roanne. Amid the consternation, mourning, and confusion a German servant was able to ransack the Governor's baggage and make off with a number of valuables, including the manuscript of his memoirs, which Dr. Rabelais had packed in a trunk of the mule-train. Next day the Doctor proceeded sadly, with the aid of another physician, to embalm the hero's body. Duly encoffined, it was borne in slow procession under Lorens' direction to Le Mans, where the obsequies were celebrated in that cathedral with the magnificent flying buttresses on March 9 with suitable splendour. Among the nobility, gentry, and notables present have already been noted Messire Loys de Ronsard from Anjou, one of the four pallbearers, and his young son Pierre, whose fame is destined to outsoar even Rabelais'.

If it is ever possible to catch Dr. Rabelais in tears, this must be the unique occasion. Recalling it years later in the Fourth Book in a discourse on the death of heroes, he makes mysterious reference to "the many dreadful Prodigies that we saw five or six days before he died", but omits to describe any of them. He yields us nevertheless a glimpse of the stricken Du Bellay household gathered round his idol's dying-bed, naming a few and himself among them.

. . . and many other Friends and Servants to the Deceased, all dismay'd, gaz'd on each other, without uttering one word; yet not without foreseeing that France would, in a short time, be depriv'd of a Knight so accomplish'd and necessary for its Glory and Protection, and that Heaven claim'd him again as its due.

Such moods of awe, reverence, recognition of true nobility, recollection, and almost worship are not so frequent in the Doctor as to be easily overlooked. His feeling for Guillaume du Bellay might be said to be the nearest thing to a religious emotion, perhaps, that he ever knew.

He now found himself unemployed once more, and soon to be needing a patron again, the ever-dependable Geoffroy d'Estissac being himself in his last illness and due to succumb within four months. What the Doctor did with himself for the two years following Guillaume du Bellay's funeral is not known. Another of those periodical vanishing-tricks has taken place. From the references to Poitou which stud the Third Book, on which he must have been engaged for a large part of this period, M. Plattard has conjectured that he retired to that province, if not to his native Chinnonais. Judging from a dimmish joke on his forthcoming title page it might also be that Dr. Rabelais had been lately botanising in the Iles d' Hyères, off Toulon, notable for their richly varied vegetation, and in that peaceful retreat putting the last touches to his manuscript. Most likely, having hastened to the dying-bed of his old benefactor and friend he was hospitably detained by Louis d'Estissac, the bishop's heir, who seems to have shared his uncle's esteem for the Doctor and to have continued some of his benefactions.

Early in 1546 *The Third Book of Pantagruel* appeared, bearing the imprint of a Parisian publisher. For the first time the author is named, with one more novelty, on the titlepage.

Tiers livre des faictz et dicts heroiques du noble Pantagruel; composez par M. Franc. Rabelais, docteur en medicine, et calloier des Isles Hieres. L'auteur susdict supplie les Lecteurs beneuoles soy reserver à rire au soixante et dixhuytiesme liure. A Paris: par Chrestien Wechel, en la Rue Saint Jacques, à l'escu de Basle, et en la rue Sainct Iehan de Beauuoys, au Cheval volant, M.D. XLVI. Avec privilege du Roy pour six ans.—In-8.[1]

[1] "The Third Book of the heroic Doings and Sayings of the noble Pantagruel, composed by M. François Rabelais, doctor of medicine and Patriarch of the Iles Hyères. The said author implores well-disposed readers to reserve their laughter

More lies behind the royal "privilege" or copyright-grant than the formula conveys. On the eve of publication an advance copy of *The Third Book of Pantagruel* had been read to the king at the Louvre by Pierre Duchâtel, Bishop of Tulle and Lector-Royal, and His Majesty, rocking with laughter, had sworn that Dr. Rabelais was the merriest devil in his dominions. In this mood he was well disposed to help the author. Nothing was more probable than that the Sorbonne would brand the Third Book with the same censure as its predecessors, and it seemed to the king, who did not greatly love the theologians, a good jest to spike their guns. His sister Marguerite approved Dr. Rabelais' hilarities equally—two years later she returned to deep Catholic devotion—and is said to have so intimated to the Sorbonne. Thus it happened that the Third Book came on the town backed by royal approbation of a practical kind, and Dr. Rabelais could rub his hands. Whether he had yet been presented to the king, or if he was presented round about this time, or if he ever was, is impossible to ascertain. Many leading authorities assume it even thus early.

3

"Up, my Lads, to this Wine; spare it not! Drink, Boys, and trowl it off at full Bowles!" With a rousing hail to customers of goodwill and a resounding, half-playful curse dismissing the recalcitrant, the Prologue to *The Third Book of Pantagruel* announces the tapping of a new barrel. And this time Dr. Rabelais has certainly, as we say, rung the bell. Every connoisseur of Rabelaisiana will, I hope, agree that the Third Book represents a peak, a vintage-year. Gone is the tedious giant-*motif*, with which the Doctor was plainly bored long since. Pantagruel's towering frame has seemingly shrunk to match those of his companions, Gargantua can now occupy an ordinary chair without comment or explanation. Gone are those recurring song-and-dance performances celebrating the Renaissance Dawn; gone likewise the

---

till the seventy-eighth volume. Published at Paris, by Chrestien Wechel in the Rue St. Jacques, at the Shield of Bâle, and in the Rue St. Jean-de-Beauvais, at the Flying Horse, 1546. With Royal privilege for six years.—Octavo."

Calloier, a mystery-word, is believed to be derived from two Greek words meaning "good priest", then applied to the higher monastic clergy of the Greek Orthodox Church; but this is only a contemporary guess.

gibes at the theologians and, barring a couple of brief outbreaks, the obsession with monkish imbecility and turpitude. In the newest act of the Pantagruelian Comedy the stage is entirely Panurge's, and he himself has exchanged the monkey-tricks of *Gargantua* for far more intelligent and entertaining gambols. Moreover, the Third Book has something approaching a coherent plot.

Before the Prologue in every edition after 1549 stands a dedication to "the Spirit of the Queen of Navarre"; ten lines of verse composed by Rabelais at Marguerite's death in the December of that year. It is to be noted from this otherwise not noteworthy tribute that the Doctor has at last emerged a fullblown literary type. His new work, which (he pretends) has not been brought so far to the notice of the "abstracted Soul, ravish'd with Ecstasies", seems to him well worth quitting Paradise for.

> Woulds't thou not issue forth, for a short space,
> From the Divine, Eternal, Heavn'ly Place,
> To see the Third Part, in this Earthly Cell,
> Of the brave Acts of good Pantagruel?

Follows the Prologue, one long burst of high spirits, after which the Doctor plunges immediately into his story.

Having defeated the Amaurotes, subdued Dipsodie, and in the opening chapter transported, in the best manner of our modern civilisation, ninety millions of the inhabitants to Utopie, Pantagruel bestows on Panurge the barony of Salmygondin. The three-year revenue of this estate Panurge is able to squander in fourteen days, defending this policy in four successive chapters of dextrous and amusing paradoxes, economic and other, so skilfully and even brilliantly argued and so stamped with the hallmark of the Schools as to testify—probably the last thing Dr. Rabelais desired—to mental training received at La Baumette. There is incidentally a passage in Panurge's praise of debtors which any languid Algy or Eustace of Oscar Wilde's might utter, given a trifling change of idiom, while toying with the Chambertin and ortolans:

You can hardly imagine how glad I am when every Morning I perceive my self environed and surrounded with Brigades of Creditors, humble, fawning, and full of their Reverences; and whilst I remark that as I look more favourably upon and give a chearfuller Countenance to one than to another, the Fellow thereupon buildeth a Conceit that he shall be the first despatch'd, and the foremost in the Date of Payment, and valueth my Smiles at the rate of Ready Money. It seemeth unto me that I then act and personate the God of the Passion of Saumur, accompanied with his angels and Cherubims.[1]

To me these four chapters represent a display of hilarious verbal pyrotechnics surpassed only by Chesterton, a master of the *genre* whose exploitation of the paradox as an intellectual weapon is so regrettably wasted on those members of what Barbey d'Aure-villy calls "the antlered dull" for whom the froth topping the Atlantic wave has, apparently, no connection with the depths below. Across the gulf between them, and for all his native chastity of mind, Chesterton recognised and saluted the genius of Rabelais; masculine and merry as his own, though measured side by side for cerebration with the author of *The Everlasting Man* and *Saint Thomas Aquinas* the Doctor looks small enough. And in his generosity, it occurs to one in passing, Chesterton may have flattered Dr. Rabelais a trifle by comparing him to a navvy using obscene language to express disgust at obscene conduct. If such a motive inspires the jovial Doctor it is not often, to me at least, discernible in his works.

So we come to the main theme of *The Third Book of Pantagruel*. Seized suddenly by an overpowering urge to marry, and simul-taneously terrified by the ever-looming shadow of cuckoldry, Panurge in his dilemma seeks the advice of Pantagruel, who has three suggestions; the throwing of dice, the use of the *sortes virgilianae* or "Virgilian lottery", at which we have already glanced, and divination by dreams. These having been tried in vain, Pantagruel recommends the aged Sybil of Panzoust—we are suddenly not in Utopie but Touraine—in a neighbouring village. The Sybil likewise disappointing him, Panurge proceeds to question Goatsnose, a dumb man, Raminagrobis, an old poet, Her Trippa, an astrologer, Friar John of the Chops, in very good form, Hippothadée, a theologian, Rondibilis, a physician, Trouillogan, a "pyrrhonic" philosopher, and Triboulet, a pro-fessional fool, with an interlude involving Bridlegoose, an old doddering judge. Since he gets every kind of answer but the one

[1] A celebrated Passion-play, then performed in Holy Week at Saumur in Anjou.

he wants, Panurge in despair vows to consult the celebrated Oracle of the Holy Bottle, whose shrine lies far away beyond Lanternois, or Lantern Land, at the end of a long journey by sea and land, "replenished and fraught with eminent Perils, full of innumerable Hazards, and every way stored with evident and manifest Dangers". With this project Pantagruel readily agrees, and the Third Book ends in bustle and expectation and the noise of the building and fitting of a fleet of ships, "to the number of those which Ajax of Salamine had of old equipped in Convoy of the Graecian Soldiery against the Trojan State", for one of those voyages of adventure which provided any Renaissance story-teller of imagination with half his plot in advance.

From even this swift outline may be gathered what opportunities Panurge's quest provides for rich entertainment, mingling light-hearted bawdy (and plenty of it) and the usual ration of classical allusions with pure grotesquerie, some searching psychology, plenty of satire, and shrewd scientific analysis of a sex of which Dr. Rabelais had now acquired unlicensed experience. Of that endless theorising on an inexhaustible topic under Maître Tiraqueau's laurels in his Fontenay days he had plainly retained a great deal. Is it any slur on Dr. Rabelais' possible capacity, of which we know nothing, for inspiring and returning a tender passion to suspect that during his late amours he had kept a notebook or two, by now enriched with many curious observations, physiological and psychological? One may pick up knowledge, as Pantagruel reminds Panurge in rhyme, from anything—a fool, a pot, a flagon, a mitten, or a slipper:

> D'un sot, d'un pot, d'une guedoufle,
> D'une moufle, d'une pantoufle . . .

And hence even a woman. Inevitably the vision rises of the Doctor disentangling himself firmly from a pair of plump white arms to jot something down—one foible of the *gens scientifica* overlooked, so far as I know, by every satirist interested in the type.

Panurge's string of advisers in the Third Book leave practically no phase of feminine peculiarity undiscussed, and the physician Rondibilis, speaking for the Faculty, seems at first to leave him with less hope than any of them. "Shall I be a cuckold?" is Panurge's eternal cry. To which Dr. Rondibilis answers in decisive terms.

> My noble Friend, I am married, and you are like to be so speedily. Therefore be pleased from my Experiment in the matter to write in your Brain, with a steel Pen, this subsequent Dicton: There is no married man who doth not run the hazard of being made a Cuckold. Cuckoldry naturally attendeth Marriage; the Shadow doth not more naturally follow the Body, than Cuckoldry ensueth after Marriage, to place fair Horns upon the Husbands' heads.

This verdict is, one might think, indisputably Dr. Rabelais' likewise. A little previously he has permitted Father Hippothadée, one of the good theologians who implant *la vraye et vive foy catholicque*, to indicate to Panurge a way of escape. "There [in Holy Writ] you will find that you shall never be a Cuckold, that is to say, your Wife shall never be a Strumpet, if you make choice of one of a commendable Extraction, descended of honest Parents and instructed in all Piety and Virtue." It might be expected that Dr. Rondibilis, *hilaris et facetus*, would proceed immediately to make hay of this pious theorising. But no. Surprisingly, he comes at length to a corollary. Nature—one may see Hippothadée's eyebrows go up at the word—has of course blundered to some extent in fashioning such a frail imperfect sex, and above all by endowing it with a physiological handicap, described by Plato as an "animal" and discussed by Rondibilis with clinical terseness, which only a woman of sterling virtue, *preude femme*, can overcome. Hence a perpetual menace of cuckoldry. And the genial physician pauses. One may detect a broad smile as Panurge bursts out in despair.

> Odsfish (quoth Panurge), have you no preventive Cure in all your Medicinal Art for hindring one's Head to be hornygraffed at Home, whilst his feet are plodding Abroad?
> Yes, that I have, my gallant Friend (answered Rondibilis), and that which is a sovereign Remedy, whereof I frequently make use my self.

It is indeed a remedy, and nobody needed it more than the typical Renaissance cuckold-elect, whom we gather from Brantôme's pages to have been, at least in France and Italy, a tiger of ridiculous jealousy and suspicion, swift to stab and strangle and even capable—as in the classic case of Gesualdo di Venusia —of publicising his misfortune, when it duly arrives, by flinging a couple of naked corpses into the street. To him Dr. Rondibilis speaks as to Panurge. He must eschew all *turquoiserie*, all prowlings, pryings, and lockings-up, all "Waylayings, Ambushes, narrow Observations, and malicious Doggings", which merely drive a perverse sex into the arms of the god Cocuage. In a word, says Rondibilis, addressing husbands everywhere, they must be continually amiable (*favorable*) to their wives, show them love, converse with them sociably at all times, and never leave them destitute of companionship. "Now I have said, and you have heard my Cure."

Sound doctrine enough, and we perceive thereby that Dr. Rabelais has considerably altered his attitude for once towards the sex-relation. Women are no longer exclusively toys, amusing but treacherous, cuckoldry is no more the ritual joke it was, matrimony is a partnership to be respected and cherished. Is it possible, as a recent commentator suggests, that this change is largely due to the Doctor's late unauthorised dalliance in the *Pays du Tendre*? He may quite well have learned something in his Lyons bower, though this was not the way for a man under vows to go about it (and I may be excused for finding the word "marriage" applied to his term of concubinage as grotesque as the notion of mortal sin must be to the broadminded don concerned). Yet finally, Hippothadée agrees with Rondibilis, citing our mother Eve as the all-time example, on the "contrary Disposition" of the feminine sex and its natural longing for things prohibited. This being the Doctor's last word on the subject, one may regret that he never knew St. Thomas More, an authority on happy Christian wedlock who could have opened his eyes considerably.

The laconic Trouillogan we have already met. The only effect of his "pyrrhonic" ripostes is to leave Panurge palsied with rage "like a fond Dotard, raving, wagging, and shaking his Hands, dandling, lolling, and nodding with his Head, like a Cow bellowing for her Calf". The aged Sybil of Panzoust—they show her cave today near the village, but in the Third Book she inhabits "a straw-thatch'd Cottage, scurvily built, naughtily movabled and all besmoaked"—proves all too sybilline, and her farewell gesture is vulgar in the extreme. Her Trippa, the master-astrologer who can read all the stars but cannot perceive his wife, "a pretty snug Hussie", cuckolding him under his very nose, turns out another broken reed. Dumb Goatsnose's answers to Panurge by signs are construed by Pantagruel in cheerless fashion. Friar John of the Chops has a great deal to say, or rather roar; merry, lewd, and quite uncomforting. The old French poet Ramino-grobis is found dying, beset by mendicant friars, rejecting their offices with truly Rabelaisian ferocity, and capable only of scribbling incomprehensible advice in inexplicable verse. Old Mr. Justice Bridlegoose, who decides lawsuits by throwing dice, is eloquent enough, but his maunderings in legal jargon have no bearing on Panurge's problem. Finally the fool Triboulet, after whacking Panurge on the nose with a hog's bladder, replies in a brief and mystic enigma ("Beware the monk, Buzançay horn-pipe!"), over the significance of which Panurge and Pantagruel wrangle exhaustively without coming to any conclusion. No wonder, therefore, that Panurge at last makes his vow to get an answer at all costs from the Holy Bottle.

One thing only, to which we shall come shortly, clogs the verve of the Third Book, nearly every episode in which is packed with what might be called the Rabelaisian Quintessence, and into which a great deal has been read, as usual, of which the author probably never dreamed. It is evident, nevertheless, that Dr. Rabelais' butt is the absurd Panurge with his egotisms, gullibilities, vacillations, cowardices, rages, jealousies, boastings, and other marks of the Natural Man. I have seen it affirmed that in the Third Book Panurge personifies "the non-practical medieval mind", which the Doctor naturally scorned. The implications of "non-practical" have a peculiar savour, best appreciated after an hour or two spent in some stupendous cathedral, Chartres, Burgos, Beauvais, Seville, or in perusal of a page of the *Summa*.

Whatever Panurge may have stood for, at any given moment, to his creator, the Third Book is all his. In a moment of Hellenic frenzy the Doctor might even have called it *The Panurgiad*. All the "fat", in theatre jargon, is Panurge's. The once gigantic and dominating Pantagruel has become merely his compère and "feed", uttering at intervals didactic sentiments of painful banality. Thus, remonstrating "very gently in strong Arguments"

G

with Panurge after he has squandered three years' revenue of
Salmygondin in a fortnight, Pantagruel points out that if he
persists in this unthrifty course and does not become a better
manager "it would prove altogether impossible, or at least hugely
difficult, at any time to make him rich", a truth it takes no
B.Sc. (Econ.) to descry. And again, when Panurge on the eve of
deciding for marriage takes to wearing a gown and a cap with
spectacles tied to it, Pantagruel delivers opinion that although a
fantastical taste in dress, such as that formerly affected by "Here-
tical Persons and Schismatical Sectaries"—one wonders how the
Queen of Navarre liked this—shows a "contempt of common
Custom" which he dislikes, such whims are in themselves neither
good nor bad, since they do not come from the thoughts or the
heart. Did Pantagruel not play up so indefatigably to Panurge
in his trials and adventures one might almost describe him in his
present incarnation as a bore and a blot, unlike Friar John, who,
though his own role is also somewhat diminished, is in rattling
bawdy form for the most part. For art's sake one is compelled
here to single out a very minor member of Pantagruel's entourage,
namely Carpalim, who rarely opens his mouth but suddenly
steals some of Panurge's best thunder, opening Chapter XXXIV
with the most unexpected and engaging of lines:

When I was (quoth Carpalim) a Whoremaster at Orleans . . .

And such, it seems, Carpalim was, and an expert moreover in
"bringing young beautiful married ladies into the Snares of
Adultery" by convincing them of their husbands' jealousy, an
unfailing formula. "If this belief once enter into their Noddles,
their Husbands will infallibly be Cuckolds." Here Friar John
for once fails to burst in and annex a theme which might be described in popular language as right up his street; not because he
is stricken dumb by Carpalim's brilliance but because his creator
has not brought him on the scene at all, his last appearance being
in Chapter XXVIII, where he tells Panurge the good old smoking-
room story of Hans Carvel's ring. In the Third Book Dr. Rabelais
has nevertheless advantaged the Friar with an alluring new form
of self-expression in the shape of long near-rhymed lists of merrily
abusive epithets. For these our English language is so constructed

that in translation rhythm and rhyme alike are completely lost, as may be immediately demonstrated. "Speak, thou jaded Cod," roars Friar John at Panurge, and dashes straightway into his derisive chant:

Faded C.
Mouldy C.
Musty C.
Paultry C.
Senseless C., etc., etc.

In the original the Friar begins: "Escoute, couillon mignon", proceeding:

C. de renom,
C. paté,
C. naté,
C. plombé,
C. laicté,
C. feutré,
C. calfaté . . .

And so on for fifty more lines or so without pausing. This innovation, for readers who do not feel uncomfortable on recognising the formula, derived from the Litanies, is always diverting, and shows the Doctor once more to be a master of the language. And, of course, of French.

A serener note, as it were from the wood-wind and a bird-call, announces the entry on the stage of Mr. Justice Bridlegoose. There are faint hearts who complain that the imbecilities of this pillar of the Law, extending through five chapters packed with the jargon of the Courts, precedents, and citations, and affording Dr. Rabelais a comprehensive swing at the French judicial system, its delays and its officials, are overdone. This may be so in places. Law is one of the Doctor's subjects, and he possibly tends to labour the jest on which the Bridlegoose sequence is based. In his old age the judge, being what is called nowadays "a trifle gaga", has taken to deciding all judgments by throwing the dice, translating the *alea* in *alea judiciorum*, a legal locution meaning "hazards of judgment", literally as "die". Summoned before President Trinquamelle and the Parlement of Myrelingues on appeal from a recent decision of this kind, the aged buffoon no doubt rambles a trifle in justifying his method, though fairly lucid on the criminal side:

> Yea, but (asked Trinquamelle) how do you proceed, my Friend, in Criminal Causes, the culpable and guilty Party being taken and seized upon *flagrante crimine* ?—Even as your other Worships use to do (answered Bridlegoose). First, I permit the Plaintiff to depart from the Court, enjoining him not to presume to return thither till he should have taken a good, sound, and profound Sleep, which is to serve for the prime Entry and Introduction to the legal carrying-on of the Business. In the next place, a formal Report is to be made to me of his having slept. Thirdly, I issue forth a Warrant to convene him before me. Fourthly, he is to produce a sufficient and authentick Attestation of his having thoroughly and entirely slept, conformably to the *Gloss*. 22, *Quest*. 7, *Si quis cum* [etc., etc., etc.].

Thus the case slowly grows and ripens, with ever-increasing bagfuls of nourishing documents, and when the pile on either side is sufficiently high Judge Bridlegoose reaches for his dice, and justice is done. And although Panurge, forgetting his marriage-problem for a moment, broods sceptically over Bridlegoose's run of luck, there may be bruised and embittered victims of the Law even today who will maintain with Pantagruel that the Bridle-goose way is as good as any other.

So we come to the only material flaw in the Third Book, to which I have already referred. It embraces the four final chapters, in which Dr. Rabelais, suddenly bitten by his hobby of botany, goes off into four long, discursive, allusive, boring orations in praise of a mysterious herb called Pantagruelion, which swiftly develops into a symbol of human activity and social discipline; as Moland aptly describes it in his glossary, "a kind of positive talisman, a materialist Holy Grail". The least botanically-minded reader is very soon able to identify it as nothing more exotic than the herb *cannabis*, or common hemp. Immense quantities of Pantagruelion, to which Dr. Rabelais attributes a score of virtues and properties and the inspiration of human ingenuity on an extensive scale, are taken aboard Pantagruel's fleet for the voyage to the Holy Bottle; for what purpose is not clear, since we never her of it again. Certainly, I think, the Doctor penned these four chapters in his cups. Such is their rambling eccentricity that our good Sir Thomas Urquhart, ex-hausted by his Rabelaisian labours and now at the end of them, turns cloudy French into cloudier English and gets himself finally into such a tangle ("and that so much the rather . . .") that one is glad to think of him with his boots off at last, night-gowned and slippered, drinking a posset and getting to bed. The honest man! He is said, God rest his Episcopalian soul, to have died of merriment at the news of Charles the Second's return.

Whatever magic qualities the herb Pantagruelion possesses, therefore, the seabound Pantagruelists will make no use of it, even to test its incombustibility in the experiments with roasting eggs and cremating corpses recommended by Dr. Rabelais. It might be said that there is very little in the Pantagruelion chapters to captivate the average reader unless he happens to practise one of the more recondite of the liberal professions. At this the Doctor glances with elephantine coyness.

> Others have been heard most wofully to lament, at the very instant when Atropos was about to cut the Thread of their Life, that Pantagruel held them by the Gorge. But (well-a-day), it was not Pantagruel; he was never an Executioner. It was the Panta-gruelion, manufactured and fashioned into a Halter, and serving in the Place and Office of a Cravat.

The proportion of public hangmen among readers of the Third Book in the sixteenth century, as now, must have been relatively small. They should be grateful to Dr. Rabelais for bringing them in. The gentlemen in inky ruffles who compiled their manual of professional deportment, the Newgate Calendar (that improving work) in the eighteenth show no scientific curiosity concerning the rope itself, though the production of Pantagruelion was then at a peak.

> Scarce can our Fields, such Crouds at *Tyburn* die,
> With Hemp the Gallows and the Fleet supply . . .[1]

For by-products interesting the dope-industry, finally, Dr. Rabelais has no esteem, warning his readers in fact that the herb Pantagruelion taken into the system is offensive to the stomach and that its exorbitant heat engenders "grievous, hurtful, smart,

[1] Johnson: "London, a Poem", 1738.

and noysom Vapours", and bequeathing the hopheads in gross and detail to De Quincey, who preferred the juice of the poppy, christened "laudanum" incidentally by our old acquaintance Paracelsus. Even then I think the Doctor could have handled the topic more buoyantly.

Let not the weaker brethren despair. This botanical aberration is unique and temporary. Dr. Rabelais has still another volume of vintage Pantagruelism up his unfailing sleeve.

4

"Sonnez, clairons! Chantez, coucous!" Exhilaration over the launching of yet another successful book, bearing his name at last, flaunting the royal privilege on the title-page, approved by the mystical Queen of Navarre, and instantly acclaimed a comic masterpiece by the cognoscenti, died, alas, all too swiftly. Within three months of the publication of *The Third Book of Pantagruel* Dr. Rabelais' horizon was heavy with thunderclouds and a chilly east wind was whistling round his ears.

Three blows had fallen, in quick succession. The king, his newest protector, had fallen gravely ill and was reported unlikely to recover. Royal privilege notwithstanding, the Sorbonne had examined the Third Book and condemned it like its predecessors, this time on graver grounds than obscenity. Finally, and perhaps a greater shock still, the truculent and now impossible Dolet, having overstepped the mark at last, had been arrested, tried, condemned for atheistic propaganda, and burned at the stake in the Place Maubert in Paris in the March of this year, 1546, friendless and defiant, amid the vociferous approval of Catholics and Calvinists alike all over France, and, as Mr. Christopher Hollis notes in his study of Erasmus, with "an especially jolly hip-hip-hooray from John Calvin of Geneva".[1]

And the Sorbonne had now attached Dr. Rabelais himself with heresy, a charge in the present circumstances fraught with acute forebodings. It turned out to be not merely a question of what the Doctor will assert at the top of his voice to be a printer's blunder, the substitution for *âme* (soul) of *âne* (ass) in a sentence

---

[1] The inscription on the present statue in the Place Maubert, erected by the Third Republic, perpetuates Dolet's denial of immortality.

of Chapter XXII, "Son âne s'en va à trente mille panerées de diables"—"His ass goeth infallibly to thirty thousand panniers-full of devils"; in the original a recognisable pun which actually makes no difference to speak of. This grievance, authentic or not, will still be rankling a half-dozen years hence, when he dedicates the Fourth Book to that enigmatic personage Cardinal Odet de Châtillon, his latest patron and admirer:

> This, my Lord [Rabelais is harping on the late charge of heresy] embolden'd me once to tell you, as I was complaining of it in your Presence, that if I did not esteem my self to be a better Christian than they show themselves to me, and if my Life, Writings, Words, nay, Thoughts betray'd to me one single Spark of Heresie . . . I would then like the Phoenix gather dry Wood, kindle a Fire, and burn my self in the midst of it.

> You were then pleas'd to say to me, that King Francis, of eternal Memory, had been made sensible of those false Accusations; and that having caused my Book (mine, I say, because several, false and infamous, have been wickedly laid to me), to be carefully and distinctly read to him by the most learned and faithful Anagnost [reader] in this Kingdom, he had not found any Passage suspicious, and that he abhorr'd a certain envious, ignorant, hypocritical Informer, who grounded a mortal Heresie on an N put instead of an M by carelessness of the Printers.

Which is all very well, and he had certainly suffered intolerably from pirate publishers; but the Doctor glides in discreet silence over a much more serious offence, occurring in the same context as the alleged printers' blunder which some unknown enemy had exploited. We may glance again at Chapter XXI of the Third Book for a moment.

Pursuing his despairing quest and attended by Friar John and Epistemon, Panurge pays a call on the old French poet Ramina-grobis (said to be drawn from a mediocre versifier named Guillaume du Bois, known as "Cretin"), in the town of Villomer. The aged Raminagrobis receives them in his bedchamber; he is lying at the very point of death, but "looking chearfully, with an open Countenance and Behaviour full of Alacrity". Having politely presented him with gifts suitable to one *in articulo*, namely a gold and sapphire ring and a Socratic white cock, which perches forthwith on the bed-tester, crowing "stentoriphonically", Pan-urge puts his ritual question. To this Raminagrobis, having asked for pen, ink, and paper, scrawls a reply in a couple of French verses of puzzling obscurity.

> Prenez la, ne la prenez pas,
> Si vous la prenez, c'est bien faict;
> Si ne la prenez en effect
> Ce sera oeuvre par compas.[1]

Dr. Rabelais and Urquhart may now take over:

These lines he gave out of his own Hands unto them, saying, Go, my Lads, in Peace, the great God of the highest Heavens be your Guardian and Preserver, and do not offer any more to trouble or disquiet me with this or any other Business whatsoever. I have this very same day (which is the last both of May and of me), with a great deal of labour, toil, and difficulty, chased out of my House a Rabble of filthy, unclean, and plaguily pestilential Rakehells, black Beasts, dusk, dun, white, ash-colour'd, speckled, and a foul Vermin of other hues, whose obtrusive Importunity would not permit me to die at my ease; for by fraudulent and deceitful prick-lings, ravenous harpy-like Graspings, and suchlike unwelcome Approaches, forged in the Shop of I know not what kind of In-satiabilities, they went about to withdraw and call me out of those sweet Thoughts, wherein I was already beginning to repose my self, and acquiesce in Contemplation and Vision; yea, which the good God hath prepared for his faithful Saints and Elect in the other Life, and State of Immortality.

Yet another routine-variation on a Rabelaisian dominant, the passage appears at first glance; this time, perhaps, a trifle more insulting, since Dr. Rabelais has never before classed the Mendi-cant Orders in print with vermin, and a trifle more detailed, embracing the colours of their various habits. But the circum-stances, as any intelligent contemporary reader, Catholic or otherwise, would instantly perceive, are heavy with significance. Substituting a rabble of "vermin" for the priest summoned by

[1] Urquhart:
> Take her, or not take her, off, or on
> Handy-dandy is your lot,
> When her name you write, you˙blot.
> 'Tis undone, when all is done
> Ended˙ere it was begun . . .

every normal Catholic *in extremis* to administer the Last Sacraments and speed his departure with the lovely words of the Liturgy
("Go forth, O Christian soul, from this world, in the name of
God . . ."), and causing the raging Raminagrobis to expel these
visitors with contumely and die unshriven, Dr. Rabelais would
seem by implication to involve solemn rites of his Church in a
general roar of ridicule, contempt, and hostility. He makes of
course no reference to the Viaticum, even obliquely. In some
quarters nevertheless the whole jest might easily be construed
in that sense; as in fact it was, and often has been.

Can it possibly be believed that the Doctor had any deliberate
intention thus to shock and insult the devout? In his wildest
moods he is careful never to attack any fundamental of the Faith.
That unruly pen has run away with him again, one must charitably conclude, this time rather dangerously. Just a carefree
romp, no doubt; but there might well be consequences for a
jester on such a theme who happened to be in Holy Orders.
Raminagrobis' conduct was going to be extremely awkward for
his creator to justify before an ecclesiastical tribunal. Any moral
theologian could indict the furious old dying poet to start with
for hatred and malediction of his kind, *odium proximi et maledictio*,
and wilful self-proclaimed opposition to infallible authority,
voluntarium judicium, and even at the beginning of the enquiry one
can see the Sorbonne's eyebrows going up. ("You, a priest,
encourage this? . . . What's that? Just what? *Fun?* . . .")
Nor could Dr. Rabelais fall back here on the traditional standby
of every publicist in a jam and blame his printers, still less his
proof-readers, who had certainly let Chrestien Wechel's new
author down. Today "*?taste*", or "*?R.C. susceptibilities*" would be
the marginal scribble. In 1546 "*?heretical*" would suffice.

However, the thing was done, nor was this all. The seeming
defence of the friars by Panurge, horrified at the old dying poet's
outburst, in the chapter immediately following makes things no
better; and in our English version, one might add, Urquhart's
native prejudice is given free expression. All too clearly Panurge
is only assisting the Doctor to further playfulness:

By the Virtue of God, I believe he [Raminagrobis] is an Heretick,
the Devil take me if I do not; he doth so villainously rail at the

Mendicant Friars and Jacobins, who are the two Hemispheres of the Christian World, by whose Gyronomonick Circumbilvaginations, as by two Celivagous Filopendulums, all the Autonomatick Metagrobolism of the Romish Church, when tottering and emblustricated with the gibble-gabble Gibbrish of this odious Error and Heresy, is homocentrically poised . . .

Panurge having declared finally that Raminagrobis is a blasphemer against the true Faith, it occurs to Epistemon that the old poet may actually have been referring not to the friars but to a swarm of fleas, flies, gnats, and suchlike pests infesting his chamber. This solution Panurge rejects with scorn. "He is, by the Virtue of God, an arrant Heretick, a resolute formal Heretick." And resolving to go back forthwith and ply the rebel with wholesome admonition for his soul's sake, Panurge recollects suddenly in terror that Raminagrobis' bedchamber is now, probably, swarming with devils straight from hell, and changes his mind.

To explain away all this persiflage to the satisfaction of the Sorbonne was going to be difficult. Too difficult, the Doctor soon decided, seeing he could not appeal to his dying king. He solved the problem in the familiar Rabelaisian way, vanishing this time over the frontier into the territory of the Holy Roman Empire. On March 28, 1546, we find him ensconced in the city of Metz, safe from arrest. He will remain there for many months.

VI

Disappearance Of A Learned Nose

I

WITH ITS TALL, FANTASTIC GOTHIC HOUSES, ALL GABLES, GARGOYLES, and crockets, leaning together over narrow, echoing, cobbled streets, its towers and belfries for ever showering silvery music on the air, its massy ramparts and huge fortified gates, its stocky Germanic citizenry, its picturesquely swarming Jewry, and the River Moselle flowing below, clear in those days as when mirrored in Ausonius' verse, the ancient city of Metz in Lorraine must at the time of Dr. Rabelais' entry have resembled an engraving from the pages of Hoffmann or Grimm. Once the capital of the Kingdom of Austrasia, it had for nearly six centuries, by decree of the Emperor Otto II—the same who prayed the Archbishop of Reims to "extirpate all the brutality of my Saxon blood"—enjoyed the status of a free Imperial city. Four years after Rabelais' exit the Emperor Charles V failed after a severe siege to wrest it back from a French occupying force under brilliant young François, Duc de Guise, and Metz passed permanently into the keeping of France.

Till some years ago a fair amount survived of the Metz into every corner of which, according to his lifelong habit, Dr. François Rabelais must soon have poked his inquisitive, learned, and aggressive nose,

> Ce docte Nez Rabelays, qui picquoyt
> Les plus piquans . . .[1]

But the fourteenth-century Porte des Allemands, that monumental relic, took a basting in World War II with the rest of the city, and how many medieval houses now stand in the Place

[1] "That learned Rabelaisian Nose, which stung the smartest stingers . . ." (Jacques Tahureau, 1554).

Sainte-Croix, not to speak of a showplace like the Hôtel St. Livier in the Rue des Trinitaires, I know not. The Doctor would still recognise the Cathedral of St. Étienne, where the suspended organ was new in his time, and one or two other churches, though probably not the main street of the former Jewry, "En Jurue", in which he is said on good authority to have lodged. Across the city in a more spacious quarter was the house occupied at the moment by Étienne Lorens, Seigneur de Saint-Ayl, his cordial host of Piedmont days, now one of Jean du Bellay's principal liaison-agents in the Empire; whether employed as what Renaissance diplomacy called a "nuncio", a roving attaché, or perhaps *désattaché*, without negotiating powers, or a "procurator", so empowered but without embassy status, I have not discovered. Here Dr. Rabelais could expect to find again the conversation and the hospitality he loved. Otherwise Metz had not much to offer him, boasting no humanist or literary circle. A fair proportion of the citizenry had embraced the Reform, and there was also an extensive Jewish population, in those days more likely to inspire the brush of a Rembrandt. The average Metzois spoke, and speaks, a French of sorts.

Before slipping over the frontier—how easy to take cover in those days!—Dr. Rabelais had hurriedly made his plans. The first refuge in his mind had been Strasbourg, where Jean Sturm, head of the city's high school or "gymnasium", and another of Du Bellay's agents, had promised the cardinal to do what he could for him. For some reason Sturm, having expressed indignation at the Doctor's enforced exile in both classical languages, did nothing, and Rabelais, electing to stay in Metz, bestirred himself to find an occupation. Not long after arrival we find him accordingly, on the evidence of the city's account-books, in the service of the Municipality. And in his own profession, as one would naturally assume; but there is a trifle of mild controversy over this. An authority in Metz pointed out some years ago that the one hundred and twenty livres a year Rabelais received was the salary of a "councillor", a municipal official occupying a minor administrative post and paid more than a doctor. An outstanding medical reputation may, it occurs to one, just as well explain the higher rate, itself not magnificent. A desperate letter to Jean du Bellay dated February 6, 1547, seems to me eloquent enough. Within a year of his new employment, having found it impossible to make ends meet and facing the prospect of having to throw up practice altogether, the Doctor is in a state of "anxiety and necessity" amounting to panic.

> Monseigneur, if you do not have pity on me I shall not know what to do, unless in my extreme need I take service with some- body here, with obvious damage and loss to my studies. It is not possible to live more cheaply than I am doing. However little you can spare me out of the abundance God has given you, I can manage to get on, with frugal living and honest conduct, as I have hitherto done for the honour of the House I quitted on leaving France.

This *cri de coeur* illustrates what might be called the worst economic "low" in Dr. Rabelais' career, so far as is known. It is impossible to judge his income in any given year. His successive patrons were wealthy and apparently generous. With their assistance, professional fees, many hospitable friends, an occasional sum from his publishers, and, for nearly two years, the emolu- ments from a couple of livings, he must have been for the most part comfortably off in a modest way.[1] The five handsome Aldine volumes of Galen with his autograph now preserved in Sheffield University Library, certainly no poor man's books— the present binding is not original—may, of course, have been a gift. Bibliophiles with the detective-instinct can bite their nails over a defiant little enigma here. The Doctor's books, presented to Sheffield Infirmary in 1807, with other medical works, by the first Lord Wharncliffe, had previously belonged to Dr. Alexander Cooke of Ripon (1696–1757), who had studied at Leyden and Padua.[2] Here the brief trail ends. *Omnia exeunt in mysterium*, as St. Augustine said. How the only authentic signatures of Dr. François Rabelais in existence, barring the one at Montpellier, came finally to rest in Yorkshire might be a theme for a romantic novelist. It has so far, fortunately, escaped this attention.

---

[1] To these sources of income might be tentatively added the three hundred livres a year of his canonry of St. Maur (if he still held it), and possibly one or two small benefices unrecorded.
[2] One other previous owner, "Perellus", also autographed a volume. He may, thinks Prof. Harcourt Brown, be the author of a treatise on fevers in the Bibliothèque Nationale.

In February 1547 the Doctor certainly felt the pinch. He was, he tells his patron, depending on Étienne Lorens to explain his circumstances fully; but Lorens, whose enthusiasm for the Doctor seems to have cooled, forwarded his letter without comment and did no more, having a priority-case on his hands for the cardinal's attention. Doubtless Du Bellay responded to his physician's appeal as he had done before. How much longer Dr. Rabelais continued to serve the Municipality of Metz is not known. On June 24 he drew thirty livres of salary; the rest of the register is missing. It has been conjectured that he quitted Metz round about the March of 1548. At whatever date he did so it was at the summons of the cardinal, with whom, having rejoined him probably in Paris, where under such protection no fear of arrest need perturb him, he took the road to Rome once more, some time in the spring or early summer.

Like his physician's, Cardinal du Bellay's affairs were not flourishing at the moment. Since the death of François I a few months previously his stock at Court, as we say, had dropped considerably, and he was soon made aware that the Crown had no further need of his diplomatic services, at any rate in the same field. At Henri II's direction Jean du Bellay was now returning to Rome to take permanent office as Protector of the Affairs of France at the papal Court, with authority over his French brother-cardinals there resident. And being still victimised by sciatica, the elderly Du Bellay needed his Rabelais again.

It would seem that during the late crisis at Metz the Doctor had betaken himself in desperation to his pen and had turned his spare time to good account. By the time of his recall to Jean du Bellay's service he had about one-third of a sequel to the Third Book finished. And so sorely did Dr. Rabelais need money still that on reaching Lyons this time he called on his publisher with the manuscript and urged him to publish it as it was; ending, at that moment, with an unfinished sentence midway in what was to become the present Chapter XXV—the episode following the great storm, in which Pantagruel and his companions land on the Island of the Macreons. Every harassed author alive and capable of so doing will raise his hat to Pierre de Tours, successor to François Juste of Lyons and the publisher of his dreams, for this benefactor put the Doctor's chump-end of a book on sale then and there, simultaneously with an almanac for 1548 which he had hastily slung together.

An effort to clear himself with the Sorbonne and the public explains Dr. Rabelais' haste equally. Having proclaimed in his new prologue, which he will replace by a less entertaining one, the essential purity of his works—a string of amiable fooleries, harmless entertainment for the sick and gouty, offending neither God nor man—the Doctor looses off a broadside at his critics, now increased in number by reason of a few pirated editions on the market. *Caphards, cagotz, matagotz, botineurs, papelards, butgotz, patespelues, porteurs de rogatons, chattemites, animaulx barbares, nouveaux diables engipponés*—Dr. Rabelais is at the top of inventive and untranslatable form. Overpowered by righteous indignation, he becomes comic. Hear the Master of Defamation appeal to Heaven:

> In Greek, calumny is called *diabole*. How detestable before God and the angels is this vice of calumny, by which the devils of Hell are distinguished and named! Those I mean are not, properly speaking, devils from Hell, but their apparitors and ministers; I call them black and white devils, devils of private life, domestic devils. What they have done to my books they will do, if they are allowed, to those of others . . . Seeing the public fervently longing to read my writings, they have spat in the basin . . .

Which, the Doctor is at pains to explain, refers to a custom prevalent among certain ill-disposed Greek philosophers such as Philoxenus and Gnatho, who enjoyed free meals by spitting in tavern dishes to make disgusted epicures abandon them. And he is chiefly moved in behalf of his beloved invalids, who by this means are robbed of his healing works. His fulminations against pirate publishers were, of course, justified and unanswerable, and faintly reminiscent in their fervour of a celebrated outburst by Dickens on the same topic in America three centuries after him. For this wrong Dr. Rabelais was soon to obtain redress. As for his "calumniators", not all of whom based their attack on pirated texts, as will shortly be evident, one perceives that the Doctor's most amusing entertainment-effects are not always intentional. As with the saucy comedian Foote on receiving an unexpected back-hander from Dr. Johnson, indignant incredulity lends an added piquancy to the wrath of the biter bit. It is inevitable that such glints of the eternal human comedy should escape those for whom Dr. Rabelais is a godlike figure musing apart, his head enwrapped in Olympian clouds—something, if the thought be permissible, like Rodin's *Penseur* before sitting down to conjecture who has stolen his trousers. They miss a great deal.

Having unburdened himself somewhat, and having a little ready money to jingle, Dr. Rabelais could continue his journey south with an easier mind, secure once more with a strong patron. At Jean du Bellay's attitude towards Rabelais' latest brush with the Sorbonne I think one may fairly well guess. No love being lost between the hierarchy and the professional theologians, his esteemed physician's version of the affair, spiced with a thousand quips and racy tirades against slanderers and busybodies (not to mention the crimes of printers), would probably be good enough for the cardinal, whose leniency in this matter has been much admired, not to speak of his nonchalant attitude towards Canon Law in the matter of harbouring and protecting a cleric for some time defying it. "Liberal" or lax, a politician and a diplomat before a churchman, Du Bellay is, like Mazarin and Retz and Richelieu after him, a type of prelate more comprehensible to the world than a Bellarmine, a Borromeo, or a Newman. It is interesting to speculate on his activities had he succeeded Marcellus II in 1555, as, being then head of the Sacred College and a strong candidate, he might well have done had Providence not favoured a better man.

Once more settled in Rome, Rabelais proceeded to divide his leisure between finishing *The Fourth Book of Pantagruel* and relaxation in his customary circles. At this time likewise he began a learned correspondence with that interesting character Pierre Paschal, then living in Venice: the Gascon opportunist, the dexterous exploiter some years hence of Ronsard and his fellow-poets of the Pléiade. The Paschal affair is perennially diverting. Lavishly extolled by the Ronsard group on account of a highly flattering literary *Who's Who* for which he was then gathering material in France, the hitherto obscure Paschal was soon able to climb nimbly from their shoulders into the enviable post of

Historiographer-Royal, after which no more was heard of his monumental work. By that time Rabelais was dead. He would have relished a choice piece of Ronsardian invective called *Petri Paschalii Elogium* (1559), in which the Gascon's prominent nose is suitably congratulated for its unfailing skill in smelling out advantage ("naso ad aliquid olfaciendum semper intento . . .").

Before long a notable event broke Dr. Rabelais' placid routine. At the palace in the vast Piazza dei Santi Apostoli off the Corso, where Jean du Bellay and his suite were now installed, there arrived on March 1, 1549, a special envoy from Henri, King of France and Navarre, to the Holy See announcing the birth of Louis, Duke of Orleans, his second son, at St. Germain-en-Laye on February 2. Celebrations on a suitable scale were immediately ordered by Cardinal du Bellay, not without arousing a controversy which has escaped the notice of the learned of my acquaintance. The dates proposed for the festivities, covering the second and third weeks of March, fell well within the penitential season of Lent. These French . . . ! On learning of his colleague's project Cardinal Giovanni-Pietro Carafa, a fiery reformer and martinet, at once voiced, very properly, those protests to Paul III recorded by Pastor. On record also is the equally vigorous encouragement proffered his patron by Dr. François Rabelais, in whose reaction to Lent, expressed in the Fourth Book and elsewhere, there would seem to be something pathological, unless, as with Erasmus, a six weeks' fish-diet disagreed with him. Cardinal du Bellay was able at length to convince the Pope that in the circumstances diplomacy should take precedence of discipline. A dispensation was accorded and the arrangements proceeded. Half a dozen years onward Jean du Bellay, now Cardinal-Dean in charge of the Sacred College, will again encounter the redoubtable Carafa, newly raised to the pontificate as Paul IV and starting on a purge of his cardinals first. ("So as not to cause too much upheaval, We have resolved not to break them all at once . . .")[1] This time Du Bellay, with his brethren, will bow to discipline without argument.

Meanwhile (we are back in March 1549) Cardinal du Bellay

---

[1] Paul III had already begun transforming the Sacred College by nominating men of the calibre of Pole, Sadolet, Carafa, Contarini, Aleander and Fisher, apart from offering the Hat to Erasmus. By 1557 few of these were left.

opened the festivities with three official banquets, followed by elaborate firework displays. The *pièce de résistance* followed a few days later, in the shape of a couple of spectacular sham-battles in the fashionable Renaissance style; a *naumachia*, staged on the Tiber, and a *sciomachia*, or military engagement, fought four days later on the Piazza. Temperamental Father Tiber in flood spoiled the aquatic spectacle, but the land one proved so successful that Dr. Rabelais ("You fellows that have the knack . . .") was ordered to produce a full account of it for the delectation of the French Court. The result is called *La Schiomachie et Festins faits à Rome, au Palais de Mgr. Réverendissime Cardinal du Bellay, pour l'heureuse Naissance de Mgr. d'Orléans*, addressed to the Cardinal de Guise by M. François Rabelais, Doctor of Medicine. Sébastien Gryphe of Lyons in due course published it as a thirty-page pamphlet.

There are critics, even good critics, even good French critics, who dismiss the *Sciomachie* with a sniff as a piece of commissioned hack-work unworthy of Dr. Rabelais' pen. I think they do him wrong. Called on suddenly to perform a, for him, difficult exercise in a novel art-form, namely descriptive journalism, having to supply not normal fantasy but "hard" news, forced to ride a bucking and snorting Pegasus rigorously on the curb for once and submit a wayward fancy to the discipline of what is nowadays called factual objective reportage, he acquits himself with surprising success.

As Our Special Correspondent covering this assignment I rate the Doctor high. He belongs no doubt to the old expansive school —a precursor of Russell, Stanley and Ashmead-Bartlett, a pre-Pulitzer-Prize type—but he is undoubtedly an interpreter of the *chose vue*. You hear the shouting of the crowd, the clash of arms, the hellish noise of perpetually exploding firebombs, the neighing of horses, the blare of hautboys and trumpets, the rattle of drums; you see the battle, your eyes and nostrils are full of dust and gunpowder-fumes. Incidentally diverting is the discovery that like any "feature" specialist of the modern big-circulation Press the Doctor is hag-ridden by the Woman's Angle, judging by the attention he devotes to the coiffure and costume of the tall beauty representing Diana in an early episode. She is, naturally, a blonde, with the silver crescent of the Hunting Goddess on her brow. Her golden locks, plaited on top into a laurel-wreath entwined with violets and roses, flow gracefully over her shoulders. Over a gown and farthingale—*verdugalle*, evidently the Spanish mode—of richly embroidered crimson damask, she wears a half-length smock of finest Cyprus cloth of gold, pleated "like a Cardinal's rochet", and a precious leopard-skin breastplate is attached to her left shoulder by large gold buttons. Her boots of embossed gilt leather are laced with silver *à la nymphale*, an ivory horn hangs from her left shoulder, a pearl-studded hunting-pouch is suspended by knotted silken cords, white and crimson, from her right, and she carries a silvery spear. "And the other nymphs," adds the Doctor, dismissing the bridesmaids in two lines, "much the same, except for wearing no crescent and holding handsome Turkish bows."

On the entertainment provided by Cardinal Jean du Bellay those of his guests crowding his balconies and open windows could afterwards, when they had sufficiently cleared their dizzy heads, sincerely congratulate him. Loitering in the spacious Piazza dei Santi Apostoli in a moonlit midnight I have found it not very difficult to conjure up the scene, though which of its surviving palaces Jean du Bellay occupied, if any, I have not tried to discover. Rabelais merely remarks that next to the Piazza Agonale (Navona) the Santi Apostoli is the finest and largest in Rome and that the cardinal's lodging was on "the long side"—might he have taken the Colonna for this stay, or the Odescalchi? It was at all events the grandstand for this occasion, and from the erection directly opposite the cardinal's main doors of a formidable castle designed by Captain Giovanni di Monte Melino, part brick, part painted wood, bristling with artillery and destined to be besieged, mined, and taken by assault, one may reasonably deduce that Du Bellay and his guests swallowed their fair ration of smoke and din that night. Such was the quantity of artillery-blank, rockets, mortars, bombs, *pots à feu*, and other fireworks exploded on this occasion, observes Dr. Rabelais, that the whole neighbourhood rocked and the Piazza dei Santi Apostoli was enveloped in smoke, flame and thunder.

Cardinal du Bellay certainly spared no expense on a typical festival offered by a Renaissance *grand seigneur* to a crowd representing every social degree from the Roman aristocracy, together with a sprinkling of the Sacred College and the Corps Diplo-matique, down to the lowest riffraff of the Trastevere lining the Piazza densely on all sides and occupying every available roof and window in sight. At two o'clock on the sunny afternoon of March 14, a company of the Papal Swiss Guard and a company of Colonna footmen having marched into position round the barricades to keep order, the show opened with a corrida featur-ing a quartet of fierce fighting-bulls. Two of these were despatched by toreros on foot in the Spanish manner, one by Corsican mastiffs, and the fourth, who swiftly proved a menace to the spectators, by pikemen. After a clowning interlude by the celebrated Moret, *archibuffon d'Italie,* three hundred infantry troops and a squadron of fifty cavalry, all in gala uniform under dis-tinguished command, entered the Piazza to fife and drum and ranged themselves to await the combat. Followed, to a gay symphony of hautboys, sackbuts, and flutes, the entry of the Goddess Diana and her attendant hunting-nymphs, one of whom, while tying a shoelace preparatory to the chase, was kidnapped by a party of roving soldiery and carried into the castle. With the arrival of three hundred more gaily-clad troops, horsed and foot, amid many fanfares, the battle for the captured nymph began, lasting till well beyond nightfall.

Though there seems to have been very little make-believe about the ensuing clash, vigorously conducted amid a terrific expendi-ture of gunpowder, there were no casualties worth reporting—or, to be accurate, Dr. Rabelais reports three only, not counting one horse. After a preliminary assault on the castle has been beaten off two of the attacking force are seen to lie bleeding on the stricken field. A couple of clowns, Frerot and Fabricio by name, rush forward. While one of them kneels and pretends to hear the dying men's confessions the other begins going through their pockets. The crowd having quickly tumbled to the joke, the clowns toss two men of straw into the air amid thunderous applause and scamper off; the spectators (notes the Doctor) marvelling at the way the dummies had been concealed during a hot fight. Later in the battle another lifelike dummy falls from the high tower of the castle during a virulent artillery bom-bardment, after which an enormous bomb spouting fire from thirty orifices is hurled, among other fiery missiles, from the ramparts into the attackers' ranks; a pleasing device, the joint invention of Messer Vincentio, a Roman citizen, and Messer Francesco, a Florentine, both of the Papal Bombardiers. The clown Frerot having slightly overdone his comic act by bursting the great bomb with a pike, thereby getting himself singed "black as an Ethiopian" and scarred in the face for three months to come, the castle is finally mined and stormed in a blaze of fire—it is now night—the captive nymph is released, the arms and colours of the King of France appear in triumph over the tower, and the crowd, crying "Viva Francia!", "Viva Bellay!", streams through the cardinal's wide-open doors for supper. For Jean du Bellay has thrown his palace open to all comers—*ouverte à tous venans, quelz qu'il fussent*—and in every anteroom, hall, reception-chamber and gallery is spread a banquet with wine and food on a gigantic scale.

A table in the "middle chamber" is reserved for Jean du Bellay and his personal guests, the French Ambassador in Rome, his colleague in Venice, the great banker Filippo Strozzi, twelve cardinals, Italian and French, and one or two bishops and other prelates. The rest of the nobility and gentry rub shoulders with the soldiery, the bourgeoisie, and the ragtag-and-bobtail at dozens of tables and buffets all over a palace blazing with lights and glittering with plate of gold and silver. A sung grace and the recital of a long Horatian ode in honour of the House of France, composed by Jean du Bellay, himself a good Latin poet, bring the banquet to an end soon after midnight.

> Ut tibi noctes, CATHARINA, laetas,
> Ut dies, ENRICE, tibi serenos,
> Demum ut ambobus, sobolisque fausta est
> Cuncta precata![1]

And Dr. Rabelais has an interesting note:

As for the banquet, I observed two singular things; in the first place there was no discord, argument, dissension, or any kind of tumult; in the second, though so many guests of every degree were served in so much silver, not one piece was found lost or missing.

---

[1] "Thus we unite our prayers that thy nights, Catherine, may be joyful, thy days, Henri, serene, and the offspring of you both of happy omen!"

Which tribute to the manners and integrity of the Roman populace may have raised an eyebrow or two at the Louvre. Masked dancers and a ball till dawn ensued, and two further nocturnal displays of fireworks and bonfires concluded the festivities. One may guess that Cardinal du Bellay's physician had little time for either literary work or learned dalliance for a few days and nights following.

A trifling and not unamusing Rabelaisian setback attaches to these celebrations. What Dr. Rabelais thought of contemporary astrology may be gathered from his treatment of the imbecile Her Trippa in the Third Book. He had previously expressed himself briskly on this subject in the *Pantagrueline Prognostication* of 1532, warning the public to take no notice of astrologer-fools, *ces folz astrologues de Louvain, de Nurnberg, de Tubinge et de Lyon.* An access of patriotic fervour at the news from St. Germain-en-Laye nevertheless moved him to toy with a despised art for once in behalf of "Monseigneur d'Orléans", the new little Prince of France. He sat down and drew up a life-horoscope for the child accordingly. A highly favourable one was revealed by the stars, with one reservation—"if he can avoid a somewhat threatening aspect in the western angle of the Seventh House". Within a few weeks it turned out that the Doctor had made a mistake or two in calculating his angles, trines and conjunctions. The royal baby never got anywhere near the Seventh House, dying in his cradle. Is it permissible to overhear an absent-minded murmur from one of the Doctor's more waggish intimates while refilling his goblet some later evening? "Fifteen brace of Devils seize upon the Body and Soul of this horned Renegade, Miscreant, Cuckold, Enchanter, Witch, and Sorcerer of Antichrist . . ." A quotation from Panurge's farewell to Her Trippa should have been too good to miss.

Undoubtedly Dr. Rabelais could laugh at a harmless jest against himself. But not invariably, I fancy; and not from anybody.

2

On September 22, 1549, Dr. Rabelais left Rome with his patron on the road to France, handing the *Schiomachie* to Sébastien Gryphe on his way through Lyons. Cardinal du Bellay's

considerable expenditure on loyal and propagandist celebrations
had apparently not affected his declining prestige at Court. That
interests unfavourable to him—the Cardinal of Lorraine is mentioned in this connection—had gained the king's ear he was
well aware, and, knowing the nature of the courtier breed,
doubtless without surprise. In July Henri II had directed him
to share his functions as Protector of the Affairs of France at the
papal court henceforth with a coadjutor, and an Italian at that
—Ippolito d'Este, Cardinal· of Ferrara, due to be expelled from
Rome by Paul IV in 1555 for his intrigue. After a few weeks'
experience of D'Este Du Bellay asked for his recall, and was
now on his way to present his case to the king in Paris. His
physician must have shared the cardinal's depression. Before
adding the manuscript of the *Schiomachie* to his baggage he had
done some discreet revision in Du Bellay's behalf, blending a
compliment or two to the cardinal's diplomatic successes with
an especial tribute to Guillaume "of eternal memory", his hero
still. But the future looked disturbing.

A more immediate preoccupation was darkening the mind of
Dr. Rabelais on this cheerless journey north. A Latin work
published in Paris in the previous spring, a copy or two of which
kind friends had undoubtedly ensured his receiving within a
month of publication at least, had hit him in the midriff like a
battering-ram; being, in fact, so intended. The operative part
of its overlong title was *Theotimus*, its theme the menace of bad
literature. Its pages, the work of a monk of the Benedictine
abbey of Fontevrault and a Doctor of Theology, by name and
title Dom Gabriel de Puits-Herbault, packed a punch, so to speak,
as devastating as Dr. Rabelais' own.

That Puits-Herbault gets an excessively bad Press from the
majority of the Doctor's commentators is comprehensible enough.
The monk's nerve plainly takes their breath away. For such a
fellow to venture to reply to the stream of insult launched by the
Doctor against his and every other monastic Order for years
past is, one gathers, nothing but *lèse-progrès* and treason against the
light. The name of Puits-Herbault in fact stinks so foully in
learned nostrils and is so swiftly cast aside that it is not always
easy to gather what he said.

Puits-Herbault—Dr. Rabelais is not his only target by any

means—says a great deal, no holds barred. Dr. Rabelais is a drunkard, a glutton, a cynical clown, a perverter of truth, a vendor of literary poison; such an impious and dangerous character, fearing neither God nor man, that Puits-Herbault marvels to find any prince of the Church admitting such a type to his intimacy, his proper place being Geneva. The thunder rolls formidably in the Latin:

> Totos dies nihil aliud quam perpotat, helluatur, graecatur, nidores culinarum persequitur, ac cercopissat, ut est in proverbio, miseras etiam chartas nefandis scriptionibus polluit, venenum vomit, quod per omneis longe lateque regiones dispergat . . .[1]

How Cardinal du Bellay relished the reference to a prelate of highest learning and probity favouring a lewd and shameless fellow, *impurum foedumque hominem*, would be interesting to know. As one of the Doctor's most affectionate lieges I find the situation, as Wilde said of the death of Little Nell, enough to move a heart of stone to laughter. It was in fact high time Dr. Rabelais was pulled up. The monastic Orders, among whom, at this as at any period, were plenty of men of saintly character, some as learned as himself, had endured him with exemplary patience and in silence. Puits-Herbault had now, adopting the Doctor's own attractive technique, restored the balance.

Those who dish it out, proclaims one of the soundest of modern folksayings, should be able to take it. As we have already had one or two opportunities of observing, Dr. Rabelais, a master at dishing-out, rarely takes it very gracefully or in a very sporting manner. How M. Louis Moland is enabled to state that Puits-Herbault's counter-attack had "no effect whatsoever" I cannot discover. It certainly reached one of its principal objectives. Rumbling and objurgating three years later,

> And with a face as red and as awry
> As Herod's hangdogs in old tapestry,

the Doctor will be still nursing his wrath in the dedication to Cardinal Odet de Châtillon of the completed Fourth Book. So atrociously and unreasonably has he been handled by "cannibals,

---

[1] "Spending his days in nothing but boozing, gormandising, gobbling Greek, snuffing up the kitchen-smells . . ." The remainder is impolite.

misanthropes, and enemies of mirth", he assures his patron, that for a time he determined to write no more. He changed his mind, nevertheless, and for Puits-Herbault and his following a special fate is reserved. In Chapter XXXII of the Fourth Book the *enraigez Putherbes* (Lat. *Putherbeus*) appear among the spawn of the bestial monster Antiphysis, the enemy of Mother Nature and of all good.

And Puits-Herbault is in distinguished company, the eminent Calvin having joined the spawn of Antiphysis likewise on publication of his treatise *De Scandalis* (1550). In this diatribe the Dictator of Geneva, having dealt with Étienne Dolet and one or two more notorious atheists, libertines, blasphemers, and spurners of the Gospel, who in so far as attaining spiritual life is concerned may be deemed no better than dogs and pigs ("nihil a canibus et porcis putarent se differre"), turns to excommunicate Dr. Rabelais and two more ex-cronies of the Lyons group, Bonaventure des Périers and Antoine de Gouvea ("Alii ut Rabelaysus, Deperius, et Goveanus . . .") as equally typical of those writers who, having once tasted of the Gospel, have been struck with blindness and have turned to sacrilegious derision and mockeries. Five years onward, raging still over the Doctor's answering gibe at *les demoniacles Calvins, imposteurs de Geneve*, Calvin will renew the offensive in a sermon on Deuteronomy, with direct application to the Fourth Book, its author, and his patron Châtillon. "Here is a lout mocking at Holy Scripture like this devil Pantagruel, with all his filth and scurviness! . . . Here are mad dogs vomiting ribaldry against God's majesty . . . abetted by cardinals, favoured by them and upholding them! We even see their reverences' names blazoned in these five works."[1] No doubt the Doctor would again have suitably replied; but by that time, belike, he had sheathed the pen.

He could resign himself to bidding farewell before long to Cardinal Jean du Bellay. A useful diplomatic career extending over twenty years or more had come to an end. Directed by Henri II to attend the Conclave following the death of Pope Paul III (November 10) with the other cardinals of France, Du Bellay sailed from Marseilles in that month with his brethren

---

[1] Preaching in 1555, Calvin seems to include the spurious "Fifth Book", published seven years later. Perhaps wrath affected his arithmetic.

of Guise, Châtillon, and Vendôme, leaving his physician in Paris; there were, after all, good doctors in Italy. On February 7 the Conclave rose, having raised to the Papacy Giamaria del Monte, Julius III, the b'earded and the bellicose. Towards the autumn Jean du Bellay returned to recuperate from severe illness at his rural retreat of St. Maur-les-Fossés, where Dr. Rabelais again attended him for a time. But the Doctor could begin looking for another patron. Having resigned the Bishopric of Paris in favour of his cousin Eustache the cardinal remained in retirement and a few months later returned to Rome for good, dying there in February 1560 as Dean of the Sacred College and Bishop of Ostia, aged sixty-eight.

Another patron was fortunately at hand, and an admiring and active one. In August of this year 1550 Cardinal Odet de Châtillon was able to secure the Doctor a "privilege" from Henri II authorising him to reprint his works—"no less useful than delightful"—and ordering the suppression of all the pirated editions, *corrumpuz, dépravés, et pervertis en plusieurs endroitz*, against which he had been justifiably roaring. This was a satisfactory enough riposte to the "gulligutted Dunces" and "Church-vermin" of the Puits-Herbault camp. To their increasing numbers had just been added the Platonic poet Charles de Sainte-Marthe, whose congratulations to the Fontevrault monk in his efforts against "atheists and epicureans" must have galled the Doctor all the more because of the old quarrel between his family and the Sainte-Marthes which he had woven into the Picrocholian War years before. However, he had strong backing. His latest patron stood high in favour at Court. The new reign had brought Odet de Coligny, Cardinal de Châtillon, Count-Bishop of Beauvais, and the rest of the Coligny family into prominence, and their sympathies were notorious. Already the shadow of the coming wars of religion was rising above the horizon; already two rival factions at Court were taking shape, headed by the powerful Guises of Lorraine on the Catholic side and the hardly less powerful Condés and Colignys on the other. Not many years hence Rabelais' patron—a "second Gallic Hercules" to the Doctor—would defy Rome in a spectacular manner by proclaiming himself a Calvinist and, duly excommunicated in 1563, publicly marrying Elisabeth d'Hauteville in his cardinal's robes, in which he appeared with *Madame la Cardinale* at an important Court function, and would doubtless have continued so to do, amid discreet titters, had his affairs not taken a bad turn.[1] Even now, possibly, Châtillon's ambitious brother the Admiral was meditating that *coup* which would so nearly enable him a few years hence to kidnap the Crown, liquidate the Guises, and, if Michelet's theory is tenable, set up a Calvinist republic.

Dr. Rabelais, as we need hardly remind ourselves yet again, was no fool. To attach himself exclusively to the Coligny interest might well turn out a tactical blunder. As early as 1549 he had begun to realise this and to make arrangements accordingly, if his addressing of the *Schiomachie* to Cardinal de Guise has any significance; as it obviously has. Apart from their high birth and position at Court, the Guises were closely allied to foreign royalty, Marie, sister of Duke François, having married James V of Scotland some years before and given birth to Mary Stuart, whose name so few Scotsmen can hear without a pang of shame. ("Such a Queen as every man of any gallantry of spirit would have sacrificed his life for!"—the indignant roar of Dr. Johnson drowns the hiccups of a thousand Burns Nichts). In crudely sporting terms, therefore, the Guises, champions of the Catholic cause with the mass of the nation behind them, were a much safer bet for Dr. Rabelais in the year 1550 than the Calvinist Colignys. He could, moreover, as many did, keep a foot in both camps.

That he had soon come to this sage conclusion and without offending Châtillon veered discreetly towards the Catholic party is disclosed by a legal document of January 18, 1550, emanating from the Procurator to the Bishopric of Paris and confirming to *magistro Francisco Rabelaeio, presbytero doctori medico*, the secular cure of St. Martin of Meudon, ten miles from Paris. This living was in the gift of Cardinal Jean du Bellay, who on resigning the Bishopric of Paris had reserved the right to dispose of benefices, but it could hardly escape public notice that the lord of the manor of Meudon was François, Duc de Guise, who had recently acquired the estate from the Duchesse d'Étampes. Having this opportunity

---

[1] Having figured among the defeated Calvinist commanders at the battle of St. Denis (1567), Châtillon fled to England with a price on his head, was effusively welcomed by Elizabeth Tudor, and was poisoned by one of his servants at Hampton on February 14, 1571, as he was preparing to return to France under the amnesty. In 1602 Madame failed to recover her dowry in a lawsuit.

to make up to his esteemed physician for a lost bequest, Guillaume du Bellay's brother would be all the readier to accede to the duke's application. It may be that the living of St. Christophe-de-Jambet in the Sarthe, which the cardinal added simultaneously, was likewise a Guise recommendation. At any rate the Catholic generalissimo had succumbed apparently without difficulty to that *Rabelaismus* with which we are now so familiar. According to Guillaume Colletet, a reliable person, the new curé of Meudon was on sufficiently easy terms with the Guises already to be able on his appointment to salute the duke and duchess jovially as "my good and pious parishioners". Very soon, in the second (1552) edition of the Fourth Book, would be blazoned an anecdote highly flattering to the *seigneur duc de Guise*, a gallant soldier and one probably no more averse from a compliment in print than the rest of us.

Panurge tells the story in Chapter XI; it has since been served up many times in various forms. Holding forth in the duke's presence on a certain hot engagement under his command with the Emperor's troops, a military fop named Breton de Villandry provokes at length from the duke the chilly remark that he does not remember seeing him there. To which Villandry retorts, "Faith, my lord, I was there—and what's more, in a place *you'd* never dare be seen in!" As all present hold their breath Villandry adds that he was taking cover with the baggage-train and the whole company dissolves in laughter with the duke. Such a patronage was certainly worth securing. How Dr. Rabelais could woo the Guises without antagonising Châtillon is explicable enough, no doubt. The position as between the rival parties was still fluid, and a certain type of Renaissance mind, at once labyrinthine and elusive, could accept many odd compromises. There may have been times when Cardinal Odet de Châtillon, Bishop of Beauvais, thought of turning Catholic himself.

Dr. François Rabelais meanwhile had become a parish priest. That his appointments to Meudon and St. Christophe could not have been published without evoking protests in certain Catholic quarters, as Moland and Lesellier confirm, was inevitable. Today, were it possible to conceive of a priest of Dr. Rabelais' reputation thus favoured in high quarters, it would be a scandal calling for the intervention of Rome. No doubt François de Guise, judging

the Doctor to be a valuable recruit from the Left, would assume
that at the age of nearly sixty he had finished sowing his wild
oats. The indulgence of Cardinal Jean du Bellay towards a
curious pastor of souls might be attributed to a broad outlook,
personal liking, an undoubted debt of gratitude, and perhaps the
same assumption as the duke's. The new curé at any rate was
not disturbed, and some satiric Bernanos of the period could
begin jotting down a few notes for a *Journal d'un Curé de Campagne*,
highly useful to Dr. Rabelais' biographers had it taken shape.

As it happens we have something of the sort, of quaint absurdity.
A curious sentimental folklore, most of it of nineteenth-century
provenance, has gathered round the figure of the Curé of Meudon,
by which title Rabelais is still saluted by busy French journalists
with little time for history. The vision of genial silver-haired old
Curé Rabelais settling down at last in a humble country parish
to teach the little ones their Catechism and potter round the
presbytery garden has been too much for romantic pens, which
have embellished the theme ad lib. (There is naturally a Left
Wing or Gay-Old-Dog alternative version.) The bellicose and
bacchanalian Doctor has merged into a secularised edition of the
Curé d'Ars, bathed in pink floodlight. He is gentle, kindly,
conscientious, charitable, and beloved, and all the little birds
come at his call. He is, in fact, the prototype and essence of all
the venerable old curés in the *Bibliothèque Rose*, and if he enjoys
an occasional glass of wine with the celebrated poet Ronsard,
now a bosom friend and frequent visitor, it is the most temperate
and innocent of bacchanals. A charming picture, not its least
affecting aspect being the implication that the dear old Curé
has begun to practise his religion again after some thirty years,
though I have not seen this actually affirmed in black and white.

Unfortunately there is no evidence that the famous Curé of
Meudon ever went near his parish or that of St. Christophe either.
Making a formal visitation at Meudon in June 1551, the new
Bishop of Paris, Eustache du Bellay, found the absentee Doctor
represented by his curate, Pierre Richard, though on all such
occasions the presence of the parish priest, even on his sickbed,
is essential. The alleged Ronsardian visits rest on a seventeenth-
century legend; as already observed, there is no record that
Ronsard and Rabelais ever met in their lives. And finally, even

had the Doctor turned out a St. Jean Vianney before his time, the miracle did not last long. In a document dated January 9, 1552, he resigned the living of Meudon together with that of St. Christophe-de-Jambet in the proper form (". . . *resignavit, cessit, et demisit, pure, libere, et simpliciter*"), and in the presence of an episcopal procurator and the usual witnesses.

Why the Doctor should after less than two years' tenure suddenly throw up two sinecures yielding a welcome addition to whatever income he was now making may seem at first glance one more of the Rabelaisian Mysteries. Two explanations have been offered; both, I think, sound, and possibly related. It may easily be that at this moment the new bishop, less indulgently inclined towards his notorious curé—twice censured by the Sorbonne for obscenity, a third time for heresy—than the elderly cardinal his cousin, saw eye to eye with the Guises on the desirability of the Doctor's relinquishing both his livings forthwith.

Indignation roused by his appointment was undoubtedly still unallayed. Lesellier quotes from the Vatican archives the formal application (February 1551) of one Jean Rouze, priest of the diocese of Chartres, for the living of Meudon, on the grounds that it is actually vacant in law by reason of "either the incapacity or irregularity" of the new incumbent. By January 1552 there must have been a strong body of opinion in agreement with Rouze. How did Dr. Rabelais manage now as at other times to escape being hauled before an ecclesiastical tribunal, at a time when the rigours of the Counter-Reform against scandalous clerics were already beginning? Obviously such protectors, royalty apart, as Du Bellay, Châtillon, and Guise supply the answer. Whether the Doctor had in addition, as Lesellier suggests, lately provided himself with a certificate of absolution from his major irregularities from the Grand Penitentiary in Rome I am apt to doubt. Having satisfied the conditions of the Sacrament of Penance he would of course be no longer guilty and no tribunal could touch him; but such things are not a kind of all-in insurance policy or driving-licence to be flourished at will.

At any rate his resignation from Meudon and St. Christophe would minimise further scandal now imminent. Ill-fortune had dogged Dr. Rabelais again. If, as Léon Daudet so plausibly maintains, he had been the Crown's propagandist during recent trouble with the Holy See, the Crown had let him down. On the basis of Daudet's theory, in which many good authorities acquiesce, his awkward situation may be briefly exposed. Over nearly five years from 1547 onward relations between the aggressive new Pope Julius III, an ally of the Emperor, and Henri II had become increasingly strained over matters of policy ranging from papal appointments and dues in France to the future of the Duchy of Parma, from which the Pope wished to expel Henri's protégé Ottavio Farnese. By 1551 tension had reached a peak. The Sorbonne had ruled that Henri owed the Holy See no political allegiance, Julius had deposed Farnese, Henri had dismissed the papal nuncio, the financial "usurpations" of the papacy had been denounced by leading French jurists, and a Gallican schism seemed imminent. In this year, almost undoubtedly, an intimation reached Dr. François Rabelais, Master of the King's Requests, from the highest quarters conveying permission to indulge Gallican *esprit* to the limit against the Roman Curia in the comic work on which he was engaged. Nothing would delight the Doctor more than thus to oblige his king. By the time *The Fourth Book of Pantagruel* came out in January 1552, however, the situation had changed. Pope and king were reconciled—a treaty with the Holy See was signed that April—Dr. Rabelais' over-hearty onslaughts, with the royal privilege attached, were obsolete, and he was left facing another inevitable condemnation from the Sorbonne. It was as simple as that.

The Fourth Book came on the town nevertheless as successfully as its predecessor. Three-quarters of it is merely a high-spirited Rabelaisian rollick; the Doctor does not train his guns on the Curia till he comes to Chapter XLIX, ceasing fire at Chapter LIV. And here the reader may be usefully reminded that we have changed our translator, the gifted and unreliable Sir Thomas Urquhart having yielded to the slightly less reliable and extremely rancorous Peter Le Motteux.

3

"Uretacque, hau ! Bressine, uretacque, hau! guare la pane! Accapaye, hau!"—"Helm a-lee, ho! 'Boutship with her! Helm a-lee, ho! Stand off from the leech, let her drive, ho!" A great shouting salty seawind like the voice of Master-Pilot Jamet

Brayer down the gale fills so much of the Fourth Book that one could wonder whether Dr. Rabelais might have missed his vocation after all. In the opening chapter, where Pantagruel's flagship *Thalamege* rides at anchor in the roads off Thalassa, surrounded by her escort of galleons, men-of-war, feluccas, and triremes, we are plunged at once into the excitement of the Renaissance Voyage. Blocks are creaking, gulls scream, sails go up, captains roar, bo'suns pipe, the tarry seamen with gold earrings are cursing and singing at windlass and capstan, and below in the great cabin the gentlemen clink their goblets.

"Inse, inse! Aux boulingues de contremejane!" Where did the Doctor gather his vocabulary of the sea, all authentic? He was as inland-born and bred a scholar as any man could be. His natural background is the city: Lyons, Rome, or Paris. Nowhere in any of his writings is the most fleeting glint of the sea perceptible till he suddenly bursts out like a foghorn in the Fourth Book with sailing-jargon rich and ripe. Such breezy locutions could not in his time be learned, as nowadays, from novels by maiden ladies in Hampstead or Belgravia, or indeed from books at all. In the absence of, so far as I know, any speculation on this fascinating question, I conclude that the Doctor learned his nautical patter in the one and only French seaport which fits into any of his journeyings, namely Marseilles. Here undoubtedly he must more than once have embarked or landed on the way to or from Italy with Cardinal du Bellay, and found time to pick up a technical phrase or two and a little local patois (of a flying-fish mentioned early in the Fourth Book he remarks: "At Marseilles they call it a *lendole*"). Here, strolling round the quays or refreshing himself in some tavern of the Old Port, if not actually aboard ship during a good crossing, he must have talked with the original of Pantagruel's pilot and sailing-master, Jamet Brayer, whose name is authentic—and as such, one of the very few in the Four Books, the others pertaining to friends or enemies—and added to a new notebook.[1] The gifted pencil of Joseph Hémard perfectly conveys what one imagines Brayer to look like: a hairy, lean, tough, mahogany-faced, hard-bitten old matlow in gold earrings and a stocking-cap, sketched in the act of bawling to the

---

[1] According to Louis Moland, Brayer was a well-known pilot at this time. Rabelais may have borrowed the name.

deck, a type salted no doubt by adventure in strange lands and perilous seas, fertile of oaths and yarns.

The thrills and the gusto with which the Doctor prepares to launch Pantagruel and his companions on a sea-voyage into the Unknown one may partly share by musing over a map of the Americas and the Spanish Main in Charles V's time, with its array of evocative place-names. Nombre de Dios, Hispaniola, Trinidad, Ciudad de los Reyes, Cartagena, La Guayra, Villa Rica de la Vera Cruz, Puerto de Carenos, Nuestra Señora de Guadalupe, where, on the site of Our Lady's apparition in 1531 to the Indian convert Juan Diego would shortly be rising the national shrine of the Patroness of Mexico, on which even a modern ruffian like Calles dared not lay a finger—how magical they are! In Peru, at a date when Rabelais had just entered the service of Bishop d'Estissac, the stupendous Pizarro, impassive in his steel armour under a lethal sun, was leading a handful of troops, worn by famine, disease, weather, and incessant fighting, over the snowy Cordilleras to discover and take El Dorado. On a day when Dr. Rabelais was bustling round his wards at Lyons the city of Caxamalca was stormed in a bloody battle with fifty thousand Incas and their emperor Atahualpa taken prisoner. Years earlier, as Friar Rabelais was reciting the Good Friday Office of 1519 with his brethren at Fontenay, Cortes had landed at Vera Cruz; a few months later the disaster of the *Noche Triste* had decimated his troops and avenged the capture and looting of Tenochtitlan, otherwise Mexico City; in due course the Royal and Pontifical University of Mexico and a score of monasteries, schools and hospitals were spreading civilisation in a flourishing New Spain. It is almost impossible to exaggerate the bedazzlement with which the New World and worlds still undiscovered beckoned to Renaissance eyes, even if the Spaniards had failed, most disappointingly, to locate the Fountain of Youth on the island of Bimini, off Florida.

So on a fine June day the Pantagruelists troop aboard the *Thalamege* ("The Great Ship"), evidently a typical thousand-ton galleon of the time; a tall and beautiful craft with her lofty gilded poop-lanterns, her carved and gilt-scrolled galleries, ports and bulwarks, her brilliantly-painted sails, her silken pennants and

H

streamers, and a "huge large Bottle", half-silver, half-gold, proclaiming from her stern-galleries whither the convoy was bound. In the flagship before weighing anchor, and presumably in the great cabin, Dr. Rabelais concedes a brief religious service on the Genevan pattern, ending with the singing of Psalm cxiii, the "travellers' psalm", *In exitu Israël de Aegypto*; not in the familiar Latin of the Church but in the French version lately made by his friend Clément Marot for John Calvin, *Quand Israël hors d'Égypte sortit*. And after a lavish banquet and drinking-bout in which all the leading citizens of Thalassa participate, the convoy sails, "with a merry Gale at the South-East", Master-Pilot Jamet Brayer having recommended and laid this course.

Seeing that the Oracle of the Holy Bottle lay near Cathay in upper India, his Advice, and that of Xenomanes also, was not to steer the Course which the Portuguese use; sailing thro' the Torrid Zone and Cape Bona Speranza at the South Point of Africk beyond the Equinoctial Line, and losing sight of the Northern Pole, their Guide, they make a prodigious long Voyage; but rather to keep as near the Parallel of the said India as possible, and to tack to the westward of the said Pole, so that winding under the North they might find themselves in the Latitude of the Port of Olone, without coming nearer it, for fear of being shut up in the Frozen Sea; whereas by following this Canonical Turn by the said Parallel, they must have that on the Right to the Eastward which on their Departure was on their Left. . . .

Somewhat confusing sailing-directions, thanks partly to Translator Peter le Motteux, even with his punctuation improved. M. Plattard points out that Dr. Rabelais has mingled a roving fancy with data taken from maps, and, possibly, the narrative of Jacques Cartier, who discovered Canada in 1534 while in search of a north-west passage to China. Incidentally the Doctor has buoyantly forgotten his promise at the end of the Second Book to send Pantagruel to the Antilles, in the zone of the Spanish Main; a voyage in which his public would be far more interested, and in the "Cannibal Islands"—Martinique, for one, perhaps—especially. One could wish the Doctor had remembered this plan. The bull of Paul III (1537) establishing the equality of human rights of the chocolate-skinned aboriginals of the Americas with those of their conquerors, with equal access to the Sacraments, and forbidding their exploitation, would have afforded him some scope.

However, Pantagruel and his friends are now on the high seas, with a brisk south-easterly gale behind them. The log of the *Thalamege* would probably, had it occurred to the Doctor that even a Pantagruelist flagship needed to keep one, tie any serious navigator into knots. A précis of the voyage, supposing one of Pantagruel's suite to have cultivated a diary—say the priggish Eudemon, a born diary-keeper, whom one can see making careful nightly entries under the cabin lamp in a neat, thin, niggling script—might go, at its briefest, thus:

Monday (four days out): Called at the island of Medamothy to make purchases at the fair. Many merchants from Africa and Asia. Pantagruel bought 78 pieces of tapestry, three unicorns, and a *tarand* [a fabulous animal simultaneously resembling a bullock, a stag, and a bear] as presents for his father Gargantua. These duly despatched, voyage resumed.

Tuesday (five days out): Nearing the Pole. Spoke a merchantman full of French from Xaintonge returning from Lantern Land. On board Panurge quarrels with Dindenault, a sheep-merchant from Taillebourg. Peace made by Pantagruel.

Wednesday: Quarrel resumed, Dindenault drowned by Panurge.

Thursday: Wind SSW. Went ashore on the island of Ennasin. Strange inhabitants, noses like the ace of clubs, curious customs. Unlikeable.

Saturday: Wind W. Landed on the island of Chély, received by King Panigon. Friar John missing, found at length in Panigon's kitchen. Long explanation of the reason monks love kitchens.

Tuesday: Lay off Procuration, a legal country full of catchpoles or bumbailiffs. Heard good story about catchpoles beaten silly by the Lord of Basché. Landed at length.

Wednesday: Met some typical catchpoles. Friar John half-murders one.

Friday: Spoke nine ships full of monks and friars bound for the Council of Chesil [Trent]. Delight of Panurge. Gifts to monks of seventy-eight dozen hams and other provisions before proceeding.

Saturday: Ran into terrific storm. Cowardice of Panurge. Contempt of Friar John.

Sunday: Storm worse. Panurge in panic.

Monday: Storm still worse. Panurge hysterical.

Tuesday: Storm over. Panurge resumes normal swagger.

Thursday: Landed on the Isle of Macreons, inhabited by aged and dead heroes. Epistemon's account of the death of Guillaume du Bellay.

Saturday: Landed on Sneaking Island, ruled by Shrovetide [Lent]. Xenomane's description of Shrovetide, a horrible monster.

Sunday: Off Wild Island. Pantagruel slays a giant whale.

Tuesday: Landed on Wild Island, inhabited by Chitterlings, sworn enemies of Shrovetide. P. just escapes being ambushed by them. Council of war called. Friar John supervises construction of Wooden Sow on Trojan pattern, to hold one hundred and fifty cooks.

Wednesday: Pitched battle with Chitterlings. Strange appearance of a Flying Pig, at which Chitterlings surrender. P. makes peace-treaty with their Queen Niphleseth.

Friday: Landed on Island of Ruach, where the inhabitants live entirely on wind. Curious experiences of flatulence and explosions.

Sunday: Landed on Papefigue Island. Inhabitants oppressed by Papimanes on adjoining island. Story of small devil fooled by old woman of Papefigue.

Tuesday: Land on Papimane Island, received by local bishop, Homenas. Pope-worship here prevalent. Homenas hospitable but obsessed by Decretals. Long, fervent address on this topic. Gifts on parting.

Sunday: At sea again. Adventure of the Frozen Words.

Wednesday: Landed on island ruled by Messer Gaster [Lord Belly]. Extraordinary devotion of inhabitants to guzzling and boozing. Customs and processions most bizarre. Gaster's disconcerting gesture noted.

Friday: Becalmed off island of Chaneph, full of hypocrites and mountebacks. NW gale gets up. Voyage resumed.

Sunday: Off the isle of Ganabim, inhabited by thieves and assassins. Slight difference between Panurge and the great cat Rodilardus, following one-gun salute to the Muses by whole fleet.

With which the Fourth Book abruptly ends; all too soon, one may conjecture, for the Doctor's readers, who had enjoyed many robust and breezy experiences. Of these the Great Storm, the Battle of the Chitterlings, the Adventure of the Frozen Words, and, extravagant as it is, the attack on the Curia and the Decretals in the Isle of Papimanes, are of the true Rabelaisian vintage, and I for one never tire of them.

Since the last of these episodes is, so to speak, the nub of the Fourth Book and a Royal Command performance, it may be glanced at first. The Papimanes are what would nowadays be called Ultramontanes, whom it is very easy for a satirist of no great scruple to turn into idolators of the Pope and besotted imbeciles. The Decretals are documents on which were based the legislative claims of the medieval Papacy and—according to the Doctor, allied for once with the Sorbonne—recent usurpations by the Roman Curia, opposed by the French Crown.[1] Originally the reply of the Holy See in the early Middle Ages to repeated encroachments in the spiritual sphere by emperors, kings and princes, the Decretals took the form of a code of canonical jurisprudence compiled in 1234, at Gregory IX's orders, by St. Raymond of Pennafort, a Dominican legalist. These five important volumes, to which Dante's *bête noire* Boniface VIII added a sixth and John XXII two new series forming an appendix, thenceforth provided the official interpretation of Canon Law and all papal decrees, including—which chiefly irked the secular power—those covering papal rights to nominate to benefices and reserve part of their revenues everywhere in Christendom, since the Holy See needs money like everyone else. And Dr. Rabelais' theme-song is that to the Curia and the clergy at large the Decretals are now more precious, sacred, and venerable than Holy Scripture itself. As he puts it, abetted by Le Motteux, into the mouth of the lyrical Homenas:

What was it that founded, underpropped, and fixed, and now maintains, nourishes, and feeds the devout monks and friars in convents, monasteries, and abbeys, so that did they not daily and nightly pray without ceasing, the world would be in evident danger of returning to its primitive chaos? The Sacred Decretals. What makes and daily increases the famous and celebrated Patrimony of St. Peter in plenty of all temporal, corporeal, and spiritual blessings? The Holy Decretals. What made the Holy Apostolic See and the Pope of Rome in all times, and at this present, so dreadful in the Universe that all Kings, Emperors, Potentates, and Lords willing-nilling must depend upon him, hold of him, be crowned,

[1] They are to be distinguished from the "False Decretals", published in France by one Isidore Mercator in the ninth century and proved in the seventeenth to be mostly a forgery. The object of these was to increase the independence and authority of the bishops against the civil power.

confirmed, and authorised by him, come thither to strike sail,
buckle, and fall down before his holy slipper? . . . The mighty
Decretals of God [etc., etc.].

In such a brisk farrago very few of the Doctor's Catholic
readers no doubt were qualified to winnow fact from fancy; but
when Bishop Homenas proceeds to declare that the very pages
of the Decretals are holy and miraculous they would instantly
become aware that the naughty Doctor was up to his tricks again.
Five ridiculous instances of the magic effect of these parchments,
two of them scatological, are quoted by Panurge, Friar John,
and others of Pantagruel's suite present in mischievous enthusiasm.
To each in turn Homenas cries in ecstasy: "Miracle! Miracle!"
The Curia's episcopal spokesman is in fact a perfect old fool,
albeit an amiable one. Dr. Rabelais has no personal animus
against him, even when he thrusts most vigorously in the king's
behalf, denouncing those chapters of the Decretals which have
the "aurifluous Energy" to draw four hundred thousand ducats
a year to Rome from French coffers, and allowing Epistemon to
attack Julius III, who had recently employed Papal troops in the
Emperor's behalf.

> But methinks, Gentlemen, this same Picture is not overlike our
> late Popes; for I have seen them not with their Pallium, Aumusse,
> or Rochet on, but with Helmets on their Heads, more like the Top
> of a Persian Turban; and while the Christian Commonwealth was
> in Peace, they alone were most furiously and cruelly making War.

In the end all part the best of friends, Panurge giving Bishop
Homenas nine pieces of "double-friz'd Cloth of Gold" to hang
before the grille protecting a venerated papal portrait, filling
"the Church-Box, for its Repairs and Fabrick" with gold double-
crowns, and ordering nine hundred and fourteen gold angels to
be shared among "the Lasses who had waited at Table, to buy
them Husbands when they could get them". After which Dr.
Rabelais, having sufficiently dealt in six swashing chapters with
the Temporal Power, the Curia, and the reigning Pope, turns to
something else. As usual he has overstepped the mark, and more
than one of his missiles has hit the wrong target. Between the
Pope-worship of the lunatic Papimanes and the traditional

veneration of the Catholic world for the office of the Vicar of Christ there was and is a sane and clear division—is there not a well-known story of a Roman woman who, having knelt devoutly for the blessing of Pope Alexander VI, rose up to denounce the sins of the man Rodrigo Borgia? Our high-spirited Doctor is none too concerned to respect this distinction; once again the parallel of Molière occurs. And could his putting into Homenas' mouth fantastic threats of fire and slaughter, multiplied tenfold by Le Motteux, against heretics rejecting the Decretals be construed as anything but a malicious attempt to stir up odium against a Papacy which had not long since rebuked the French for this very thing? Dr. Rabelais had, as we say, asked for trouble once more.

With relief and pleasure we quit the arena of politics for the Battle of the Chitterlings, a piece of hilarious Learish pantomime which starts off by waving the banner of allegory but soon drops it. At first representing the revolt of the natural human appetite against the tyranny of Shrovetide, or Lent—for which season, as we may recall yet again, Dr. Rabelais had a rabid distaste—the Chitterlings swiftly become chitterlings pure and simple, depicted by the glorious Hémard as savage and formidable sausages, armed to the teeth, marching in column of route with fife and drum to meet an array of Pantagruel's fighting cooks brandishing cutlery and *batterie de cuisine* and bearing savoury names like Coquelardon, Tirelardon, Myrelardon, Hochepot, Moustardiot, Boudinandière, and dozens more, rendered by Le Motteux as "Nible-lard", "Pinch-lard", "Chew-lard", "Tosspot", and so forth. Like the Horse of Troy the Wooden Sow, commanded by Friar John of the Chops, is the tactical pivot of Pantagruel's operations.

Then began the Martial Fray, higledy-pigledy. Mawl-Chitterling did mawl Chitterlings, Cut-Pudding did cut Puddings; Pantagruel did break the Chitterlings at the Knees; Friar Jhon stay'd in sight within his Sow, viewing and observing all Things, when the Patty-Pans that lay in Ambuscado most furiously sallied out upon Pantagruel.

Fryar Jhon, who lay snug all this while, by that time perceiving the Rout and Hurlyburly, set open the Doors of the Sow and sallied out with his merry Greeks, some of them arm'd with Iron Spits,

others with Andirons, Racks, Fire-Shovels, Kettles, Grid-Irons,
Oven-Forks, Tongs, Dripping-pans, Brooms, Iron-pots, Mortars,
Pestles, all in Battle Array like so many Housebreakers, hollowing
and roaring out all together most frightfully *Nabuzardan, Nabuzardan,
Nabuzardan.* Thus shouting and hooting they fought like Dragons
and charg'd through the Patty-pans and Sawsages . . .

As the ferocious Chitterlings, carved and sliced and chopped
most mercilessly by Pantagruel's troops, fight back like devils,
a portent suddenly appears in the sky, flying towards the battle-
field from the north, in the shape of "a huge, fat, thick, grizly
Swine, with long and large Wings like those of a Windmill, its
Plumes red crimson . . . its Eyes flaming like a Carbuncle, its
Ears green like a Prasin-Emerald . . . its Feet white, diaphanous,
and transparent like a Diamond, somewhat broad and of the
splay-kind, like those of Geese, and as Queen Dick's used to be
at Tholose in the Days of Yore"; by which Le Motteux means
the legendary Reine Pédauque of Toulouse, whom we have
encountered already. At the sight of this their tutelary deity
Mardigras, or Carnival, round whose neck is a gold collar in-
scribed in Greek "Hog Teaching Minerva", the Chitterlings
fling down their weapons and fall on their knees, thus enabling
Friar John and his braves to intensify the jolly massacre till
Pantagruel whistles them off. After which, hovering backwards
and forwards for a space between the two armies, the Hog Mardigras finally voids "above twenty-seven Butts of Mustard" over
the stricken field and flies away, crying: "Carnival! Carnival!
Carnival!" A treaty signed with Niphleseth, Queen of the
Chitterlings, whose name conveys a phallic jest to Hebrew
scholars, ends the affray, and Dr. Rabelais winds up on a characteristic note. A street in Paris in his time was called, he affirms,
La Rue Pavée d'Andouilles, "The Street Paved with Chitterlings",
so named from huge numbers of the fallen enemy buried there at
this time by the king's consent. Obviously this street, if he did
not have to invent it, inspired the entire farce.[1]

The four chapters devoted to the Great Storm are a prose
masterpiece I have enjoyed so often as almost to know them by
heart. The comic terrors of Panurge mingle with the bawlings

[1] The Rue Séguier in the university quarter was formerly known as the Rue Pavée.
Rabelais possibly added the Chitterlings.

of Friar John, the shrieking of the wind, the pounding crash of enormous waves, the creaks and groans of the labouring flag-ship, the cries of the seamen, and the great voice of Jamet Brayer roaring over all in extraordinary realism. In big seas the typical Renaissance galleon of large tonnage, I have read in some nautical work, was not what sailors call a "handy" ship; her tall, heavy masts with their vast spread of sail and her excessive freeboard and top-hamper in bulwarks, bows, poop, and fore and stern "castles" made her extremely difficult to handle with a strong wind abeam, and above all in gale conditions, when her heavy rolling made for strains and leaks, and sailing near the wind was almost impossible. Whatever experiences in smaller vessels Dr. Rabelais may have endured during crossings to or from Italy (and the Mediterranean can be pretty formidable when it chooses), he has managed to convey so brilliantly as to put his fellow-lands-man Shakespeare well in the shade. The opening scene of *The Tempest* represents less than one-fifteenth of the Doctor's sustained effort, and the master of King Alonso's ship shows up as the merest ninny compared with his stentorian colleague of the *Thalamege*. It does not seem to me excessive to describe Dr. Rabelais in this aspect as the Conrad of the Renaissance, though I suspect, since he liked his comfort, that he shared with Panurge such a lively distaste for the sea in its rage that he may well at some time have applied himself in his extremity to God and Our Lady, adding the same heartfelt cry—"Would it were the pleasure of the Divine Bounty that I were at this present Hour in the Close at Seuilly, or at Innocent's the Pastry-Cook over against the painted Wine-Vault at Chinon!" Which surely echoes some personal agony long remembered?

Here then begins the storm:

When the Master, whose Watch it was, observing the fluttering of the Ancient [ensign] above the Poop, and seeing that it began to overcast, judg'd that we should have. wind, therefore he bid the Boatswain call all hands upon Deck, Officers, Sailors, Foremast Men, Swabbers, Cabbin-boys, and even the Passengers, and made 'em first settle their Topsails and take in the Spreetsail. Then he cry'd, In with your Topsails, lower the Foresail, tallow under the Parrels, brade up close all them Sails, strike your Topmosts to the Cap, make sure with all your Sheepsfeet, lash your Guns fast! All this was nimbly done. Immediately it blow'd a Storm, the Sea began to roar and swell Mountain-high; the Rut of the Sea was great, the Waves breaking upon our Quarter, the North-West Wind bluster'd and overblow'd . . .

The technicalities pour out in the original as if Jacques Cartier's own sailing-master held the pen; *mejane, contremejane, triou, maistralle, epagon, civadiere, boulingues, trinquet de prore, grand artemon, grizelles, coustieres*—a bracing sequence. And here, three chapters later, the great gale begins blowing itself out:

Shoar, shoar, cry'd Pantagruel, land to, my Friends, I see Land, pluck up a good Spirit, Boys! 'tis within a Kenning, so we are not far from a Port—I see the Sky clearing up to the Northwards— Look to the South-East! Courage, my Hearts, said the Pilot, now she'll bear the Hullock of a Sail, the Sea is much Smoother; some Hands aloft, to the Main Top—Put the Helm a-weather—Steady, steady—Hawl your aftermizen Bowlins—Haul, haul, haul—Thus, thus, and no nearer; mind your Steerage, bring your Main Tack aboard—Clear your Sheets, clear your Bowlins; port, port, Helm-a-lee—Now to the Sheet on the starboard-side, thou Son of a Whore! (Thou art mightily pleas'd, honest Fellow, quoth Fryar Jhon, with hearing him make mention of thy Mother). Loff, loff, cry'd the Quartermaster that conn'd the Ship, keep her full, loff the Helm. Loff it is, answer'd the Steersman; keep her thus—Get the Bonnets fix'd—Steady, Steady . . .

More and more salt words have been tumbling out—*inse, guarant, trinquet de gabie, couetz, escoutes, bolines, malettes, amure babord*; they must have been as invigorating to dash down on paper as they are to read. And how superb, and impossible to translate adequately, are some of the long laments of Panurge:

Zalas, zalas, où sont nos boulingues? Tout est frelore bigoth. Nostre trinquet est à vau l'eau! Zalas, à qui appartiendra ce bris? Amis, prestez icy darriere une de ces rambades. Enfans, vostre landrivel est tombé. Zalas, n'abandonnez l'orgeau, ne aussi le tirados! J'oy l'agneuillot fremir! Est il cassé? Pour Dieu, saulvons la brague; du fernel ne vous souciez. Bebe bous, bous, bous . . .

One might say that here our old medical *loup de mer* surpasses even himself.

Possibly owing to its evocation of wireless and still-unsolved mysteries of the ether, the episode of the Frozen Words seems to move the most arid pedants to a fascinated grunt. Standing out to sea after the visit to the Papimanes, the *Thalamege* is driving smoothly along under a fresh breeze. On the poop-deck her passengers are "junketing, tipling, discoursing, and telling Stories", when Pantagruel rises abruptly to his feet. "Do you hear nothing, Gentlemen?" After some straining of ears they are astounded to hear, high above them in the sky, strange articulate sounds of voices, as it were of men, women, children, and even horses calling and crying together. Seized instantly and as usual with panic, Panurge creates the customary whoobub, but the sober Pantagruel, recalling certain words of Aristotle and Antiphanes and the theory of "a philosopher named Perron" concerning a mystic equilateral triangle of celestial worlds with Truth at their centre and ideas of things past and to come, as it were, falling thence on mankind as Time goes on, calls for his sailing-master. And stout, invaluable Jamet Brayer, who knows all the seas of this world, expounds forthwith:

Be not afraid, my Lord, we are on the Confines of the Frozen Sea, on which, about the beginning of last Winter, happen'd a great and bloody Fight between the Arumaspians and the Nephelibates. Then the words and cries of Men and Women, the hacking, slashing, and hewing of Battle-Axes, the shocking, knocking and joulting of Armours and Harnesses, the neighing of Horses, and all other Martial Din and Noise froze in the Air. And now the Rigour of the Winter being over, by the succeeding Serenity and Warmth of the Weather they melt, and are heard.

Almost before he has finished speaking frozen words are dropping from the sky like hail. Pantagruel catches and tosses a handful on the deck. They look like sugarplums, of many colours. Warmed in the companions' hands they melt quickly, giving off "a barbarous Gibberish"; among some handfuls are "very sharp and bloody Words", said by Brayer to return whence they came, namely to "a split Weasand". As increasing quantities fall and begin melting away together a strange clamour fills the air: "Hin, hin, hin, his, ticque, torche, lorgne, brededin, brededac, frr, frrr, frrrr, bou, bou, bou, bou, bou, bou, bou, bou, trac, tracc,

trr, trrr, trrrrr, on, on, on, on, ouououououou, goth, magoth," and
other bizarre noises. These, says Master Pilot Jamet Brayer, are
the sounds of the charging squadrons and the shock and clash
of the neighing horses on the ice. Other words go off with a
noise of fifes and clarions, drums and trumpets. Very soon one
of Pantagruel's suite—actually "I", the Doctor himself, making
one of his erratic, unheralded, and momentary entrances into
Pantagruel's presence—proposes to collect and preserve a few
"merry odd Words" in oil or straw. This Pantagruel forbids,
calling it folly to hoard what they are never likely to need, such
jests (*motz de gueule*) being never scarce among good Pantagruelists; and the all-too-brief episode abruptly ends.

An annoying anticlimax. We have been foully cheated. The
Doctor has had a superb inspiration—what could a Swift, a
Hoffmann, a Hans Andersen, or even a Barrie, not have done
with it?—and allowed it to slip negligently through his fingers.
Myself, doubtless not alone, I could find it in my heart to curse
him roundly for this, marvelling simultaneously that no master-
fabulist since his day has annexed and exploited such a theme for
whimsy, or satire, or both. "Tas de veaulx!", to echo a favourite
cry of his own . . .

Legitimate umbrage over the fiasco of the Frozen Words must
not preclude recognition, before closing the Fourth Book, of
one of those extremely rare occasions on which we discover an
unmistakably Christian sentiment, *more suo*, emanating from our
enigmatic Doctor; still and always a priest of the Catholic Church.
It comes at the end of Chapter XXVIII, concluding a discussion
in the Isle of Macreons on the deaths of heroes. Epistemon
having paid that tribute to the late Guillaume du Bellay noted
in an earlier page, Pantagruel is reminded of a strange happening
in the Greek Archipelago testified by Epitherses, father of Aemilian
the Rhetorician, and quoted by Plutarch. In a ship lying becalmed off Paxos, late one night *circa* A.D. 36, the passengers are
waked from sleep by a terrible voice calling across the sea
"Thamous!", the name of their Egyptian pilot. Thrice the voice
calls; the third time, the trembling Thamous having answered,
it orders him to spread the news on arrival at Palodes that the
Great God Pan is dead; after which the night-sky is filled with sighs
and laments. Very soon the news reaches Rome. Summoned and

examined by the Emperor Tiberius, Thamous convinces him of a fact apparently unknown to the Emperor's Chaldean astrologers, and from his scholars Tiberius—incidentally a man of culture himself—learns that according to Herodotus and Cicero the dead god was the son of Mercury by Penelope. So the story ends. Pantagruel continues:

For my part, I understand it of that great Saviour of the Faithful who was shamefully put to Death at Jerusalem by the Envy and Wickedness of the Doctors, Priests, and Monks of the Mosaic Law. And methinks my Interpretation is not improper; for He may lawfully be said, in the Greek Tongue, to be Pan, since He is our All. For all that we are, all that we live, all that we hope, is Him, by Him, from Him, and in Him; He is the Good Pan, the Great Shepherd; who as the loving Shepherd Corydon affirms, hath not only a tender Love and Affection for his Sheep, but also for their Shepherds. At his Death, Complaints, Sighs, Fears and Lamentations were spread through the whole Fabrick of the Universe, whether Heaven, Land, Sea or Hell.

The Time also concurs with this Interpretation of mine; for this most Good, most Mighty Pan, Our only Saviour, died near Jerusalem, during the reign of Tiberius Caesar.

On which Pantagruel falls silent, and in a little while tears "as big as Ostridge's Eggs" are seen flowing from his eyes. "God take me presently," adds Dr. Rabelais profanely, "if I tell you one single Syllable of a Lye in the Matter."

Irrupting thus into the Rabelaisian brouhaha like a litany into a bacchanal, Pantagruel's meditation might be called breathtaking. It has in fact caused much uneasiness, and more than one attempt has been made to minimise the shock; notably by the learned Solomon Reinach in the 1900's. According to M. Reinach there can be no question here of Pan, still less of any hypothetical Egyptian pilot, "Thamous" being the Syrian name of Adonis, whose female worshippers made nocturnal processions of mourning for his death—Adonis had already been proved a sun-myth by Mallarmé, but who, at that fruitful period, was not?—every autumn, chanting a lament in which "*Thamous! Thamous! Thamous!*" was followed by a triple cry in Greek, "The All-Great [*Panmegas*] is dead!" Hence Plutarch blundered, and the Doctor, with his application to Calvary—a sizeable blot on his copybook, one may remark without uncharitableness, in the view of some of his commentators—also. I personally take this lapse into devotion, an impulse of a unique and moving kind, to have the devotions of generations of his forbears, long since dead and forgotten, behind it. If fifty per cent of the posthumous descriptions of the Doctor's dying-bed are authentic, they were with him at the end as well.

And finally, taking leave of the Fourth Book, it is impossible not to linger a moment more over the six vivacious chapters devoted to the island of Messer Gaster—Lord Belly, "First Master of Arts in the World", whose rule is universal and whose "gulligutted Gastrolaters" are scourged by Dr. Rabelais in a quaint access of moral indignation, considering the Doctor's own notable lack of aversion from belly-furniture and the way he revels in and gloats over the colossal gormandisings and boozings of Gargantua, Pantagruel, and their boon-companions all through the Four Books. Yet even Panurge is revolted by Lord Belly's worshippers and the elaborate processions they hold in his honour, in which a couple of hundred choice dishes are ceremonially borne, all listed by the censorious Doctor as carefully as if he were delating a Mrs. Beeton to the Congregation of the Index. Denouncing these idolaters in the words of St. Paul to the Philippians, in iii. 19 (". . . whose end is destruction, whose God is their belly, and whose glory is in their shame"), he must sorely have shocked and wounded his precious pockified Blades, unaccustomed to such sudden outbreaks of austerity from a *bon vivant* of Dr. Rabelais' standing.

In the end Lord Belly gets a good mark, and very properly. He is no fool. He cherishes no illusions, he despises his ignoble gastrolaters, and, thanks to his doctors, has "the Manners to own that he was no God, but a poor, vile, wretched Creature". This truth he freely demonstrates to his besotted horde of adorers in the most practical way. Though perhaps unsuitable for repetition in a refined page, Lord Belly's disconcerting reply to the Yes-Men might be profitably commended for imitation to every Mr. Big now infesting a tycoon-ridden world.

4

Expected trouble arrived swiftly. This time it was serious. Within a month of the publication of *The Fourth Book of Pantagruel* a decree of the Parlement of Paris ordered the whole edition to be suspended for a fortnight, Rabelais' publisher, Michel Fezendat, being given notice to this effect in person, "on pain of corporal punishment".

The decree, dated March 1, 1552, runs as follows:

> Following censure pronounced by the Faculty of Theology on a certain harmful book exposed for sale under the title of *The Fourth Book of Pantagruel*, with Royal privilege, this Court orders that the publisher be summoned before it and forbidden to sell or display the said book for two weeks following: during which period the Court orders the Procurator-Royal to advise our said Lord the King of the censuring of this book, and to convey to him a copy of this ruling for decision at his good pleasure.

The principal legal tribunal of France had wasted little time on receiving the Sorbonne's report, and the suspension-period may have been extended. This month Henri II was with his army in Lorraine, occupied with operations against the Empire, France being ruled during his absence by his wife, Catherine de Médicis, as Regent. On April 18 Henri made his triumphal entry into Metz. It is believed that the Parlement's decree may have run until his return to Paris later in the month.

Immediately on the king's return somebody with influence at Court, undoubtedly Châtillon—one can hardly see François de Guise doing so, even if he had not been commanding the French forces at the time—spoke to him in Dr. Rabelais' behalf; after which it was announced that the king's good pleasure ordered the sale of *The Fourth Book of Pantagruel* to continue. The Doctor might relax again, and Master Michel Fezendat, for whose agonies every decent literary hack must feel the liveliest sympathy, could thank whatever gods the Parisian Publishers' Association then recognised. Satisfaction in some modern quarters over yet another victory for progress over reaction ("Sore hearts in the Vatican tonight, boys!"—the old story of the Ulster village football team inevitably recurs) might nevertheless, I think, be tempered by a trifle of commonsense. There is an unanswerable case for the Sorbonne's censors if it be recalled, as it cannot be too frequently, that the Four Books are the work of a clerk in Holy Orders, an old offender, a *récidiviste* who, were the same circumstances conceivable today, would have been deprived and suspended years before. They had merely done their duty, the whole printing-trade being now under supervision of the Sorbonne.[1] At the same time there is something to be said for Henri II. Having let Dr. Rabelais in for his latest misfortune, he undoubtedly owed him reparation. Misfortune it certainly was, and I doubt if the precedent of Erasmus indulging himself in spitefulness could be relied on. Apart from Erasmus' being a much greater man, his fundamental Catholicity was unquestioned, which could hardly be said for the Doctor's.

Meanwhile Dr. Rabelais had hastened amid his anxieties to turn suspension to account by weaving into a reprinted Prologue a couple of compliments which could not but leap agreeably to the royal eye: the one lauding the ancient wisdom of "ce tant noble, tant florissant, tant riche et triomphant Royaume de France", the other, killing two birds with one stone, addressed to "le bon, le docte, le sage, le tant humain, tant debonnaire et équitable André Tiraqueau, conseiller du grand, victorieux, et triomphant roy Henry Second". The posy for the debonnair and equitable Tiraqueau turned out, alas, to be thrown away. The Doctor's old friend and host had risen high in the legal world and had ceased to admire his brilliant, erratic guest of Fontenay days. Plattard has noted that in *De Nobilitate*, a treatise on the French aristocracy which Tiraqueau published in 1549, Dr. Rabelais' name does not appear in an incidental list of the leading contemporary medical figures in France. Such omission, considering the Doctor's fulsome dedication to Tiraqueau of Manardi's letters twenty years before, and the compliments scattered through the Four Books, was a most unkind cut. Worse than this had happened now. A member of the Council of the Parlement of Paris, *Conseiller à la Grande Chambre*, since 1541, Maître André Tiraqueau had signed the recent suspension-decree with eleven distinguished colleagues, being in fact, or having developed into, a Catholic of the least compromising kind. The Doctor

[1] Edict of Châteaubriant, August 1551, by the Parlement of Paris.

seems not to have been aware of this before hurrying to print his rather pathetic compliment. He must at length have realised that he could count on one of his oldest friendships no more.

However, his Fourth Book resumed its sales, under royal protection, with sufficient success ("Seen the new Rabelais?"—a masculine chorus exclusively, one may reflect in passing, since the Doctor did not write for women and was then not read by that sex) to warrant, early in 1553, the publication of the first collected edition of his works, a botched affair bearing no publisher's or printer's name and seeming to indicate that the pirates were once again hastening to cash in. What legitimate annoyance this must have caused Dr. Rabelais is not discoverable, for a very good reason. At this moment we come unexpectedly to a standstill against a wall of thick darkness the size of the Great Wall of China. From now onwards no trace of the Doctor has ever been detectable; no clue to his whereabouts or his condition thenceforth exists. The last and greatest of the Rabelaisian enigmas now confronts us. Dr. Rabelais has performed his last vanishing-trick. The Learned Nose has disappeared, picturesquely speaking, into Limbo

VII

Epilogue

EXASPERATINGLY BAFFLING AS DR. RABELAIS' SUDDEN AND FINAL disappearance from history must be (like Villon's before him) to all his friends today, it is some consolation to know that it baffled some of his contemporaries equally. Passing through Lyons towards the end of 1552 the humanist Denys Lambin heard that the Doctor was in prison; a bit of spicy provincial rumour obviously absurd, seeing the protection the Fourth Book enjoyed. The story perturbed Lambin sufficiently, nevertheless, to set him hotfoot on the trail immediately on returning to Paris in December. After inquiries in every quarter he wrote to his friend Henri Estienne, a personage of cold Calvinist integrity who disapproved of Dr. François Rabelais *in toto* but was, like other critics, interested in his activities, that he could discover no trace or echo of the Doctor, the last news of him being the resignation of his two livings. After this falls a profound silence, broken for the first time towards the spring of 1554 by a few poetic tributes and elegies proclaiming each and all that Rabelais is dead.

That such an outstanding, not to say notorious, figure in the contemporary French medical, humanist, and literary worlds, with a host of eminent friends and acquaintances and powerful Court contacts to boot, could thus vanish from circulation like a will-o'-the-wisp and expire so to speak anonymously seems incredible. But the fact is there. Plainly the Doctor must have died a natural death somewhere, and in his bed. Any fleeting mental visions of a Rabelais poisoned by monastic spies, stabbed by masked Sorbonne theologians up a dark alley—what a deprivation for the thoughtful that he never had contact with the

Jesuits—or kidnapped by Calvin's Tcheka and preached to death
by wild pastors in some dank Genevan dungeon may be reluctantly dismissed. He is assumed by most leading authorities to
have died some time in the last six months of 1553. Preferring
the date April 9, recorded in a surviving eighteenth-century
manuscript collection of epitaphs of the parish of St. Paul, in
which the Doctor died, M. Henri Clouzot may be right. M.
Clouzot likewise derives from the Prologue to the Fourth Book
the interesting and ingenious suspicion that for all his shout of
"hale, and cheery, and sound as a Bell", Dr. Rabelais may have
been in this year 1552 a sick man.

Pondering the Fourth Prologue afresh, one finds the plausibility
of M. Clouzot's suggestion growing swiftly. The Doctor's words
have a curiously familiar ring. His chief theme, recurrent and
urgent, is the essential priority of perfect physical health ("Without health life is not life," quotes Dr. Rabelais from one of his
beloved pagans, Antiphron the Sicyonian). The voice is so like
the voice of some evangelist of the Fitness Church booming from
the popular Press today that one half-expects the Doctor to slip
in a word about the new laxative to which he personally owes his
rosy cheeks. And suspicion increases. It is, I dare aver, axiomatic
that no normal healthy man fusses over health unless he is being
paid for it. Given this, it takes no titled specialist to diagnose
from such a manifesto that by the year 1552 one or both of those
dread bloodhounds on the trail of the elderly Renaissance epicurean, Gout and Cirrhosis by name, may well have caught up
with the *bon beuveur* at last, as they caught up with so many of
his contemporaries. Pain was their inevitable lot, and I think
we know the Doctor too well by now to be able to believe that
he would welcome and accept it with that eager supplicating cry
heard on a December morning of this same year on the desolate
island of Chang-chuenshan off the coast of China. "Lord!
More suffering!"—Dr. Rabelais would certainly have ranked
the dying servant of God Francisco Xavier, his fellow-priest,
among the mooncalves of Papimany.

With the assumption that he died in the parish of St. Paul,
near the Bastille, and was buried in the long-vanished cemetery
of that parish we are on solid ground. It was at the time, one
gathers, neither a very fashionable nor a very sanitary quarter,

so he may have been financially in low water at the end, unless Châtillon was as helpful a patron as his predecessors. One would like to think that the gratuity from Fezendat on publication of the Fourth Book was itself enough to keep the Doctor in comfort for the rest of his life; but sixteenth-century publishers may have been less impulsive in good works than they are today. We know nothing at all about any of these things; *nada, nada, nada, nada, nada,* like the beginning of the ascent to the Mount of Perfection as the greatest of Spanish mystics portrayed it in the 1570's—and how such an association of ideas would have sent Dr. Rabelais' eyebrows up.

Concerning the manner of his death there are two conflicting schools of reportage, each posthumous. The Rabelais Legend naturally exhibits him as gasping out scepticism and mockery with his last breath. In a contribution to it by, of all people, Francis Bacon, Lord Verulam—where Bacon got it nobody knows—the dying Doctor refers to the sacrament of Extreme Unction, just received, as "greasing my boots for the last journey", which might incidentally convey no gibe at all. In another story he receives a messenger from Cardinal Odet de Châtillon with cryptic words. "Tell Monseigneur in what state you find me. I go to seek a Great Perhaps (*un grand peut-être*). He is at the magpie's nest—tell him to stay there. As for you, you'll never be anything but a fool." Finally, of course, comes the great last laugh and the old allegedly-sceptical cry, "Draw the curtain, the farce is played!", which many a Franciscan preacher had uttered before him. On the other side we have the versions, likewise late—that is to say, towards the 1600's—of Antoine Duverdier in his *Prosopographie*, of the usually reliable Guillaume Colletet, and of Guy Patin, this last quoting the thoroughly integritous Fay d'Épesse, whose magistrate-father was among Rabelais' intimates. All these echoes testify that Dr. Rabelais yielded up his errant soul to God and died a penitent and a Catholic, *touché de repentance, en fidèle chrétien,* like Felix Randal in the poem.

> Sickness broke him. Impatient he cursed at first, but mended,
> Being anointed and all; though a heavenlier heart began some
> Months earlier, since I had our sweet reprieve and ransom
> Tendered to him. Ah well, God rest him all road ever he offended!

Anyhow Dr. Rabelais was dead, at the age of round about sixty, before the spring of 1554, when the poets began publishing their elegiacs. It is significant that in the best-known of these Pierre de Ronsard, then aged thirty, paints the Doctor very closely after the Puits-Herbault portrait: a red-nosed Silenus, all belching and booziness. A little of Ronsard's long *jeu d'esprit*, one of his lesser ones, will illustrate the approach:

> Si d'un mort qui pourri repose
> Nature engendre quelque chose,
> Et si la generation
> Se faict de la corruption,
> Une vigne prendra naissance
> De l'estomac et de la panse
> Du bon Rabelais qui buvoit
> Tousjours ce pendant qu'il vivoit . . .
>
> Jamais le Soleil ne l'a vu
> Tant fust-il matin, qu'il n'eust bu,
> Et jamais au soir la Nuict noire,
> Tant fust tard, ne l'a vu sans boire,
> Car altéré sans nul séjour
> Ce galant buvoit nuít et jour . . .
>
> Il chantoit la grande massue
> Et la Jument de Gargantua,
> Le grand Panurge, et le pays
> Des Papimanes ébahis,
> Leurs loix, leurs façons et demeures,
> Le Frère Jean des Entommeures,
> Et d'Epistème les combats;
>
> Mais la Mort, qui ne buvoit pas,
> Tira le Beuveur de ce monde,
> Et ores le faict boire de l'onde
> Qui fuit trouble dans le giron
> Du large fleuve d'Acheron.[1]

[1] "If from a body lying rotten-ripe Nature engenders anything, if generation springs from corruption, then a vine will be born from the belly and paunch of the good Rabelais, who drank all the days of his life . . . Never the sun has seen him, however early, unless he had drunk; never dark Night at eventide, however late, has seen him not drinking; for with a thirst without surcease this gallant drank

The Latin epitaph by twenty-five-year-old Joachim du Bellay, who had known the Doctor in Rome, is shorter and soberer, concentrating nevertheless on the epicurean and Lucianesque Rabelais exclusively.

> . . . Fuit ars mihi cura medendi,
> Maxima ridenda sed mihi cura fuit.
> Tu quoque non lacrymas sed risum hic solve, viator,
> Si gratus nostris manibus esse cupis.[1]

Which theme Ronsard's friend Antoine de Baïf echoed in a verse-collection published twenty years later:

> O Pluton, Rabelais reçoy!
> Afin que toy qui es le roy
> De ceux qui ne rient jamais,
> Tu aies un rieur désormais.[2]

Jacques Tahureau's address to the Learned Rabelaisian Nose, published on May 1, 1554, I have quoted at the beginning of the previous chapter. A dash of the final sceptic of the Legend is perceptible in the concluding lines:

> Et de ceux même en mourant se moquoyt
> Qui de sa mort prenoyent quelque soucy.[3]

Nobody, it is interesting to observe, extols the doctor of medicine; in fact, the venomous Scaliger will take the opportunity of damning his dead confrère ere long for a charlatan. Nobody extols the scholar and humanist either, oddly enough, and it goes without saying that there is nobody likely to extol the friar, the monk, or the priest. The Doctor's enduring bequest to the

---

night and day . . . He sang the great club and the Mare of Gargantua, the great Panurge, and the country of the gaping Papimanes, their laws, customs, and dwellings, Friar John of the Chops and the combats of Epistemon . . . But Death, which did not drink, drew the Drinker from this world, and now makes him quaff of the wave which flows murkily into the bosom of the great River Acheron."

[1] "The cult of healing was my concern; innnitely more the cult of mirth. If you wish to please my shade, traveller, burst not into tears but laughter."
[2] "O Pluto, welcome Rabelais, so that you, King of the Mirthless, may possess one jester henceforth!"
[3] "And dying, he mocked even at those mourning for his passing."

world was, and is, the Four Books, and it is not without interest that François Duc de Guise, on taking over a naval squadron at Dieppe in 1557, christened one of his new ships *Pantagruel*. After Rabelais' death the pirates fell avidly on his works once more as they have always done. There can be no better tribute to his spell, which has worked on so many diverse kinds of intellect ever since. Many of high quality have, of course, continued to resist it equally. There have been not a few of the great whom the Doctor has failed to charm; among those saying so it is no surprise to find St. François de Sales, patron of all literary men, himself among the luminaries of classic French prose. For him as for any saint a fitting title for the Four Books would be *Introduction à la Vie Indévote*—yet what Catholic in his five senses would ever dream of taking Father Rabelais for his spiritual director?

So, at least by the end of 1553, the Doctor had ended a busy and chequered career, and his friends and admirers might well express their hopes in the manner of Donne, versified by Pope:

> I die in Charity with Fool and Knave,
> Secure at least of Peace beyond the Grave;
> I've had my Purgatory here betimes,
> And paid for all my Satires, all my Rhymes . . .

Somewhere under the Rue des Jardins-Saint-Paul in the Fourth Arrondissement, to some of whose old houses clings a curious aura of mystery and melancholy, may lie a handful of Rabelaisian dust (the inscription on the façade of No. 2 is certain of it). Among the more commonplace meditations which have occurred to me in this street is one I continue to find a stimulant. Whatever depths of scepticism, doubt, and denial the Doctor may have plumbed, especially in the days when his boon-companions were one or two of the leading *libertins* in France, he rejected the last folly of Dolet and his kind. "I believe," affirms Pantagruel in the Fourth Book, "that all intellectual Souls are exempted from Atropos's Scissors". If intact, the Doctor's skull must be still grinning at a gaggle of solemn atheists who persist in claiming him for one of their own.

But not immediately was our turbulent Doctor to be vouchsafed a quiet grave.

2

Rabelais dead ? Not so ! Between these covers
His finest wit once more expands and hovers,
Wafting this message from beyond the Portal,
To make his name more precious and immortal !

Well may the *aficionados* have rolled agreeably-astonished eyes one spring day in 1562, nine years after his death, on being handed by their booksellers a slim volume entitled *L'Isle Sonante* ("Ringing Island"), just published; a carelessly-printed little book of sixteen chapters lacking a publisher's name but flaunting the Doctor's familiar hallmark, with the above-quoted verse in French introducing it. These four lines are cryptically signed *Nature Quite*. In four centuries nobody has succeeded in penetrating behind the mask.

Contemporary suspicions have been adopted by the best modern scholarship. *L'Isle Sonante*, styled by those who accept it *The Fifth Book of Pantagruel*, is almost certainly a Calvinist tract. The second edition of 1564, expanded to forty-eight chapters, a few of them less virulently anti-Catholic than the opening ones, does not shake the conclusion that the deceased Doctor had been exploited by a propagandist lacking his verve and buoyancy and, most notably, that fundamental bonhomie underlying all his truculence. *L'Isle Sonante* is a bitter book, full of hate; a gift, one need scarcely add, to Translator Peter Le Motteux, whose embellishments go beyond decency. The accents of Geneva ring from its pages very clearly—or rather, the accents of some French camp-follower of Calvin employing tactics to which the stern and upright Henri Estienne, one of the two or three "possibles" to whom its authorship has been tentatively attached in desperation, would certainly never have stooped.[1] I have been able to find no record of its being condemned by the Sorbonne, a fate inevitable and far more deserved than by any of the Four Books. Greater issues were preoccupying the French nation at the time. Censure and even suppression by decree of the Parlement of Paris may have gone unnoticed.

Whether or not somebody had gone through Dr. Rabelais'

---

[1] See Appendix C: Ringing Island.

private papers at his death and abstracted a few of his rough notes for a sequel to the Fourth Book, *L'Isle Sonante* was launched at what may be called, for its author's purpose, the psychological moment. Early in 1562 the long-impending civil war broke out at last, despite feverish last-moment struggles to avert it by Catherine de Médicis, again Regent of France during the minority of Henri II's recent successor, the boy Charles IX. The stout queen-mother, half a Medici, half Auvergnat—the Shopkeeper's Daughter, as some of the French nobility called her, looking down their finely-shaped noses at her family's commercial enterprise—is being at last awarded her due by French historians. With all her imperiousness, Italian love of intrigue, and frequent lack of scruple, Catherine was neither foolish, bigoted, hasty, nor cruel. As Lucien Romier puts it, all she wanted was peace, "the safeguard at all costs of the Monarchy's prerogative and her children's inheritance".

These were now in danger, a singular experiment by Catherine having failed to destroy the roots of conflict. Her attempt to bring about agreement on the Sacrifice of the Mass and other fundamentals at what is called the Colloquy of Poissy (1561) is unique in history; the assembly of Catholic and Calvinist divines soon broke up in tumult, as anyone could have foreseen. After a bloody clash between rival factions in the following March at Vassy, immediately claimed by one side as a massacre instigated by the Duc de Guise, the Calvinists of France took arms under Louis de Bourbon, Prince de Condé, that hump-backed, ambitious, talkative, amorous little nobleman, about whom the Parisian populace were soon singing a derisive song.

> O ce petit homme tant joly!
> Toujours cause et toujours rit,
> Toujours baise sa mignonne,
> Dieu garde d'mal le petit homme![1]

With twenty thousand well-armed troops behind him Condé wasted no time in first steps to the throne. Orleans was occupied, the cathedral sacked and burned, and Calvinist appeals for help

[1] "O, what a charming little man! Always talking, always laughing, always kissing sweethearts true—God keep the little man from rue!"

sent out to Germany and England. South of the Loire meanwhile many of the nobility and gentry had seized gladly on a pretext for settling old feuds, and whole towns were soon to be involved by the furious Gaul on either side. To Paris, the principal Catholic stronghold all through the war, François de Guise had recently removed from Fontainebleau the queen-mother and the boy king, whose lives were now in peril.

In this year 1562, therefore, the moment—on one side—was ripe for a little brisk anti-Roman propaganda over the signature of the celebrated Rabelais, his break with Geneva and Calvin's fearful counterblast notwithstanding. The main outlines of *L'Isle Sonante* were obviously indicated. At the end of the Fourth Book Dr. Rabelais had left Pantagruel and his companions dangling their legs off the Island of Ganabim, with their voyage to the Shrine of the Holy Bottle only half completed. They were now to up anchor again and attain their goal.

So the tall galleon *Thalamege* and her escort sail, and after three days out the ears of the flagship's passengers are bombarded by a confused noise coming over the sea, "not unlike the Sound of great, middle-siz'd, and little Bells rung all at once, as 'tis customary at Paris, Tours, Gergeau, Nantes, and elsewhere on high Holidays"; one of Dr. Rabelais' pet aversions, we may recall. These are the myriad bells of Ringing Island, on which they land a day later to be greeted by a "diminutive little old Hermit" named Braguibus. Having served them a meagre meal —it is, he explains, one of the fasting or Ember Weeks—the hermit Braguibus hands them over to one Master Aeditus, "a little quear old Fellow, bald-pated, with a Snout whereat you might easily have lighted a Card-match, and a Phiz as red as a Cardinal's Cap", who is to be their guide and cicerone.

Master Aeditus is not the only queer inhabitant of Ringing Island. They soon discover it to be the home of hundreds of strange opulent singing-birds in magnificent bell-hung cages, male and female, all of varied colours and marvellously human in appearance and habit; the males being classified by Aeditus as Clerghawks, Monkhawks, Priesthawks, Abbothawks, Bish-hawks, and Cardinhawks, the female species as Clergkites, Nun-kites, Abbesskites, Priestkites, Bishkites, and Cardinkites. There is also a "mongrel Species" called Knighthawks, strongly resembling the Knights of Malta, owning rich Commanderies and "embroidered over the Phiz with Carbuncles, Pushes, and Pockroyals", due to their being "pretty apt to be toss'd on the Salt Deep", as in fact the Turk knew to his cost. Ruling over all is the great Popehawk, a species by himself, living apart and viewed only with difficulty. All these fortunate birds live in luxury, gluttony, and idleness on offerings from their dupes abroad, their only activity being to sing loudly in chorus whenever a bell on each cage is rung. Their ranks are recruited mainly from the "younger Fry" of large families, metempsychosised into birds by mumbled incantations; not one of these but is "either crooked, crippled, blinking, limping, ill-favoured, deform'd or an Unprofitable Load to the Earth" before transformation. On this theme the author of *L'Isle Sonante* lingers with relish. Not a few lay choirmasters should appreciate his description of the Church's plainsong, monastically rendered, as "bellowing out some Cataretes and Scythropys, curs'd, lamentable, and wretched Imprecations as were usually offer'd to the Arimanian Daemon". Under the Calvinist dispensation in France, it may be remembered in this connection, all psalms and hymns were and are sung in the vernacular to tunes other than plainsong, and doubtless so exquisitely that the listener's soul, like the soul of Fray Luis de León ravished by the music of Francisco Salinas, sails on a sea of sweetness.

> Aqui la alma navega
> Por un mar de dulzura . . .

Yet at a Sunday-afternoon Vespers sung by the Benedictines of Solesmes, Montserrat, Sant' Anselmo in Rome or Ampleforth in Yorkshire, it has occurred to me to suspect the author of *Ringing Island* of a trifle of exaggeration. He fails, moreover, to make as much of this onslaught as he might have done. Tempestuous Friar John, who so heartily expresses Dr. Rabelais' view of plainsong when he storms into choir in the First Book to interrupt the Office with news of the invaded vineyards ("But these responses that you chant here, by G——, are not in season! . . .") misses his cue and stands dumb as a fish.

Even thus early in the book, I think, disappointment and suspicion must have set in for many of the critical. During Master

Aeditus' exposition so far a few questions and comments have come from Panurge, Friar John, and Pantagruel. From these we perceive how strikingly the three companions have deteriorated since Dr. Rabelais left them. All Pantagruelism has evaporated. Pantagruel himself, diminished almost to insignificance, rarely opens his mouth. The aggressive Panurge is about as Panurgeish in the old gay way as a gunman with dyspepsia, and the flamboyant crest of Friar John is considerably cut, as his latest style reveals:

> After we had pretty well staid our Stomachs with some tight Snatches, Fryar Jhon said to Aeditus: For ought I see, you have none but a parcel of Birds and Cages in this Island of yours and the Devil-a-bit of one of them all that sets his Hand to the Plough, or tills the Land whose Fat he devours. Their whole Business is to be frolick, to chirp it, to whistle it, to warble it, to sing it, and roar it merrily Night and Day. Pray then, if I may make so bold, whence comes this Plenty and Overflowing of all dainty Bits and goods Things which we see among you? From all the other world (return'd Aeditus), if you except some part of the Northern Regions, who of late Years have stirr'd up the Jakes. Mum! they may chance ere long to rue the Day they did so; their Cows shall have Porrage and their Dogs Oats; there will be Work made among them, that there will. Come, a Fig for't, let's drink . . .

When at long last the travellers are privileged to take a private glimpse of the great Popehawk, just before quitting the island, we see how Panurge has changed also.

> Pantagruel earnestly desir'd to see the Popehawk, but Aeditus told him, it was not such an easie matter to get a sight of him. How (ask'd Pantagruel), has he Plato's Helmet on his Crown, Gyges's Ring on his Pounces, or a Chameleon on his Breast, to make him invisible when he pleases? No, Sir, (return'd Aeditus), but he is naturally of pretty difficult Access; however, I'll see and take care that you may see him if possible. With this he left us piddling; then within a quarter of an Hour came back, and told us the Pope-hawk is now to be seen. So he led us, without the least Noise, directly to the Cage, wherein he sate drooping, with his Feathers staring about him, attended by a Brace of little Cardinhawks and six lusty fusty Bishhawks. Panurge star'd at him like a dead Pig,

examining exactly his figure, Size, and motions. Then with a loud
Voice he said, A Curse light on the Hatcher of this ill Bird; o'
my Word, this is a filthy Whoophooper! Tush, speak softly (said
Aeditus) by G——, he has a Pair of Ears, as formerly Michel de
Metiscone remark'd. What, then (return'd Panurge), so hath a
Whoopcat. Sho! (said Aeditus), if he but hear you speak another
such blasphemous Word, you had as good be damn'd. Do you
see that Basin yonder in his Cage? Out of it shall sally Thunder-
bolts and Lightnings, Storms, Bulls, and the Devil and all, that
will sink you down to Peg-Trantums an hundred Fathoms under
Ground. 'Twas better to drink and be merry, quoth Fryar Jhon.

A partly unquotable passage for a seemly page follows, Panurge
having suddenly spied what he takes to be a "Madgehowlet"
under the Popehawk's cage. "What damn'd cousening, gulling,
and Coney-catching have we here?" On being convinced by
Aeditus that the bird is not a female one—surely an extraordinary concession—he resumes:

May we not hear the Popehawk sing (ask'd Pantagruel)? I dare
not promise that (return'd Aeditus) for he only sings and eats at
his own time. So don't I (quoth Panurge); poor Pilgarlic is fain
to make every Body's time his own; if they have time, I find time.
Come, then, let us go drink if you will.

Abandoning the Popehawk's presence then, and without
ceremony, they perceive on the way to their drinking-bout
"an old greenheaded Bishhawk, who sat moping with his Mate
and three jolly Bittern-Attendants, all snoring under an Arbor.
Near the old Chuff stood a buxom Abbesskite, that sung like any
Linnet". And Panurge waxes truculent again:

Quoth Panurge: This Pretty Cherubin of Cherubins is here breaking
her Head with chanting to this huge, fat Ugly-face, who lies grunting
all the while like a Hog as he is. I'll make him change his Note
presently, in the Devil's Name. With this he rang a bell that hung
over the Bishhawk's Head; but, tho' he rang and rang again, the
Devil-a-bit Bishhawk would hear; the louder the sound, the louder
his snoring. By G—— (quoth Panurge), you old Buzzard, if you
won't sing by fair Means, you shall by foul. Having said this, he
took up one of St. Stephen's Loaves, *alias* a Stone, and was going to

hit him with it about the Middle. But Aeditus cryed to him, Hold, hold, honest Friend! Strike, wound, poyson, kill, and murther all the Kings and Princes in the World, by Treachery or how thou Wilt, and as soon as thou wouldst; unnestle the Angels from their Cockloft; Popehawk will pardon thee all this. But never be so mad as to meddle with these Sacred Birds, as much as thou lov'st the Profit, Welfare, and Life not only of thy self, and thy friends and Relations alive or dead, but also of those that may be born hereafter to the thousandth Generation.—Cat-so! let us rather drink then, quoth Panurge. He that spoke last spoke well, Mr. Antitus, quoth Fryar Jhon; while we are looking on these Devilish Birds, we do nothing but blaspheme, and while we are taking a Cup, we do nothing but praise God. Come on then, let's go drink; how well that word sounds.

This is not the Panurge of the "Papimany" chapters of the Fourth Book—the Panurge of relative courtesy, of relative respect at least for the papal office, and of final generosity; still less the Panurge of the Third Book, shocked by the aged Raminogrobis' rejection of the Church's last rites and vowing to save his soul despite himself. Panurge has changed into a Calvinist type, full of bile and acridity, who might have helped to write the Placards and sack Orleans Cathedral. A great deal more than the old *panache* has gone.

Nothing more in Ringing Island need detain us overlong. The heat is turned for a space on the lawyers of the Cour des Comptes on the Island of Apedeftes or Ignoramuses; a breed detested by *la Religion* as the tools of Rome, so it would seem from some bitter lines by Agrippa d'Aubigné, the only front-rank poet French Calvinism has yet produced. Thence the Pantagruelists sail to the Isle of Tools, in which all the trees bear lethal but apparently unsectarian cutlery; thence to the Isle of Sharping, tenanted by gambler-devils characteristically up to Romish goings-on; for having been allowed, after "sweetening up the Syndics of the Place", to view the celebrated relic of the *Sang Real*, or Holy Grail, Pantagruel and his companions are shown, amid a blaze of candles, and with a thousand "antick Tricks", nothing more impressive than "the ill-fac'd Countenance of a roasted Cony". So and thence they sail on to the Island of the Furred Cats, another nest of Popish lawyers, ruled by the terrible

Grippeminaud, or Gripe-men-all. The diabolical activities of the Furred Cats exceed even those of Rome itself, as the author, ably seconded by Le Motteux, hastens to warn us in advance.

> If ever Plague, Famine, War, Fire, Earthquakes, Inundations or other Judgments befal the World, do not attribute them to the Aspects and Conjunctions of the Malevolent Planets, to the Abuses of the Court of Romania, or the Tyranny of Secular Kings and Princes, to the Impostures of the false Zealots of the Cowl, Heretical Bigots, False Prophets, and Broachers of Sects, to the Vilany of griping Usurers, Clippers, and Coiners, or to the Ignorance, Impudence and Imprudence of Physicians, Surgeons, and Apothecaries . . . but charge 'em all wholly and solely to the inexpressible, incredible, and inestimable Wickedness and Ruin which is continually hatch'd, brew'd, and practis'd in the Den of these Furr'd Law-Cats.

The blast for competitive sects may be noted; it was a constant theme with Geneva as with every rival citadel of the Reform at this period.

Bidding farewell to the Furred Cats at last after an uncomfortable stay—Grippeminaud incidentally scares Pantagruel more than his companions—the travellers arrive at the Island of Quinte-Essence, or Kingdom of Entelechy, from the Aristotelian ἐγτελέχεια, "perfection"; a vogue-word with the literary horde at this period, applied in his youthful enthusiasm by the great Ronsard ("N'estes-vous pas ma seule Entelechie?") to his first love, Cassandre. "Entelechie" is the name of Queen Whims, a god-daughter of Aristotle who rules Quinte-Essence and heals the incurable with a song. The officers of the Household are likewise adept at whimsy feats, such as turning blackamoors white by rubbing their bellies with a basket, protecting the moon from wolves, milking he-goats, teaching cows to dance, curing the syphilitic (somebody has remembered the Doctor's pet theme) with a touch from a wooden shoe, and netting cock-lobsters from the wind; not to omit a valuable exercise since developed on a modest scale by Hollywood, namely the metamorphosis of "old, weather-beaten, over-ridden, toothless, blear-eyed, tough, wrinkled, shrivell'd, tawny, mouldy, decrepit Hags, Beldams, and walking Carcasses" into exquisite young beauties, "juicy, tight, brisk, buxom, proper, kind-hearted, and right as my Leg".

For the wonders of Entelechy so charm the sour author of *Ringing Island* that he breaks here, as Dr. Rabelais did on occasion, into his story himself. His tedious next three chapters, describing at excessive length the dinners, balls, and "tourneys" of Queen Whims and her Court, have at least the merit of keeping his mind for a space off Rome.

From the Kingdom of Entelechy Pantagruel and his company sail on to the Island of Odes, another un-propagandist and rather agreeable episode, all too brief. In this island the roads run literally up and down and are terrified of the highwaymen infesting them. Returning to their ship the Pantagruelists meet three of these gentry on their way to be broken on the wheel, and see a fourth "burn'd with a ling'ring Fire" for beating a defenceless road and breaking down one of its sides. After which the attack on Rome is vigorously resumed with the landing on the Isle of Sandals, tenanted by an order of grossly lecherous, gluttonous, idle, cynical, monosyllabic and altogether revolting "Semiquaver Fryars", representing the old Rabelaisian formula raised to the n-th and injected with most un-Rabelaisian venom. After two lengthy chapters of spite the summing-up snarl is left to Epistemon. "Truly, truly, this Rascally Monastical Vermin all over the World mind nothing but their Guts, and are as ravenous as any Kites." Following which one more of the master's inhibitions is exploited and magnified in the shape of a long diatribe against Lent, at the end of which Epistemon again sums up savagely:

> All Distempers are sow'd in Lent; 'tis the true Seminary and native Bed of all Diseases; nor does it only weaken and putrefie Bodies, but it also makes Souls mad and uneasie, for then the Devils do their best and drive a subtle Trade, and the Tribe of Canting Dissemblers come out of their holes. 'Tis then Term-time with your cucullated Pieces of Formality that have one face to God, and another to the Devil; and a wretched clutter they make with their Sessions, Stations, Pardons, Syntereses, Confessions, Whipping, Anathematizations, and much Prayer, with as little Devotion . . .

How such an outburst could be attributed to Rabelais passes comprehension. The mark of the sixteenth-century Calvinist pamphleteer at his most malignant is stamped on every phrase.

Their next port of call is in the Land of Satin, where the scenery is of woven tapestry, like its fantastic and heraldic birds and animals, and all the perpetually-blooming trees, shrubs, and fruits are of "Damask and flower'd Velvet". Here the Pantagruelists encounter tiny, blind, palsied, misshapen, chattering old Gaffer Hearsay, with his sevenfold tongue and myriad ears, keeping an open-air school for a score or more of every species of historian, traveller, geographer, and encyclopaedist down the ages from Herodotus, Pliny, and Pomponius Mela via St. Albert the Great and Marco Polo to Jacques Cartier, himself apparently among the world's yarn-spinners. Having sufficiently observed all this, Pantagruel and his companions re-embark and press on, and at length make Lanternois, Lantern Land, whose lighthouses are seen flashing from far out at sea. Here, introduced by two "Lanterns of Honour", they have an audience of the dazzling Queen Lantern at the palace and are invited to sup with the Court on "large Christmas-candles", the Queen and the Lanterns of the Blood-Royal being served with thick waxen torches, whereby all present on finishing supper shine most brilliantly. Next day, piloted by a Lantern of the nobility, they reach the Island and the Temple of the Holy Bottle, as impressive with costly marbles and precious stones as may be imagined, involving nine descriptive chapters. Here the Noble Priestess of the Bottle, Bacbuc by name, receives and admits them, by proper degrees, to the Shrine.

And having brought its voyagers to their desired goal, *Ringing Island* collapses disconcertingly with the "pff" of a dying toy balloon. All Pantagruel, Panurge, and Friar John get from the Holy Bottle in the way of a message, after their arduous exertions and a deal of elaborate initiation in the temple itself, is the word "Trinc". This *fin mot* is interpreted to them in due course by the Priestess Bacbuc in these terms:

"Trinc" is a Panomphean Word, that is, a word understood, us'd and celebrated by all Nations, and signifies "Drink". I don't say Drinking, taking that Word singly and absolutely in the strictest Sense. No, Beasts might then put in for a Share: I mean drinking cool delicious Wine. For you must know, my Beloved, that by Wine we become Divine; neither can there be a surer Argument, or a less

I

deceitful Divination. Your Academics assert the same when they make the Etymologie of Wine, which the Greeks call $OINO\Sigma$, to be from *Vis*, Strength, Vertue, and Power; for 'tis in its power to fill the Soul with all Truth, Learning, and Philosophy.

If you observe what is written in Ionian Letters on the Temple Gate, you may have understood that Truth is in Wine. The Goddess-Bottle therefore directs you to that divine Liquor; be your self the Expounder of your Undertaking.

From which it may be observed that although the Oracle of the Holy Bottle, unlike most oracles, has expressed itself briefly and clearly, its priestess has taken a different line. "Drink [secular] knowledge," the Oracle is interpreted as meaning by the learned in chorus, no doubt accurately. "Drink, then do what you fancy you want to do," seems to be Bacbuc's gloss in simple language; but the effort to discover what the author exactly implies has given the learned many headaches, and every explanation seems to have occurred to them except what seems a reasonable one, namely that the Doctor's unknown successor had himself not the faintest idea of what he was driving at, being possibly drunk at the time. And to me the fiasco, in two senses, of this climax, which even kindly M. Plattard calls "disappointing" (". . . dreadful Mysteries, as well in what concerneth our Religion as matters of the publicke State, and the life oeconomical"—oh, Doctor!), is one more morsel of evidence that Dr. Rabelais did not write the so-called "Fifth Book". He has his own woolly periods, but he could have contrived a better finale than this.

So, at any rate, *L'Isle Sonante* ends, not with a bang but a whimper, and the Pantagruelists—a trifle chapfallen as I see them, since they might just as well have stayed at home—take leave of the Holy Bottle and its Priestess and make their way through a country "fair as Touraine" to the port where the ships are waiting, and embark for home. It can hardly be said that their pilgrimage has achieved much. Panurge in fact has not put his great question to the Holy Bottle after all—or at least in so many words, having merely recited before the shrine, "between two Stools placed there for that purpose, his Arse upon the Ground", some formal lines taught him by Bacbuc:

O Bouteille,
Pleine toute
De mystères,
Je t'escoute:
Ne diffères,
Et le mot profères
Auquel pend mon coeur . . .

Which Le Motteux renders:

Bottle! whose Mysterious Deep
Does ten thousand Secrets keep,
With attentive Ear I wait,
Ease my Mind and speak my Fate . . .

Getting no answer in any case but "*Trinc*", he is left none the wiser, and as for the Priestess Bacbuc's unhelpful variations, one might well imagine a deceived and infuriated Panurge telling her what to do with them in blunt and soldierly terms. However, this reasonable development is evaded by the author of *L'Isle Sonante*, and Panurge, poor dupe, is allowed to hug the illusion ("Ere long, my Friends, I shall be wedded . . .") that the Holy Bottle has solved his problem. One may add that his manners, never good, have badly deteriorated since approaching the Holy Bottle, like Friar John's. Under the influence of a draught of "miraculous Liquor" drawn from the Sacred Fountain and offered by Bacbuc in a huge silver flask resembling a breviary, the pair of them break in her presence into a *fureur poëticque* of rhyming doggerel at once dull, blasphemous, and dirty. And in what fashion—undescribed—the noble Priestess receives Friar John's cry of "Sweetheart, do but teach me how the Devil you make it!" one would be interested to know. With, perhaps, a playful shove? A saucy slap? The Friar's cry smacks woundily of Captain Foulenough making the pace at a cocktail-party. The strangest thing of all is (to me) that so much witless stuff can be approached and discussed by men of intelligence as solemnly as if it were a priceless new codex of Plato. Might this be part of Heaven's punishment for burning too many joss-sticks before the Great Renaissance Thinker's shrine?

3

It was reserved for a leading critic of the 1840's, Paul Lacroix, to charge Dr. Rabelais with an even more serious literary crime than *L'Isle Sonante*. To anyone who has battled his way through Béroalde de Verville's breathless, graceless, anonymous work *Le Moyen de Parvenir*, compared by Arthur Machen to a Gothic nightmare composed exclusively of gargoyles, Lacroix' attempt to attach it to the Doctor's achievement will seem fantastic as a flight of Cocqcigrues.

De Verville is a minor Rabelais gone to seed; epicurean, sceptic, practitioner in indiscriminate mockery on the same Lucianesque plan; "libertine and debauchee", says the sober Guillaume Colletet. Born and bred a Calvinist—his father, a Genevan pastor and a man of culture, was a friend of Scaliger's—he later turned Catholic in his own interests, took Orders, and succeeded in 1593, despite Tridentine discipline, in slipping into a canonry of Tours Cathedral. His principal and only surviving work, *Le Moyen de Parvenir* ("The Way to Attain"), may be described as one of the world's greasier literary offerings, *livres de haute graisse*, or what secondhand booksellers catalogue as "curious". It consists of a hundred and eleven bizarre and disconnected dialogues, each decorated haphazard with a fancy title—*Mappemonde, Apostille, Elegie, Reprise, Folie, Plumitif*—having no bearing on anything whatsoever. Some critics give De Verville a good mark for vivacity and piquancy (his French is correct enough if sometimes none of the clearest), others consider him an obscene bore and blackguard. His scores of characters, all bearing historic names, classic and contemporary, devote themselves to capping pornographic anecdotes of a crude and jocular kind, padded out with obscure pedantry, some heavy badinage, and a myriad puns, mostly bad. Some of the stories are quite racily told, but an awful monotony is the prevailing note. Before long the victim feels like one doomed to listen to a huddle of Rotarians in a smoking-car on some endless train-journey through the deserts of Arizona. The Canon of Tours is the perfect prototype of a boozy bond-salesman out of a novel by Thomas Wolfe or Sinclair Lewis.

To M. Paul Lacroix came the theory that having discovered

in his father's library a bawdy manuscript by Rabelais, one of many circulating "under the mantle" at Court in the time of François I, Béroalde de Verville annexed and published it, with alterations and additions, as his own. Why a stiff Calvinist precisian like De Verville *père* should harbour such stuff M. Lacroix does not explain, and his attribution of this hypothetical manuscript to Dr. Rabelais is based on nothing more than a scrap of vague contemporary gossip. His singular fancy was blown to pieces without difficulty by Paulin Paris. The most cursory attention to *Le Moyen de Parvenir* reveals what a vapid mixture it is compared with the master's prose, and M. Paris' own theory that De Verville merely jotted down at night stories picked up during the day and eventually slung them together *ad lib.* seems reasonable enough. Many of his themes are filched from previous storytellers like Aretino, Poggio, Noël du Fail, Bonaventure des Périers, Sorel, Bois-Robert, and others; more than one from Rabelais himself. Ninety per cent of them naturally involve priests, monks, friars and nuns, but Calvinism and its pastors take a few knocks as well. The amiable Canon practises neither religion (or any other), and guffaws at the practitioners of both.

It would be unfair to dismiss *Le Moyen de Parvenir* as a total ragbag. Here and there at long intervals a glimmer of entertainment emerges—for example, towards the end of Dialogue LXXXIV ("Suite") in which the gay and swaggering Frostibus, Lieutenant-General of Hell, enters to drink with the company, at this moment including Sappho, Arnobius, Asclepiades, the Emperor Nero, Valden, and Dr. Martin Luther, whom he greets with a clap on the shoulder as an old friend. Ordered by Luther to (literally) get the hell out of it, Frostibus addresses the surly Reformer with easy charm. "My dear Luther, my captain, my friend—will you do me the favour of not damning any more souls? All my devils beg of you to lay off. Otherwise our accommodation people will have to start booking places in Purgatory. We've so many in hell already that quite a lot of my poor Staff devils have to sleep out." The elegant Frostibus is not quite so concise as this. De Verville is a master of verbiage. He sticks more to the point, for what that is worth, in Dialogue XCIX ("Histoire"), in which he brings Dr. François Rabelais himself into the company of Luther, Euclid, Poggio, the Spanish theologian Alfonso de Castro, Pyrrhus, Merlin, and one or two more. Dr. Luther is just finishing an anecdote about a baron and a needy musician; a dull story, but for once, by some miracle, a clean one.

RABELAIS: You've only half told that story.
LUTHER: 'Sblood, you're a fine bishop! In the name of a thousand devils, what's it got to do with you?
PYRRHUS: What's that you're saying? My old friend Rabelais has certainly been a bishop, and why not? He's as good as a lot of others that are or will be. Don't you know that only bishops and archbishops can administer confirmation, by the noble powers they have? Let me tell you our good Father Pseudo-Evangelico-Papistico-Anabaptistico here confirmed the mother of Gargantua, first named "Galemelle" by a late Bishop of Paris [Du Bellay] and renamed by Father Rabelais "Gargamelle".

So much for the learned Lacroix' attempt to implicate our Doctor in the kind of book he might conceivably have written in a mental home, but hardly otherwise. At the same time Béroalde de Verville's gibe—from which I have omitted two extra words, *Giesitaner-Briterono,* which doubtless had some contemporary significance but convey no meaning to me—demonstrates at least that if Dr. Rabelais' zigzags are noticeable to us, they were equally so to his own age; likewise, that forty years after his death his characters needed no explanatory footnote, which is not the lot of every popular romancer. It is perhaps remarkable, given his fame and the number of contemporary plagiarists, that barring *L'Isle Sonante* and the Lacroix-Verville fantasy no serious attempt has ever been made to saddle Dr. Rabelais with any rubbish of his own period or round about it, though a swarm of Calvinist hacks, particularly one Pierre Viret of Geneva, borrowed many of his themes—the "Papimany" one, naturally—and imitated his style, often closely. Two pieces queried or rejected by most competent critics seem to me on the other hand the sort of thing the Doctor might easily have written. One is a long stretch of French decasyllabics in the jargon of the Limousin Scholar, the other a diverting squib called *La Chresme*

Philosophale, "The Cream [or 'Chrism'] of Philosophy"; a sequence of a dozen parodies of the questions set for, and disputed publicly at the Sorbonne by, candidates for a final degree. Each beginning with the formal *Utrum,* they are for the most part in the language of Cloud-Cuckoo Land, and untranslatable. One of the more intelligible may serve as a specimen.

Whether a Platonic Idea flying clockwise under the Orifice of Chaos could expel the squadrons of the Democritic atoms . . .

His finest effort in this style, involving the diet of a chimera bombinating in a vacuum, he had used for the catalogue of the Library of St. Victor in the First Book. Its perennial value as a footnote to what is called the Best Contemporary Thought is patent.

So much for attempts to saddle the Doctor with literary crime. One can hardly omit mention, before passing on, of a curious contemporary artistic inspiration for which he was held—by what might be called an "interested party"—responsible, namely that collection of a hundred-odd fantastic drawings called *Les Songes Drôlatiques* ("Droll Daydreams") *de Pantagruel,* of which I once possessed a copy. Exploiting the sales of *L'Isle Sonante,* the Parisian publisher Richard Breton rushed these drawings out in 1565, claiming in the preface to have received them from the inventor, his old friend Maistre François Rabelais, in person, as his final work: an obvious trade-taradiddle which would hardly deceive a baby. The artist is not attempting to illustrate the Doctor's work but simply allowing a lush and eccentric fancy to play with whatever nightmarish impulses occur, in the manner of Hieronymus Bosch or of Cranach producing pictorial anti-papal propaganda for Luther. Most of the figures of the *Songes* are comic, some monstrous, some lewd; snouts and bellies and other organs of every size and shape predominate; grotesquely leering half-human birds of a vaguely-Cocqcigrue species play bagpipes, ring bells, and brandish pikes or toasting-forks; saucepans drool and flourish spoons; the noses and feet of monks and men-at-arms end in flutes, arquebuses, chamberpots, and so forth. The collection would make an admirable Christmas gift for a psychiatrist specialising in rich women's traumas. I believe the *Songes Drôlatiques* have their place in the early history of caricature. Master Breton's attempt to exploit Dr. Rabelais might be said to entitle them to an equally high place in the early history of publicity.

That the Doctor has, Balzac excepted, no modern prose imitator on the grand scale is not surprising; and there are times when, to me at least, even Balzac's masterly pastiche looks like a Gothic cathedral cleverly contrived in cast iron, stamped on every buttress with the hallmark of the romantic 1830's, and conveying the spirit of the Four Books about as much as Doré's grandiloquent illustrations convey the countryside of Touraine; one of the first disillusions of a Balzacian pilgrim must be the absence of mountains and abysses from the environs of Tours. Only a genius of Balzac's stature and vitality could have stridden in the Doctor's wake with such relative success, but how often does one not detect a bead or two of sweat glistening on the great Balzac's brow! How often do not some of the characters of the *Contes Drôlatiques* seem to be on the verge of doffing wigs and costume and wiping off the greasepaint in some theatre of the Boulevards before catching the last omnibus to Montmartre! With more native *élan*, I think, Léon Daudet was wont to enliven the leader-columns of the *Action Française* between two world-wars with a little invective which seems to me still of the true Rabelaisian vintage, fresh from the Caballine Fount.

> This gallimaufry of aged spinsters withered on the stalk, of pro-fessors of Patagonese, of babblers, of Cocqcigrues, of pastors frocked and unfrocked, of cockatoos in delirium, of unemployed typists, of peanut-merchants, of Red Indians, of squaws, of sangniers and sangnieroids,[1] of spirits with ectoplasm and protoplasm, of gastero-podic molluscs, of New Zealand slugs, of frock-coated tree-dwellers, and other brachycephalous troglodytes . . .

Thus Daudet's celebrated description, *circa* 1930, of the then-existent League of Nations, and from "the great swinge and rudeness of his poise" may be perceived that at least one French literary swashbuckler since Rabelais' day has been able to bend

---

[1] Referring to the "Christian Democracy" movement of the period, headed by Marc Sangnier.

the bow of Achilles. But whether the breed survives seems
doubtful.

4

As will hardly have escaped the notice of any reader who has
managed to continue thus far, the Rabelais emerging from these
pages differs, as promised, considerably from that viewed by a
group of scholarly figures on all-fours before the Doctor's shrine.
Many of these men of worth appear to me to be in a state of
hypnosis. The Renaissance, or perhaps their Renaissance, has
bedazed them. The least of its myriad pedants—Greek scholars
being then ten a penny, and after all any man of intelligence
and energy is capable of becoming a Greek scholar in a year or
two if he puts his whole mind to it—appear to them ten feet
high and the Doctor himself a portent and an oracle. Some
of the learned seem in fact, if one may say so politely, to
have eaten of that insane root which takes the reason prisoner,
and I am sufficiently lacking in reverence to find the spectacle
diverting. It may be that Dr. Rabelais would have done so
likewise.

He would simultaneously, I think, perceiving a strange lacuna
in the results of their labours which is common to practically all,
incline to agree with a remark of Étienne Gilson. Having done
a great deal of research in a field of Rabelaisiana in which he is
so far alone, M. Gilson is entitled to the observation that "before
commenting on a given text one should put oneself in the position
of understanding it". The insouciance with which not a few of
the learned assess and pass judgment on Dr. Rabelais' religious
position, quite plainly without having stooped to the slightest
acquaintance with Catholic theology, is to me an abiding amusement. Though young Rabelais undoubtedly never devoted one
scornful glance to a single page of the *Summa*, sufficient was retained in the language of the Franciscan schools during his La
Baumette days to enable M. Gilson to discover a few obvious
Thomist echoes in the Four Books; not to speak of echoes of
St. Bonaventure, Hugues de St. Victor, and Roger Bacon. To
M. Gilson's *Rabelais Franciscain* I would refer anyone welcoming
surprise and enlightment on this point. Of the theology absorbed
through his pores during the formative years at La Baumette

Dr. Rabelais never got rid. Hence, no doubt, some of his irritation with the theologians. Nothing, in some of the Doctor's moods, could have been more annoying.

I find other reasons to diverge from the learned. One, a serious one, is that so many of them seem not to know, or even to have imbibed from encyclopaedias, anything about high spirits. Why a master of red-blooded tomfoolery should prove an irresistible magnet for the glummest and most frigid types of don was for some time a puzzle to me, but is so no longer. The fascination of extremes, the little prim man swept inevitably into the clutch of a large flamboyant mate, even if he finds himself compelled at length to liquidate her, as Dr. Crippen did his Cora —surely this is explanation enough? Nevertheless, I resent these academic vultures. They should keep their claws off my beloved Doctor. Their proper meat is Mother Nature's prigs, Comte, Mill, Amiel, Emerson, Goethe, and suchlike (incidentally Emerson is unique—did he not have the courage once to admit that he and his friends were worse than fish?). One can endure the ritual darkness-into-light refrain and other nail-bitings and retrograde lunes—"mainte lune retrograde vos ongles mords avez", says Queen Whims of the Isle of Quinte-Essence to the Pantagruelists—but at attempts to express Panurge to three places of decimals it is time, I think, to draw a firm line and cry *holà*. Such a Rabelais is not mine, nor I think anybody's outside a laboratory.

Between my betters and myself the difference is, I find reluctantly, fundamental. The learned see a majestic Renaissance superman trailing clouds of glory and dispensing power and wisdom; I see a highly cultivated, brilliant, jolly, slightly alcoholic, quick-tempered member of the French professional bourgeoisie talking gloriously at high speed and occasionally making an ass of himself; for example, when expressing contempt for the enormous culture of the Middle Ages, which no man of sense could do in his right mind, and damning a monastic system which saved our whole civilisation once, and may have to do so again. No doubt the extravagant eulogies lavished on the Doctor from time to time by poetic friends are partly to blame for academic over-adulation. The routine Renaissance compliment-formula is surpassed only by the Chinese, and should not be

taken at face-value. He was undoubtedly a fine doctor of medicine, though I find medical histories do not echo the excited
fioriture of a Dolet or a Macrin, possibly because of the number
of much greater doctors flourishing contemporaneously. He was
undoubtedly a fine scholar, but fine scholars were common in
his day as blackberries, many of them as skilled as he in rein-
forcing their statements with a queue of imposing authorities
cited offhand in support. This is a consecrated trick of the trade,
practised now as then. Like Gibbon's performance with bogus
footnotes, it terrifies and subdues the reader very effectively unless
he is of that querulous, doubting, suspicious, and detestable type
which follows these things up.

I had more than once vaguely suspected our Doctor of reeling
off such lists without, possibly, having read all the authorities
he quotes, but since the point did not seem to occur to any of the
learned, suspicion seemed shameful and was allowed to fade.
The discovery at length that M. Henri Clouzot, having been
visited by the same doubts, had gone to the trouble of consulting
a few sources and caught Dr. Rabelais red-handed neither
shocked, therefore, nor grieved; it was fun, like catching one's
favourite uncle in the wine-cupboard at 3 a.m. Thus M. Clouzot,
in his critical and comprehensive preface to the Works (1922):

> Then there are the citations. What a multitude of authorities he
> quotes! His erudition seems enormous, beyond measure, and so it
> actually is. But look a trifle more closely. You will see that Rabelais
> often does not make his own researches but simply derives his
> citations from ancient polygraphs or contemporary humanists.
> Is it the story (III, 37) of the fool and the cookshop-proprietor?
> He invokes "Jo. André", a Papal rescript, the Panormitan, Barbatia,
> and Jason, omitting only to mention Tiraqueau, from whom he
> has lifted all his references. Is he discussing the legitimacy of a
> child born after its father's death? He appeals to Hippocrates,
> Pliny, Plautus, Varro, Censorinus, Aristotle, and Aulus Gellius;
> but he does not tell us that the authority last-named has furnished
> him with all his learned baggage.

Gare le moine, cornemuse de Buzançay! And Dr. Rabelais goes
perhaps to rather cynical lengths when he steals without acknow-
ledgement from Erasmus, More, Villon, and a dozen more sources

contemporary and ancient. As M. Clouzot affectionately remarks: "If one did not know the habits of the Sixteenth Century one might consider him the most audacious and conscienceless of plagiarists." But like his fellow-thieves Shakespeare, Molière, and so many more of the Immortals the Doctor enriches some of his loot a hundredfold and stamps it with his own seal.

Only those who have hoisted him on a pedestal as a great Renaissance intellectual force can be disconcerted by such things. As the long-suffering reader will hardly need reminding again, I read him for gorgeous entertainment and his Olympian moods affect me not at all. To appreciate the enormity of his comic genius one does not, I think, need textbooks by dons or instruction by diagram, and to be informed, for example, that the Doctor lacks the Critical Spirit, as he certainly does, like Flaubert and Dickens, distresses me in no way. As for his obscenities, I have already ventured to suggest that by and large and relatively they are as devoid of moral obliquity and harm as a manure-heap swept by breezes on a farm. Compared with sly immoralists like Sterne and Anatole France or a corrupter of youth like André Gide, Dr. Rabelais is a monument of probity. Like some of his medieval predecessors, and with a medical training to boot, he sees the comic side of the bodily functions, and no doubt tends to labour the joke overmuch in some aspects; but of itself it has no corruptive influence. Modern delicacy, and the priggish humbug thereto attached, carries a Manichee stink which is far more obnoxious. "Why," cried St. Vincent Ferrer, preaching on the Sixth Commandment, "should I be ashamed to name what Almighty God has not been ashamed to create?" On the same topic St. Odo of Cluny is equally frank; Huysmans has compared his celebrated analysis of the physical lures of women to a fishmonger's skinning of a rabbit. The terrible monk was far from jesting, but Gilson quotes a practical joke by a Florentine friar, Fra Detesalve, which Panurge himself might have conceived and carried out. To read Dr. Rabelais through the spectacles of the twentieth century is ridiculous, and if anything could possibly increase my esteem for Madame de Sévigné it would be the fact that this highly-bred great lady, with three saints in her family and an exquisite wit of her own, was one of Dr. Rabelais' *afición* in the chill and Jansenist seventeenth.

Which leads to the reflection that any roll-call of Dr. Rabelais' most illustrious admirers down the ages demands a footnote it rarely gets. That the large majority are sceptics, agnostics, atheists, or Protestants is natural enough, the Doctor having disliked not a few things they dislike themselves; nor would most of these notables trouble to distinguish, as Gilson and to some extent Plattard have distinguished, between what the Doctor attacks in *la chose catholique* and what he does not. Certainly this would never occur to a Voltaire, a Diderot, a Hugo, a Clemenceau, or an Anatole France; it may well have done so to Racine, Boileau, Chateaubriand, and Mme de Sévigné, as it did to Belloc and Chesterton. The Catholic Rabelaisian minority is in fact in a position to bring to the notice of the other side several misconceptions concerning the relations between the Doctor and his Church, and to produce evidence. I have never seen the flattering Brief of Paul III explained away. It was certainly not signed in ignorance of Dr. Rabelais' literary performances, and the fact that Paul III was no easygoing, art-loving Renaissance Pope of the type who could put up with an Aretino is not without significance. There is also, if it may be mentioned again, the argument of the Index, the latest edition of which (1948, supplement of 1954) lies before me. Satiric writers of celebrity listed by Rome as harmful to the simple and uninstructed, in whole or part, include Gide, Sartre, Voltaire, Diderot, Anatole France, and—since 1819—Sterne, but not François Rabelais. Old-fashioned thinkers to whom the Doctor is still "the man who wrote against the doctrines of the Church" might therefore revise their judgment with profit. The point that the Doctor never did anything of the sort was made within fifty years of his death. It has not as yet been made strongly or widely enough to attract the attention of those who do not welcome the idea; among them, it seems, being the late eminent politician Jaurès, whose verbs, as somebody said, were all in the future tense, and in whom Dr. Rabelais' Swinburnian paeans glorifying Man and his works in the Third Book roused such enthusiasm that he more than once acclaimed the Doctor publicly as a fellow Left Wing Socialist and a herald of the Red (or Pink) Dawn. To put these things right takes time.

So, *beuveurs très illustres et verolés très precieux*—how the great laughing voice rings down the centuries—the moment has come to bid Dr. François Rabelais farewell. I am well aware that I have not done him full justice, in the academic sense, in these pages. It is a sobering experience to turn again to the works of the learned and to perceive what they can make of the Doctor's lightest burp; thus fulfilling his own intention when he began to impress his public in the 1540's with the claim that behind all his "jests, mockeries, lascivious Discourse, and recreative Lies" were hidden solemn and awful secrets, adding mysterious hints of allegory and "Pythagorical Symbols". If a vulgar current phrase is permissible, my beloved Dr. Rabelais was shooting a line. There is nothing startling behind the buffoonery. For Renaissance thought one goes not to Rabelais but to More, Erasmus, Vivès, and their high company. And his pet theme is futile. Read otherwise than for pure entertainment, those per- petual attacks on his favourite Aunt Sally are merely silly and ignoble. Finer men than he were going to a horrible death in the garb he was deriding, and counting it an honour. "Cheerfully to carry the cross you shall lay upon us, never to despair of your recovery while we have a man left to enjoy your Tyburn, or to be racked with your torments, or consumed with your prisons— the expense is reckoned, the enterprise is begun; it is of God, it cannot be withstood"—the manly voice of one of Dr. Rabelais' English brethren shames into silence the jester who never de- liberately exposed himself to peril in any cause and was never without a powerful protector when he needed one. As *farceurs* go, even Henry VIII's fool Will Somers was ten times the man Dr. Rabelais was.

He is no godlike character, but who (barring the worshippers) deems him one? For every pint of wisdom he pours out a quart of nonsense, but who cares? Pen in hand he is incomparable. He is unique. He is magic. He is magnificent. He is gigantic. He dealt with the precise French language as no man has ever done before or since. Rightly is he called the father of modern French prose. His genius is like Niagara. Once having fallen under his spell it is impossible to throw it off. The Doctor's most baroque perversities—aptly might his memorial-card have quoted the *Tua nos, Domine, medicinalis operatio a nostris perversitatibus clementer expediat* from the Mass of the Seventh Sunday after

Pentecost, which he must have recited more than once at Fontenay—can offend only those handicapped in life's battle by lack of humour and charity alike.

A great artist, a supreme master . . . I wish (to echo the sigh of the biographer of Mr. Emmanuel Burden, merchant of the City of London), I could have written of him in nobler terms.

APPENDIX A

The Exchange of Habits

IN RABELAIS' "SUPPLICATIO PRO APOSTASIA", ADDRESSED TO Pope Paul III in 1536, the operative clause begins "presbyteri secularis habitu assumpto", etc.—"having assumed the habit of a secular priest he roved about, during this period devoting himself diligently to study at the Faculty of Medicine". This covers nine years' technical vagabondage and self-excommunication. How soon after leaving Geoffroy d'Estissac's employment did Rabelais discard his Benedictine habit?

In the absence of any evidence whatsoever the best conjecture seems to be that the exchange occurred during his first visit to Paris. M. Clouzot's theory that Rabelais assumed the secular habit immediately on beginning his wanderings, "now exercising his sacred functions, now utilising his medical knowledge in houses of his Order", raises one or two bristling difficulties. Flouting Canon Law and unable to produce any such passport as the equivalent of a modern *celebret*, Rabelais would hardly have been permitted to exercise "sacred functions" even if he had wanted to; at this time, moreover, would he have acquired sufficient medicine to practise, apart from the fact that ~very house of his Order had its *infirmarius* to begin with? I fall back, therefore, on the main body of theory, namely that if he did cast up at the Benedictine hostel in Paris, which would imply a Benedictine habit, he changed his lodging before long, assuming the secular habit he retained, unlawfully, till Paul III's Brief of absolution permitted him at his own prayer to resume that of St. Benedict. Into this hypothesis the discovery of his intrigue with the Parisian widow fits with the neat click of a jigsaw-puzzle piece.

The somewhat different troubles of Erasmus, a Canon Regular of St. Augustine and, like Rabelais, a clerk in Holy Orders, are interesting. Having been authorised to leave his monastery to become secretary to the Bishop of Cambrai in 1493, and having obtained permission, on going abroad, to exchange his surplice for a linen scapular "after the Parisian fashion", Erasmus was in due course nearly mobbed during a plague-epidemic in Bologna, where he was mistaken in the street for one of the attendants on the sick in strict quarantine. He then left off his scapular, and becoming worried at length about this, obtained papal absolution with a dispensation to wear either the correct Augustinian or a secular habit, as he chose. Visiting London in his Augustinian habit a little later and being warned that this dress was not popular with Henry VIII's myrmidons, he took advantage of his dispensation to discard it finally for that of a secular priest, which he wore to the end of his life.

Erasmus' anxiety to avoid scandal, in his own words—though Plattard rather oddly makes him "fling his Augustinian frock to the nettles"—and regularise his position may be contrasted with the laissez-faire of Dr. Rabelais, though the Doctor likewise knew moments of perturbation on this score. It may be observed, incidentally, that no penance incurred by cocking a snook at Canon Law for nine years is mentioned in the Brief. Penance would normally be a condition of absolution; and if dispensed in Rabelais' case, one more instance of Paul III's notable clemency towards him.

APPENDIX B

The Gargantua Puzzle

"PANTAGRUEL" WAS PUBLISHED TOWARDS THE END OF 1532. IN the Prologue Rabelais heartily commends to the reader a comic work, recently published, dealing with "the inestimable deeds of the great Gargantua". Of this "Gargantuine Chronicle" he adds that "the Printers have sold more in two months time than there will be bought of Bibles in nine years". Is he referring, with an apparently proprietorial air, to the anonymous rustic tale which inspired him to write *Pantagruel,* or to some *Gargantua* of his own already published?

Exhaustive and exhausting debate on this topic has produced no solution. The anonymous *Gargantua* came out some time in 1532; the Rabelaisian *Gargantua,* as we know it, in 1535. It is difficult to believe that Rabelais is claiming, even obliquely, authorship of the crude and heavy-handed little work of 1532. There may, on the other hand, be something in the theory that being attracted by its possibilities he had added a few facetious and experimental strokes to one of its many early editions. A publisher of the period would have no objection to employing embellishments by hacks to help sales along. In such case Rabelais would have had some interest in commending the anonymous *Gargantua,* to which *Pantagruel* claimed to be a sequel. His own *Gargantua,* meanwhile, may have been already on the stocks.

If the position is confusing, we may remind ourselves that the Doctor was fond of mystifications and masquerades. It has seemed to me most convenient to assume simply, with a number of good authorities, that he was referring in the *Pantagruel* prologue to the anonymous *Gargantua* of 1532, and to leave it at that.

APPENDIX C

Ringing Island

THE FIRST DISCOVERABLE CONTEMPORARY OPINION ON THE QUESTION whether *L'Isle Sonante* is Rabelais' work or not is conveyed in Étienne Tabourot's *Bigarrures* (1572), in which the alleged Fifth Book is referred to as "attributed to the inimitable Rabelais"; a significant reservation, which later in his pages (observes Plattard) Tabourot seems to have forgotten. Thirty-two years later Antoine Duverdier declared in his *Prosopographie* that *L'Isle Sonante* was the work of "a student of Valence". In the 1570's Duverdier had been attached for some time to the Du Bellay household, where he must have learned a great deal about the Doctor's doings, though he says nothing about his end. "His misfortune was that everybody wished to set his hand to pantagruelising," says Duverdier, "and many books have appeared in his name." In 1604 another adverse opinion was published —that of Louis Guyon, a Treasury official in the Limousin, in a work called *Divers Leçons*. Guyon is categoric. "I protest that he [Rabelais] did not write it, for it was composed a long time after his death. I was in Paris when it was written, and I well know who was the author of it. He was not a doctor." Guyon maintains, in addition, that Dr. Rabelais never in the strict sense attacked the Church, which is perfectly true. It is unfortunate that Guyon does not give the real author's name. No doubt he had his reasons for refraining.

Contrary opinions at much the same period are those of Guy Patin and Le Duchat, who thought the style and spirit of the book were those of the Doctor. This impression was contradicted at length in the 1840's by the critic Paulin Paris, who found in *L'Isle Sonante* none of the old Rabelaisian gaiety or other characteristics. Paris, moreover, discovered that the manuscript now in the Bibliothèque Nationale is not in Dr. Rabelais' hand. Later criticism has pointed out an allusion in *L'Isle Sonante* to Scaliger's attack on Rabelais, published in 1557, three or four years after the Doctor's death.

While judgment apparently remains still suspended among the learned, there seems every reason to accept Villey's hypothesis that the first edition of *L'Isle Sonante* was a Calvinist pamphlet hastily put together and rushed out as propaganda in 1562 at the beginning of the wars of religion, nine years after Rabelais' death. Enough of it has been quoted in these pages, I think, to leave no doubt of this intention and to justify the exclusion of *L'Isle Sonante* from the Rabelaisian Canon.

Efforts to discover the identity of the mysterious "*Nature Quite*", author of the introductory quatrain, have completely failed. Of three possible authors suggested vaguely from time to time a priest named Jean Quentin (of whose name "Nature Quite" is an anagram) has been ruled out by Plattard owing to his having been Orator for the Clergy at the States-General of 1566, therefore no ally of anti-Catholic propagandists. No. 2, a doctor named Jean de Mayerne, known as "Jean Turquet", may be dismissed likewise under Guyon's declaration above-recorded. No. 3, Henri Estienne, could never, though the stiffest of Calvinists, have descended to such stuff, as his character amply demonstrates.

Bibliography

Over and above authorities acknowledged elsewhere, the following works have been found useful during the writing of these pages:

DANIEL-ROPS: *L'Église de la Renaissance et de la Réforme*, Vol. IV (*Une Ère de Renouveau : La Réforme Catholique*), 1955.

DE ROCHEGUDE, Marquis, et DUMOLIN, Maurice: *Guide Pratique à travers le vieux Paris*, 1923.

DE VERVILLE, Béroalde: *Le Moyen de Parvenir*, ed. Lacroix, 1840.

DES PÉRIERS, Bonaventure: *Cymbalum Mundi*, ed. Jacob, 1858.

DUBECH, Lucien et D'ESPEZEL, Pierre: *Histoire de Paris*, 1926.

DUCHARTRE, Pierre-Louis: *La Comédie Italienne*, 1929.

GILSON, Étienne: *Rabelais Franciscain (Les Idées et les Lettres)*, 1932.

HOURS, Joseph: *Oeuvre et Pensée du Peuple Français*, 1945.

LESELLIER, J.: Contributions to vols. iii (1936) and v (1938) of *Humanisme et Renaissance*, ed. Lefranc.

MOLAND, Louis: *François Rabelais* (The Works, the Correspondence, the Latin texts of the Papal Briefs, the *Pantagrueline Prognostication*, glossary, etc.), n.d.

PASTOR, Baron Ludwig von: *Lives of the Popes (Geschichte der Päpste)*, 1886–1930; vol. xi, tr. Antrobus.

PLATTARD, Jean: *L'Oeuvre de Rabelais*, 1910.

——, *Guillaume Budé*, 1923.

RICHAULT, Gabriel: *Histoire de Chinon*, 1926.

ROMIER, Lucien: *Histoire de France*, 1950.

Rule of St. Francis of Assisi, The : London, 1933.

VALOIS, Marguerite de: *L'Heptameron des Nouvelles*, ed. Jacob, n.d.

Index